# Medieval Religious Rationalities

Inspired by the social theories of Max Weber, David d'Avray asks in what senses medieval religion was rational and, in doing so, proposes a new approach to the study of the medieval past. Applying ideas developed in his companion volume on *Rationalities in History*, he explores how values, instrumental calculation, legal formality and substantive rationality interact and the ways in which medieval beliefs were strengthened by their mutual connections, by experience and by mental images. He sheds new light on key themes and figures in medieval religion ranging from conversion, miracles and the ideas of Bernard of Clairvaux to Trinitarianism, papal government and Francis of Assisi's charismatic authority. This book shows how values and instrumental calculation affect each other in practice and demonstrates the ways in which the application of social theory can be used to generate fresh empirical research as well as new interpretative insights.

D. L. D'AVRAY is Professor of History at University College, London. A fellow of the British Academy since 2005, d'Avray has published widely on his research interests in medieval history.

# Medieval Religious Rationalities

## A Weberian Analysis

D. L. d'Avray

CAMBRIDGE
UNIVERSITY PRESS

CAMBRIDGE UNIVERSITY PRESS
Cambridge, New York, Melbourne, Madrid, Cape Town, Singapore,
São Paulo, Delhi, Dubai, Tokyo, Mexico City

Cambridge University Press
The Edinburgh Building, Cambridge CB2 8RU, UK

Published in the United States of America by Cambridge University Press,
New York

www.cambridge.org
Information on this title: www.cambridge.org/9780521186827

First published 2010

Printed in the United Kingdom at the University Press, Cambridge

*A catalogue record for this publication is available from the British Library*

ISBN 978-0-521-76707-1 Hardback
ISBN 978-0-521-18682-7 Paperback

To Julia

# Contents

# Preface and acknowledgements

This book is a sequel to its sister volume *Rationalities in History*, though either can be read without the other. Anyone who does look at both will see that a common structure informs them. This is because they were shaped by the same Weberian questionnaire. While the sister volume attempts on a small scale to do with a few ideal-types what Weber did for analytical world history, the present volume applies the same ideal-types to Western medieval 'establishment' religion. The aim is not to prove general laws or pass value judgements: ideal-types do not work like that. They generate empirical investigations into forms of thought and practice which otherwise easily remain amorphous in our conception of the period.

To begin my acknowledgements with institutions, I must thank the British Academy for the Research Readership during which I began this project long ago, the Alexander von Humboldt Stiftung for research visits to Munich funded by its programme for former fellows, and my UCL department for letting me teach unusual courses. As for individuals, the whole book is indebted to Bonnie Blackburn, Richard Kieckhefer and Julia Walworth. Patrick Zutshi, Peter Clarke and Barbara Bombi advised me on papal government. Claudia Maertl and Markus Wesche provided bibliography on Pius II, and John Bell on legal formality. This book and the sister volume have both been shaped by discussions in the Blooms- bury Sacred Law Group and above all with UCL students on the 'History and Sociology of Rationality' course, whom I cannot thank enough for their ideas and stimulation. John Sabapathy taught them with me and read the whole book, to its great profit. The publishers' anonymous readers were nearly always right, and have earned my gratitude. The staff of Cambridge University Press were more than helpful throughout.

# Abbreviations

BAV    Biblioteca Apostolica Vaticana
BL    British Library
Bnf    Bibliothèque nationale de France
*PL*    *Patrologia Latina*, ed. J.-P. Migne, 221 vols. (Paris, 1844–64)

# 1 Preliminaries

## (A) RATIONALITIES AND IRRATIONALITIES

Rational thought is like oxygen in an atmosphere filled with many other gasses, from which this study isolates it artificially as an 'ideal-type' – one which designates ways of thinking mingled with, but distinguishable analytically from, the other less rational kinds. 'Ways of thinking' is in the plural here because there are different kinds of rationality. The question that this study tries to answer is: how did different forms of rationality – four to be precise – relate to and react with one another in the Middle Ages? The resulting analyses of medieval forms of thought run parallel with the more general analyses in the sister volume on *Rationalities in History*.[1] The categories are from Max Weber – hence the subtitle. (It must not be misunderstood. Do not expect a 'rise of Western rationality' essay, nor discussion of whether the 'Protestant Ethic and the Spirit of Capitalism' had medieval origins, nor a literature survey of earlier work on Weber and the medieval West.[2]) In this Weberian spirit, a pluralist approach to rationalities informs both studies: modern Western rationality is only one species (others being, say, Hinduism, or the ideology of the classical Greek city state), of one genus (the other main genus being instrumental rationality, found in all cultures and not to be identified crudely with the modern Western value system). Weber makes this clear, though he is not always understood in this way. Nonetheless a core concept of rationality must logically precede exploration of the variety of rationalities and irrationalities.

---

[1] d'Avray, *Rationalities in History*.
[2] Notably Schluchter (ed.), *Max Webers Sicht des okzidentalen Christentums*; Kaelber, *Schools of Asceticism*.

Rationality will be defined here as: thinking which involves some general principles[3] and strives for internal consistency,[4] where the key causes of the idea or action are different from the reasons the person or people would give for it, even to themselves.[5] It could be argued that 'Rationality', used in this way, is too general a concept to be useful, especially when beliefs and practices such as magic,[6] which nearly everyone in modern academic life feels to be mistaken, are not automatically excluded as irrational. The path taken in this book is to break down the general category into a small number of key sub-concepts which enable recognition of different sorts of rationality and their interrelations. The following forms of rational thought will be defined with the precision that is possible because they are conceptual tools or ideal-types (rather than phenomena existing in a pure form in the world): value rationality, instrumental rationality, formal rationality and substantive rationality. The interactions between these ways of thinking will then be elucidated. The many other possible meanings of 'rationality' in everyday language need not be activated, just as computer software delimits the range of possible pathways to give direction to the analysis of data.

Before turning to these ideal-types of rational thought it must be stressed that 'rationality', however broadly defined, leaves much – some would say most – of medieval history unexplained. Vast areas of thought and action can be described as at least partly irrational, not only so far as the Middle Ages is concerned, but generally. 'Partly irrational' implies 'partly rational', so, strictly, one should speak of 'diminished rationality' rather than irrationality; but for convenience the latter will be used for both.

Irrationality is not easy to detect precisely because people are unaware of it. Their own utterances as reflected in the sources may direct attention away from the real explanations of their thoughts and actions. A full typology of unconscious causation cannot be attempted here but a lightning sketch is possible.

Transposition of motives into another register is one kind of irrationality. It is worth treating one example rather more fully than others to show that in principle the influence of irrational causal factors can be

---

[3] 'Everything in nature acts in accordance with laws. Only a rational being has the power to act in accordance with the *idea* of laws, that is, in accordance with principles' ('Ein jedes Ding der Natur wirkt nach Gesetzen. Nur ein vernünftiges Wesen hat das Vermögen, *nach der Vorstellung* der Gesetze, d. i. nach Prinzipien, zu handeln') (Kant, *Grundlegung zur Metaphysik der Sitten*, 56).

[4] Taylor, 'Rationality', 87.

[5] Elster, *Sour Grapes*, 15–16; Davidson, 'Paradoxes of Irrationality', 176, 181 and n. 6.

[6] Kieckhefer, 'The Specific Rationality of Medieval Magic'.

demonstrated empirically. The following case is one of the unpleasant stories in Rudolf von Schlettstadt's collection of *Memorable Stories* compiled around 1300.[7]

Rudolf asserts that a Jew procured a consecrated host from a 'perverse Christian' and invited some (Jewish) friends round to watch him experiment on it. He stabbed it and blood poured out; stabbed it again and it began to cry like a young boy. He went on hurting it and the child – the boy Jesus – went on crying out, until neighbours became concerned. They called over a butcher called 'Rindflaisch', who was passing. He thought that the Jews must have just killed a child, and yelled outside the door. That gave the Jews a chance to hide the host. When a mob had assembled and broken down the door the host was nowhere to be found. The Jews were nevertheless tried. They produced Christian witnesses (presumably character witnesses since there was no material evidence either way) but they were condemned nonetheless.[8]

It is worth setting aside the repugnance a modern reader naturally feels for the whole story in order to assess as clinically as may be how much of this behaviour can be described as rational in one sense or another. A modern agnostic might feel that the belief in the eucharist is as absurd as everything else in the story. That would surely be a mistake. The doctrines of the real presence and of the mass were so closely integrated into the set of interlocking beliefs constituting medieval (not to mention subsequent) Catholicism that to dismiss the eucharist as irrational would be a personal value judgement without explanatory power. What about the rest? Two beliefs about the Jews are intertwined here: that they murdered small boys and that they desecrated hosts. Modern scholars can safely assume that neither belief was warranted by actual facts. Consequently, either deception or irrationality of some sort must have played some part in the original creation and first dissemination of these deadly myths.[9] Further downstream in the delta of their reception one cannot be so sure that it was irrational for ordinary people to believe the myths, if it was thought to be common knowledge that Jews did such things. By *c.* 1300 one could say that it was erroneous, but rational, to regard Jews as likely suspects if such crimes were known to have been committed. The modern historian may know that these expectations were mistaken, find them hateful, and set about tracing the great harm they did, but they cannot be dismissed as 'irrational'.

---

[7] Rudolf von Schlettstadt, *Historiae Memorabiles*, 12. For background to the following discussion see Rubin, *Gentile Tales, passim*.
[8] Rudolf von Schlettstadt, *Historiae Memorabiles*, no. 6, pp. 49–51.
[9] For the origins of the host desecration myth see Rubin, *Gentile Tales*, ch. 2; for the ritual murder myth see McCulloh, 'Jewish Ritual Murder'.

Whether it was rational to assume the guilt of Jewish suspects in a particular case is another matter. In the story just summarised it would appear that the only evidence was the sound of a child crying out – even if we believe everything that Rudolf tells us. No hosts were found. Nothing is said about a confession from the 'perverse Christian' who allegedly procured the host for the Jews. So even if we accept the facts as recounted, we are looking at irrational hysteria as the explanation of the condemnation of the Jews who had been accused. When we come to the end of the story, however, we move even more clearly into the realm of the irrational.

Before the Jews had been led to the place of punishment, the poor people entered the houses of the Jews, threw their things around, and turned their houses upside down. The peasants of the neighbouring villages, hearing and seeing this, followed their example, seized the Jews who dwelled among them, snatched their goods, and burned the houses and bodies of the Jews to ashes.[10]

The sack of Jewish households in the town, and *a fortiori* the murder by arson of Jews in the neighbouring villages, can be confidently described as irrational even after every possible allowance has been made for alterity, other cultures, etc., because no medieval beliefs implied a conviction that those particular rural Jews had actually desecrated hosts. What then were the real motives? Perhaps we can do no more than speculate, but it is worth noting that in this Rhineland social context, religious indignation against people whose failure to accept Christianity seemed incomprehensible and who were the object of ugly general rumours could have been the legitimation for economic resentment of Jews.

The other types of irrationality (in a needless to say far from exhaustive survey) may be treated more briefly. There are types of thinking that are non-rational[11] rather than irrational. Sometimes routines are followed out of inertia, even at the expense of efficacy: this is what Weber called 'traditional' action.[12] A late medieval case would be the survival at the papal court into the fourteenth century of a system by which senior household officials were remunerated in kind.[13] This would have made

[10] Rudolf von Schlettstadt, *Historiae Memorabiles*, 51.
[11] My use of non-rational should not be confused with that of Gavin Langmuir when he talks of 'nonrational thinking', using the word to mean what Weber calls 'value rational': see Weber, *Wirtschaft und Gesellschaft*, vol. 2, p. 12, and cf. Langmuir, *History, Religion and Antisemitism*, 152 n. 18. As will become clear, I strongly endorse Weber's (as against Langmuir's) characterisation of such thinking as rational. The conceptual match between Weber and Langmuir, behind the verbal difference, is nevertheless worth noting.
[12] Weber, *Wirtschaft*, vol. 2, p. 12.
[13] Dehio, 'Der Übergang von Natural- zu Geldbesoldung an der Kurie'; Baethgen, 'Quellen und Untersuchungen', esp. 142–3, passage beginning: 'Mit andern Worten,

sense in an earlier period when popes travelled round their estates living off the produce as other early medieval rulers did, but not at a time when the food and drink had to be purchased and surpluses wasted or resold.

Another possible instance (which admittedly needs further research) of the diminution, either by inertia or an absence of coordination, of organisational rationality seems to be embodied in the following passages from a formulary of the fourteenth-century papal penitentiary (included in a fifteenth-century manuscript belonging to the Cardinal Penitentiary himself:[14] '[the Cardinal Penitentiary] can absolve participants in tournaments and those who have gone to watch them from the sentences imposed on such people by the same lord pope John XXII'.[15] A couple of pages on something very similar is repeated:

Again, the same lord pope granted that the [Cardinal Penitentiary] might have the power to absolve participants in tournaments and those who have gone to watch tournaments from the sentences which he promulgated against such people in certain places.[16]

The repetition is untidy, suggesting a certain degree of administrative disorganisation, but there is another more serious problem. Pope John XXII had in fact lifted the ban on participation in tournaments that he had inherited from his predecessors, and in the decretal by which he absolved anyone who had incurred excommunication through involvement in them he begins with a disarming admission, typical of his approach, that canon law decrees can get it wrong and may need to be removed.[17] It seems unlikely that John XXII subsequently changed his

die ganzen an die Kurialen verteilten Mengen' (p. 142) and ending 'keine andere Verwertungsmöglichkeit dafür hatten!' (p. 143); Frutaz, 'La famiglia pontificia'.

[14] MS Biblioteca Apostolica Vaticana Lat. 3994, described in Göller, *Die Päpstliche Pönitentiarie*, 71–2 (ownership of the Cardinal Penitentiary Nicolaus Albergati: p. 71). For further bibliography on the Apostolic Penitentiary and its formularies, see below, p. 155.

[15] 'potest absolvere hastiludiantes et eos qui ad vendendum [videndum *recte?*] astiludia iverunt a sententiis latis per ipsum dominum Iohannem papam xxii contra tales' (MS BAV 3994, fol. 30$^r$).

[16] 'Item concessit idem dominus papa quod possit absolvere hastiludiantes et eos qui ad videndum hastiludia iverunt a sententiis quas ipse in tales in certis locis promulgavit' (MS BAV 3994, fol. 31$^r$).

[17] 'Since, where future events are concerned, fallible human judgement can be so mistaken that what careful thought, based on a reasonable estimate of probability, at the time judged useful, sometimes happens to turn out instead to be harmful, it often happens that decisions made advisedly are reversed still more advisedly on more mature consideration' ('Quia in futurorum eventibus sic humani fallitur incertitudo iudicii, ut, quod coniectura probabili exnunc interdum attenta consideratio utile pollicetur, reperiri damnosum quandocunque contingat, nonnunquam quod consulte statuitur ex sanioris inspectione iudicii consultius revocatur') (Extrav. Jo. XXII, 9; Friedberg, *Corpus Iuris Canonici*, vol. 2, p. 1215. Cf. Keen, *Chivalry*, 94, and ch. 5 *passim*, for general context.

mind back, and if *per improbabile* he did, his decree removing the ban was out in the world, to end up eventually in the *Corpus Iuris Canonici*, which remained the law of the Catholic Church up until 1917. Thus the Penitentiary had a formulary that contained rules that appear to contradict canon law. Unless some more logical explanation is produced by future research, this looks very much like a contradiction within the system. Perhaps the man who drafted the formulary did not do his homework, and attributed to John XXII rules that he had in fact abolished.

Sometimes emotion overrides reason, even if the person is aware of it.[18] The power of emotions like anger and lust to overcome rational calculation hardly needs to be illustrated with medieval examples, except when excessively sophisticated over-interpretation conceals a simple truth. In a famous case described by Gregory of Tours a feud is resolved by compensation payments, after which the former foes seemed to enjoy each other's company. One day, at a dinner party, the guest remarked on the gold and silver abounding in the host's house, and commented that he had it thanks to the murder of his relatives, for which the guest had paid compensation. According to Gregory the host said to himself in his heart (which Gregory could hardly have accessed) that people would call him a weak woman unless he avenged his relatives' death, so he slew his guest.[19] An account of the incident in terms of symbolic communication has been offered by an eminent scholar;[20] this may be over-interpretation of the debacle that ruined the carefully crafted settlement of the feud: one could simply say that a man made an offensive joke and provoked a fit of rage, getting himself killed.

Next, one could mention mental illness, such as depression, schizophrenia, and perhaps anorexia. Without being unduly culture-bound, we can assume the existence of some such phenomena in the Middle Ages. Postpartum depression, for instance, probably transcends cultures, and examples from the medieval period can be documented.[21] Carolyn Walker Bynum's study of fasting points out that some of the women who found themselves unable to eat recognised that the cause was *accidia*, a sort of depressive sloth.[22] As for cases where the victims did

---

[18] Cf. Weber, *Wirtschaft*, 12: 'affektuell, insbesondere emotional' ('by affect, especially emotionally').

[19] Gregory of Tours, *Historia Francorum*, 7.47 and 9.19, in Dalton, *The History of the Franks*, vol. 2, pp. 321–3 and 387. The case owes some of its fame to the classic discussion of it by Auerbach, *Mimesis*, ch. 4.

[20] Althoff, 'Zur Bedeutung', 381–2.

[21] Murray, *Suicide in the Middle Ages*, vol. 1, pp. 256–7; Atkinson, *Mystic and Pilgrim*, 209: 'The insights of modern psychology are helpful, for example, in interpreting the illness that Margery suffered after the birth of her first child. The description resembles "postpartum psychosis".'

[22] Bynum, *Holy Feast and Holy Fast*, 203.

not themselves recognise depression as the cause of their quasi-anorexic behaviour, Bynum recognised that 'psychodynamic factors' cannot be eliminated from explanation of such patterns of behaviour, even though the general thrust of her argument is that fasting should be understood inside its own religious culture as a way of imitating the sufferings of Christ.[23]

Bynum showed how cautious one must be about classing the self-starvation of religious women in the later Middle Ages as a kind of 'anorexia', as Rudolf Bell did in a controversial book.[24] Instead Bynum plausibly argued that the religious culture set a high value on self-abnegation; men had more freedom than women to choose to give up sex or wealth; food was one thing women controlled, so one thing they could choose to give up.[25] Still, it is arguable that some of the fasting described by Bell and Bynum went beyond what can easily be explained in terms of the religious values of the day.

It is hard tidily to map the murky area where people lose all awareness of the real springs of their action, and motivation is transposed from one register to another – though such processes must be among the strongest forces in history. The following attempt to label some of the species is necessarily crude.

(i) Frustrated ambition may transpose itself into other more altruistic registers. A good example of how it could be transmuted into volatile religious 'extremism' may be Margery Kempe (c. 1373–post-1438), the upper-bourgeois housewife who 'got religion' in a big way and whose enthusiastic and emotional piety seemed overdone, not to say irritating, to many of those around her. Clarissa Atkinson has applied the findings of the social anthropologist I. M. Lewis to Margery:

religious 'extremism' (trance, possession, ecstasy and the like) . . . provides a sanctioned form of resistance or aggression or escape from narrow and unsatisfactory lives. . . . Bizarre behaviour (trance, babbling, 'fits', or possibly tears) manifests the closeness of the spirits. Shamans are not revolutionaries or even reformers; most often they are not conscious of dissatisfaction in themselves or in their group or class. Lewis points out that possessed persons do not necessarily (or characteristically) question authority or attack the status system in which they find themselves. Their anger or rage is expressed without conscious awareness of the effects of hierarchy. . . . Very often, the shaman is distinguished by some

---

[23] 'Thus whatever physiological and psychodynamic factors may have influenced medieval behaviour – and I dismiss neither set of factors – cultural setting was crucial' (*ibid.*, 206); 'I will, then, leave aside the fact that some of the fasting behavior of late medieval women can be described by the modern psychological and medical term *anorexia nervosa* and address, rather, the question of why so much medieval religious behavior and the religious language of these women revolved around food' (*ibid.*, 207; note the word 'fact').

[24] Bell, *Holy Anorexia*.      [25] Bynum, *Holy Feast, passim.*

special affliction or illness. . . . Margery's tears constituted such an affliction and became a mark of special favour.[26]

Margery lacked the opportunities of the men around her:

there was obvious conflict between the social (and domestic) role of John Kempe's wife and John Burnham's daughter and the ambitious, restless, powerful personality of Margery Kempe. . . . Margery Kempe was the daughter of a public figure. Her brother followed their father into public office . . . It must have been obvious very early that Margery's energies could not be expressed in commercial or political life.[27]

Religion may have provided an outlet:

According to Lewis's notion of the social and psychological functions of ecstatic religion, the creation and continuing legitimation of the shamanistic vocation permits its adepts to experience a sense of power, significance, and liberation from unsatisfactory lives. Such ecstasy may or may not be 'hysterical'; it certainly is not a maladaptive neurotic state but an effective and fairly common means by which depressed or deprived people improve their lives. *Obviously it is not a conscious strategy* [my italics].[28]

If Atkinson is right, Margery's ostentatious piety is an example of the common case of piety which is functional, but irrational: an important distinction which defuses many of the apparent paradoxes of rationality analysis. Call behaviour functional when it helps the person or group in some way, and irrational when the real cause is different from the reason which the person or group sees as the explanation of the behaviour. Of course there is no reason why both conditions should not be fulfilled at the same time. There may even be a necessary connection between them. Suppose we accept Atkinson's assessment of Margery Kempe: had Margery not repressed any awareness of the real motivation for her behaviour she could not have carried it off with conviction. Such interpretations are speculative, even unprovable. Analysing irrationality tends to involve more guesswork than analysing rational action. But hypotheses about irrationality cannot always be avoided. The alternative is to take everyone's understanding of his own behaviour at its face value.

(ii) Wishes can father judgements for which there is insufficient objective warrant – as when Western visitors to the Soviet Union in the 1930s left their critical faculties behind and saw the society they wanted to find.[29] Medieval examples are not hard to discover. The Crusade of the

---

[26] Atkinson, *Mystic and Pilgrim*, 213–14.    [27] *Ibid.*, 212–13.    [28] *Ibid.*, 215.

[29] 'A deadening of the senses is evident in their blithe discussion of the treatment of local officials held culpable for the famine and in their response to the culling of the old Bolshevik élite in the show trials from 1936. . . . Their defenders were forced to

Children in 1212[30] and the Crusade of the Shepherds in 1251[31] may fit under the rubric of wishful thinking: a rational assessment would have warned those involved that they had no chance of success. In both cases large numbers of people believed that they could reach and make a military difference in the Middle East when they had no empirical warrant for that assessment. The 'boys' who went on the Children's Crusade hoped to cross to the Holy Land dry shod.[32] The Crusade of the Shepherds

> was an enthusiasm of the peasantry, rooted in the countryside, but in contact with important urban centres, which saw socially marginal, often youthful, agricultural labourers, landless shepherds, cowherds, dairy maids, household servants – later to be joined by assorted riff-raff (*ribaldi*) . . . who were setting out to aid and avenge King Louis, and to rescue the Holy Land from the clutches of the Saracens.[33]

Was this hope warranted in the light of what they knew or believed? It seems hard to deny that wish-fulfilment played a role.

(iii) Anger may be aroused by one thing and direct itself at another, often a person or group. The transmutation of anger towards Muslims in the near East into massacres of peaceful European Jews in the First Crusade seems to be an example of the way in which aggressive emotions and desire for vengeance can be switched from a less accessible to a more accessible object. In the confusion of motivations were doubtless mixed together mental confusion – a blurring of lines between one kind of infidel and another[34] – and greed for the Jews' money. Self-deception about the real motivation must have facilitated these acts of composite irrationality. We have detailed descriptions, notably by Albert of Aachen.[35] He reports that 'the pilgrims rose in a spirit of cruelty against the Jews who were scattered throughout all the cities, and they inflicted a most cruel slaughter on them . . . claiming that this was the beginning of their crusade

---

treat their soviet infatuation as a senile aberration, but it was never that. They saw what they wanted to see, no doubt, but the soviet Russia they saw was the closest approximation in practice to their exemplary socialist society – the Webbian design that they had sketched, with little deviation, over a period of fifty years.' J. Davis, 'Webb, Beatrice', 824.

[30] Dickson, 'The Genesis of the Children's Crusade (1212)', translated from an earlier French version. See now his *The Childrens Crusade*.

[31] Dickson, 'The Advent of the *Pastores* (1251)'.    [32] Dickson, 'Genesis', 7.

[33] Dickson, 'The Advent of the *Pastores* (1251)', 250.

[34] Riley-Smith, *The First Crusade and the Idea of Crusading*, 54–5.

[35] Albert of Aachen, *Historia Ierosolimitana*, i. 26–7, pp. 50–3; on p. 50 nn. 60, 61 and 65 the editor lists other sources for the attacks. For a modern account see Asbridge, *The First Crusade*, 84–8.

and service against the enemies of Christianity',[36] and that after the pogrom in Cologne the aggressors divided 'a substantial sum of money among themselves'.[37]

(iv) Frustration can turn into blind aggression, as with the orgy of violence that ensued after the capture of Jerusalem during the First Crusade.[38] There it seems to have been a matter of releasing pent-up frustration in shocking ways. There is a study to be done on the sociology and psychology of post-siege atrocities.

The foregoing could all be grouped under the rubric of 'psychological irrationality', because psychological causes which the actors did not themselves understand and which were different from the reasons they presumably gave themselves explain their behaviour. They involve a degree of self-deception or the switching of emotions from one object to another, without those who feel them understanding what is happening.

There are surely other forms of the transposition of motivation, but we must turn finally to the kind of irrationality which consists in the coexistence within the same mind, or society, of ideas which are incompatible with each other to a greater or lesser degree. A special case is behaviour which is directed towards a rational end but which contradicts the legitimisation offered to others: logical rather than psychological rationality. A case in point would be the crusading taxes levied on the Church by permission of the Pope by Philip VI of France in the 1330s, well studied by Franz Felten. Whatever people today think of the crusading movement, it was well integrated into the culture of the time, and one should hesitate to call a tax to fund a crusade irrational, however much one may feel the cause to be wrong from a modern observer's standpoint. As it happens, however, there are clear signs that the French king planned to use the money not for a crusade but for consolidation of his kingdom,[39] with an eye on the possibility of conflict with England.[40] There were no accounting controls to ensure that the money was spent on the stated object,[41] and the King had even arranged to make it easy for him to be absolved from any moral obligation to go on crusade.[42] He was able to obtain these enviable conditions by in effect blackmailing the then Pope, John XXII, with a veiled threat to treat him as a heretic for his

---

[36] Albert of Aachen, *Historia Ierosolimitana*, i. 26, p. 51.    [37] *Ibid.*

[38] *Ibid.*, vi. 23, pp. 430–3, and vi. 30, pp. 440–3; Asbridge, *The First Crusade*, 316–17.

[39] Felten, 'Auseinandersetzungen um die Finanzierung eines Kreuzzuges', 96: passage beginning 'Selbst wenn die Herrscher' and ending 'Mittel zu verschaffen'.

[40] *Ibid.*, 92: passage beginning 'Schon im Sommer 1335' and ending 'weil kein Silber beschafft werden konnte'.

[41] *Ibid.*, 90: passage beginning 'Die Kontrolle' and ending 'Rechenschaft schuldig'.

[42] *Ibid.*, 91: passage beginning 'der Papst verzichtete' and ending 'des Kreuzzuges rechtfertigte'.

theological theories about the afterlife; this was a formidable threat because there was a theory that a heretic ipso facto ceased to be Pope.[43] Strengthening the kingdom and defeating England were also rational objectives in the framework of *Realpolitik*, to which the French monarchy was no stranger. The quasi-'irrationality' consists in the incompatibility between the rational intentions, as evidenced by the details of the permission forced out of the Pope, and the legitimisation of the tax.

Irrationality is hard to study. Even in cases like the one just analysed, when the motivation is rational *per se* and only illogical when put side by side with the public justification, one has to cut against the grain of sources designed to conceal rather than to reveal. When people conceal irrational motivations from themselves, the problem is aggravated by their own failure to understand their actions. The historian needs to understand them better than they did themselves. The study of irrationality needs a rare combination of conceptual and empirical skills. It can be done – Lyndal Roper's studies in the Augsburg Stadtarchiv are one example from a neighbouring period of what can be achieved[44] – but must be left to others.

## (B) DEVELOPMENTAL INTERPRETATIONS

Medievalists have begun to pay attention to the history of rationalities.[45] The topic has been most thoroughly addressed by scholars interested

---

[43] Dunbabin, *A Hound of God*, 181–5. Dunbabin and Felten are best read together: she brings out the magnitude of the pressure on the Pope, he puts the King's claims to want the money for the crusade in perspective.

[44] Roper, *Oedipus and the Devil*.

[45] Bartlett, *Trial by Fire and Water*, and Kieckhefer, 'The Specific Rationality of Medieval Magic', were aware of anthropological and philosophical discussion of Rationality long before most medievalists. Althoff, 'Zur Bedeutung symbolischer Kommunikation', explores the instrumental rationality discernible in symbolic actions: see esp. pp. 371–2. Though Althoff's application of the concept of *Zweckrationalität* is full of interest (one or two rather forced examples aside), I have the impression that he does not realise how widely Weber himself applied it to medieval civilisation: on p. 371 he comes close to using Weber as an 'Aunt Sally'. He seems to have mistaken Weber's category of 'traditional action' as a characterisation of pre-modernity, which is definitely not Weber's meaning. Cf also n. 4, where he says that 'Weber analysed the medieval situation primarily with reference to the City' ('Mittelalterliche Verhältnisse analysierte Weber vor allem im Bereich der Stadt') – but what about Weber's brief but remarkably perceptive analyses of canon law and papal bureaucracy (discussed in the second part of this book), or of monasticism? For a Weberian treatment of the last of these themes, as well as of Cathars and Waldensians, see Kaelber, *Schools of Asceticism*, a serious and thought-provoking contribution. For the rationality of chivalry see Laudage, 'Rittertum und Rationalismus', esp. p. 314: 'The contradiction between the knightly ideal of the court and rationally orientated action is palpable here, but it was resolved through an attitude that I would like to call Honour Rationality' ('Der Widerspruch zwischen höfischem Ritterideal und vernunftorientierten Handeln ist hier mit

in the rise of Western rationality as a developmental process, if not progress. The present study should not be mistaken for another investigation of this theme. It is an important story. There is a deep-rooted and persistent mythical history according to which reason was dormant and superstition rampant in the Middle Ages, a situation initially but only partially rectified by the 'Renaissance and Reformation', and finally remedied properly by the rise of science and the Enlightenment. That caricatural denigration of medieval culture is likely to survive even the most powerful refutations, such as the demolition of it by Edward Grant.[46] Polemics apart, Grant provides a synthesis of the rise of advanced rational thinking in medieval universities. He argues that

It was in the esoteric domain of university scholasticism that reason was most highly developed . . . it was permanently institutionalised in the universities of Europe. Reason was interwoven with the very fabric of a European-wide medieval curriculum and thus played its most significant role in preparing the way for the establishment of a deep-rooted scientific temperament that was an indispensable prerequisite for the emergence of early modern science. Reason in the university context was not intended for the acquisition of power over others, or to improve the material well-being of the general populace. Its primary purpose was to elucidate the natural and supernatural worlds. In all the history of human civilisation, reason had never been accorded such a central role, one that involved so many people over such a wide area for such an extended period.[47]

Händen zu greifen, aber er wurde aufgelöst in einer Haltung, die ich als Rationalismus der Ehre bezeichnen möchte') (and p. 296 for the provocation to Barbarossa's honour). 'Reflexion und Inszenierung von Rationalität in der mittelalterlichen Literatur' was chosen as the theme of the 2006 Wolframgesellschaft Tagung. Hyams, *Rancor and Reconciliation in Medieval England*, makes productive use of Rational Choice Theory. Nörr, 'Von der Textrationalität zur Zweckrationalität', is important, but note that he is uses 'Zweckrationalität' in a more specific sense than the one that will be developed here.

[46] For strongly argued criticism of the caricature see Grant, *God and Reason in the Middle Ages*, ch. 7; media discourse is a lost cause but even historians of later periods do not always have sufficient resistance to this 'meme'-like schema of rationality's emergence from medieval darkness: one finds traces of the triumphalist schema in so fine a book as Israel's *Radical Enlightenment*, p. vi: '[the Renaissance and the Reformation] are really only adjustments, modifications to what was essentially still a theologically conceived and ordered regional society . . . By contrast, the Enlightenment . . . not only attacked and severed the roots of traditional European culture in the sacred, magic, kingship, and hierarchy, secularizing all institutions and ideas, but (intellectually and to a degree in practice) effectively demolished all legitimation of monarchy, aristocracy, woman's subordination to man, ecclesiastical authority, and slavery, replacing these with the principles of universality, equality and democracy.' Jürgen Habermas's developmental schema belongs to the same broad school: for a clear summary see Giddens, 'Jürgen Habermas'.

[47] Grant, *God and Reason*, 3.

Theology plays an integral part in Grant's grand narrative of medieval rationality:

Ultimately, theology became thoroughly analytical and philosophical. It was almost as rationalistic as natural philosophy, on which it came to depend so heavily. Theologians had come a long way from the earlier form of theology that was concerned with moral instruction, contemplation of the divine, and what may be called the 'theology of the heart'. It is almost as if they were determined to understand the mysteries of the faith and to explain them rationally.[48]

This is in harmony with fact that much of the most creative work in medieval philosophy arose precisely out of preoccupation with theological problems. The second part of John Marenbon's *Later Medieval Philosophy (1150–1350)* is focussed on the problem of intellectual knowledge (as a detailed illustration of academic philosophy in the period). He points out that the most creative and original work was done by theologians, who were more mature and less respectful of ancients' authority than were their counterparts in the Faculties.[49] They analysed the nature of intellectual knowledge in the context of the Trinity and of minds without matter, such as souls between death and the end of the world, angels, and God.[50] Marenbon's great contribution was to bring out the connection between a kind of philosophical rationality which seems modern and a context so alien to that of most modern philosophers.

Work on the rationalising content of later medieval thought complements a study by Alexander Murray of the rise of reason viewed as a broad general mentality, and of the social and economic origins of this process. Murray argues that:

Two currents . . . literary and mathematical, combined to feed a more regular concept of nature. The more regular this concept grew, the greater was its tension with inherited notions of miracle. The numerous old exceptions to natural laws, like magnets and eclipses, tended to fade away before the natural philosophy of the twelfth and thirteenth centuries, which showed they were not exceptions at all. Miracle was increasingly left on its own, in tension with an otherwise regular nature. The tension was variously expressed. A principal way was by disbelief in miracles and other divine interventions.[51]

---

[48] *Ibid.*, 213.
[49] Marenbon, *Later Medieval Philosophy*, 190: 'Independence in speculation was usually the preserve of the theologians, both because they were more mature and highly trained, and because a good deal of the ancient and Arab texts was incompatible with their doctrinal aims and presuppositions'; *ibid.* 143: 'The great changes in later medieval understanding of the intellect all came from the theologians.' See also Marenbon's *Medieval Philosophy*: the argument about philosophy and theological problems does not stand out in such sharp relief here, as it takes its place alongside a larger set of other themes.
[50] Marenbon, *Later Medieval Philosophy*, 94.
[51] Murray, *Reason and Society in the Middle Ages*, 11.

He gives what is in effect a sociological explanation of this rise of rationality. To quote a recent summary:

'rationality' was produced by two kinds of 'up-and-down-social mobility'. On the one hand, there was the rise of the schools – in the sense of the intellectual centres that would turn into universities. They became a path to social ascent for clerics (as they have become since then for ambitious men and women generally), and by accident made the cult of rationality current among the elites thus created. . . . The proto-university schools filled a vacuum created by the assault on simony, the previous path to a successful career in the Church. Murray remarks that simony in the sense of purchase of church office with money had itself increased drastically in the immediately preceding period, which no doubt helped to provoke the reaction of the reformers. This increase can in its turn be explained by the rise of the money economy, and it correlates with an increase in the number of robberies. . . . In a parallel development, the rise of commerce fostered the spread of practical arithmetic and calculation among merchants ambitious for profit, thus developing another sort of 'rationality'. So it was the rise of the money economy rather than that of natural science that gave 'reason' its elevated status in the West.[52]

In short, the rise of rationality derived from an intensified social mobility which had been encouraged by academic study (a path to social promotion) and mathematics (a tool for merchants and a way to get rich).

The tension between rationality and religion gets more emphasis in Murray's synthesis than in Grant's or Marenbon's. Still, Murray does not present it as irreconcilable:

It is unimaginable that European civilisation could have developed as it did, as both religious and scientific at once, if no *modus vivendi* had been found between the concepts here in tension: God's direct intervention in nature, and natural laws. Aquinas . . . here as elsewhere, was foremost in finding the resolution. [Aquinas's ideas about miracles will need to be discussed again, in both chapters 2 and 3] . . . By the end of the thirteenth century the concept of miracle had thus moved into a new conceptual environment. It can be compared to an old church in a modern city: the church itself remains unchanged, but looks quite different because of the buildings which rise around it. In Aquinas' time the age-old belief in miracle, similarly, was hedged round by the rising suburbs of reason.[53]

As these extracts show, the (later) medieval contribution to the 'rise of rationality' in the West has already been perceptively studied. Their authors correct a story in which 'Western Rationality' is the central figure. The types of rationality which Grant, Marenbon and Murray discuss are still considered rational today: academic problem-solving, rigorous philosophical analysis, mathematics, and the idea of nature as subject to law. In this context one should mention also the remarkable account

[52] d'Avray, 'Alexander Murray', 14.    [53] Murray, *Reason and Society*, 12.

by Peter Biller of the development of demographic thought in the two centuries before the Black Death.[54]

To all these findings one might add a thesis attributed to Max Weber according to which the medieval papacy was 'the first rational bureaucracy of World History'.[55] Here 'rational' should probably be understood to mean something like 'governed by an internally consistent body of rules and principle'. The attribution to Max Weber is a little misleading. Weber's list of the large bureaucracies of history begins with ancient Egypt.[56] Then again, the medieval papacy's administrative system lacks many important features of bureaucracy as Weber defines it, as will be argued below in a later chapter.[57] Nevertheless, as will be shown in detail in the same chapter, papal administration did fit into a system of legal rationality which had much in common with the legal formality of modern Western states: it had their legal formality without a comparable bureaucratic infrastructure, for which office charisma and ingenuity had to substitute, making a very unusual combination in world-historical terms.

Another Weberian theme, 'taking the magic out of the world', here applied to the prohibition of trial by ordeal and the introduction of natural sciences to European universities, is taken up in an important recent book by Robert Bartlett,[58] one of whose lines of thought converges with Grant's. ('One of', because the book also subverts the idea of progress towards rationality, pointing out that mass witch persecutions start only right at the end of the medieval period.[59]) Bartlett rightly emphasises the role of the friars and above all Thomas Aquinas in developing a clear framework for thinking about the differences between 'natural' and 'supernatural'[60] – a prerequisite for giving the autonomy of the natural order its due. He suggests that 'the medieval period could be viewed not

---

[54] Biller, *The Measure of Multitude*, e.g. p. 419. Incidentally, this book is also very helpful as a guide to the reception of Aristotle's *Politics*: *ibid.*, 296–325.

[55] Schluchter, 'Einleitung. Religion, politische Herrschaft, Wirtschaft und bürgerliche Lebensführung', 57, the passage beginning 'Rationale Leistungen' and ending 'der Weltgeschichte'.

[56] Weber, *Wirtschaft*, vol. 2, p. 564.

[57] Drawing especially on the work of Schwarz, *Die Organisation kurialer Schreiberkollegien*.

[58] Bartlett, *The Natural and the Supernatural in the Middle Ages*, 32–3.  [59] *Ibid.*, 33.

[60] *Ibid.*, 12–17. To balance this account, note the comments of Watkins, *History and the Supernatural in Medieval England*, 18–19: he argues that a rough and ready distinction between 'natural' and 'supernatural' existed long before the precise academic formulation of the idea. See also *ibid.*, 233–4: 'the "rise" of practical reason, just like the rise of speculative reason, did not roll the supernatural back in a straightforward fashion but rather created new contexts in which it was obliged to work'. The difference between Watkins and Bartlett is one of emphasis, rather than a contradiction.

as the cartoon "Other" to modern pragmatic rationalist society but as a stage on the path to it'.[61]

All this tends to push the decisive phase in the development of rationality in the West back to the Middle Ages, but it could still fit quite neatly into a developmental grand narrative. The present study, however, is not about this developmental schema. It can accommodate the kind of findings just discussed well enough, but the approach is not the same: it is more synchronic than diachronic, and it is not focused on the origins of modern rationality. The Weberian ideas that have stimulated much of this research are from a different sector of his thought than the one to which Bartlett alludes. Instead, the present study takes its initial questionnaire from his categories of rationality – though the book is not meant to be an exposition of his thought and uses his concepts with some freedom, as he would surely have wished.

## (C) A NON-DEVELOPMENTAL WEBERIAN APPROACH

A developmental reading of Weber is common,[62] and legitimate so long as no one imagines that Weber identified Western rationality with Rationality *tout court* or assumes that he thought rationalisation could only take the Western form. As will shortly become clear, he was not of that opinion (even if the original impetus for his analyses of world history may have come from a desire to discover what was distinctive about Western rationalisation and why). The principal inspiration for the present study is his opus magnum *Wirtschaft und Gesellschaft*,[63] which is structured synchronically and analytically rather than diachronically as a grand narrative.[64] So too is this book. Though much of the material comes from the last

---

[61] *Ibid.*, 32.

[62] E.g. Schluchter, *The Rise of Western Rationalism*; Boudon, 'A propos du relativisme des valeurs', esp. 884–95, thinks he finds in Weber the idea of 'progrès moral' (p. 893): towards the ideas that all individuals should be treated as citizens, that slavery is unacceptable, of the separation of powers, and of democratic institutions' – ideas coated by Boudon with very un-Weberian positive value judgements; note, however, important qualifications on pp. 892–3.

[63] *Wirtschaft und Gesellschaft*, first published in 1921; I use the fifth edition, ed. Winckelmann (Tübingen, 1972). Though the English translation by G. Roth and C. Wittich, *Economy and Society: An Outline of Interpretive Sociology*, 2 vols. (Berkeley, 1978) is in general a good one, I have provided my own translations of the passages quoted, which has enabled me to work directly from the original and which gives the reader a chance to compare independent understandings of Weber's complex prose.

[64] To pre-empt the predictable argument about the importance of narrative, grand or otherwise, it should be stressed that no one is calling this in question: but synchronic analytical frameworks can be right for some investigations, as for instance it was in most of F. W. Maitland's legal history.

three medieval centuries,[65] the principle conclusions are not confined to that period or indeed to the Middle Ages. They mirror and illustrate in detail the conclusions of the comparative sister volume on *Rationalities in History*.

## Ideal-types

*Wirtschaft und Gesellschaft* is a kind of *Summa* of ideal-types for the study of world history: they are meant to be corrected against the complexities of past societies. They are rather like the 'Identikits' of facial features (ears, foreheads, noses, mouths, etc. of different types) that the police used to employ to help witnesses reconstruct the appearance of a criminal for them (before police artists and computer software took over the job). Ideal-types need to be constantly corrected to bring them closer to concrete past reality; they derive from comparative reading and are applied back to the specificities of a given period, in the genre of Weber's studies in the sociology of particular religions.[66] There has been no question here of following Weber's conclusions in *Wirtschaft und Gesellschaft* in a doctrinaire way, but rather of seeing how far generalisations about rationalities constructed both from his writings and from comparative reading find echoes in medieval religion.

Weber's generalisations use custom-built concepts and causal schema which make no claim to do justice to the intricate phenomena of the history,[67] but which point attention in useful directions. One can think of ideal-types in terms of a questionnaire: does one find anything like X,

---

[65] Partly because data is much more plentiful and partly, it must be admitted, because of my own limitations: but it would be misleading to present the findings of this book as if relating to the later period only.

[66] *Gesammelte Aufsätze zur Religionssoziologie*, vol. 2: *Die Wirtschaftsethik der Weltreligionen*, vol. 2: *Hinduismus und Buddhismus* is particularly important for the present study.

[67] 'Ideal-types are a mental constructions, which are not to be identified with historical reality and certainly not with 'reality' *tout court*; still less are they there to serve as a pattern towards which reality ought to be orientated as towards an exemplar; instead, their significance is that of purely notional concepts, of limiting cases, against which reality is measured or compared in order to bring out more clearly certain important components of its empirical contents' (passage beginning '[the ideal-type] ist ein Gedankenbild' and ending 'mit dem sie verglichen wird') (Weber, 'Die "Objektivität" sozialwissenschaftlicher und sozialpolitischer Erkenntnis', in *Gesammelte Aufsätze zur Wissenschaftslehre*, 146–214 at 194. 'It is true that there is nothing more dangerous than to mix theory and history up together . . ., whether this intermingling takes the form of a belief that one has pinned down, in those theoretical conceptual constructions, the "true" contents – the "essence" – of historical reality, or of using these constructions as a Procrustean bed' ('Nichts aber ist allerdings gefährlicher als die . . . Vermischung von Theorie und Geschichte, sei es in der Form, daß man glaubt, in jenen theoretischen Begriffsbildern den "eigentlichen" Gehalt, das "Wesen" der geschichtlichen Wirklichkeit fixiert zu haben, oder daß man sie als ein Prokrustesbett benutzt') (*ibid.*, 195).

and does it tend to derive from Y or to cause Z? Then empirical research takes over: not to 'prove' the generalisations, or even to falsify them à la Karl Popper by counter-examples, but to correct them, refine them and give them concrete specificity. So the answers to the questionnaire should not necessarily or even usually be 'yes' or 'no', but 'up to a point' – with an attempt to specify up to what point. When Weber presents a simplified schema, he is inviting us to try it on for size in empirical investigations, and to alter it – not the same as 'falsifying' it – without compunction when it does not quite fit the data.

Thus, for instance, he analyses the different kinds of ascetic techniques generated by different world religions.[68] It is really a common-sense procedure, though the range of world history scanned in order to juxtapose a variety of value systems with their respective techniques of asceticism puts his oeuvre in a class of its own, so that his sociology becomes something like a world history on analytical rather than narrative principles. He is implicitly distinguishing the core values from the ascetic practices, while proposing that the former produce the latter. Here value rationality shapes instrumental rationality; it should be constantly kept in mind that in this study this latter concept is not reserved for amoral, cynical or purely pragmatic and utilitarian calculations – it can be applied equally well to Buddhist[69] or Christian[70] ascetic practices, or those of other religions. This usage is thoroughly Weberian, as the following significant passage shows:

Indian asceticism was technically probably the rationally most highly developed in the world. There is hardly any ascetic method which was not exercised in virtuoso fashion in India and very often rationalised into a theoretical technical science, and only here where many forms were carried all the way to their ultimate logical conclusions, which are often simply grotesque for us.[71]

The words 'technisch' and 'rational' together make it clear that he is speaking of instrumental rationality. The 'for us' alludes to the different value framework of modern Westerners.

---

[68] E.g. Judaism: Weber, *Wirtschaft und Gesellschaft*, vol. 1, p. 372, and Puritanism, *ibid.*, 329.

[69] For the instrumental character of Buddhist asceticism see Gombrich, *Theravada Buddhism*, 94 (on the reaction to an attempt to treat certain ascetic practices like absolute values). Freiberger, *Der Orden in der Lehre*, 239, argues that in early Buddhism there was, alongside the view that monasticism was the path to salvation, a contrary view that it could be achieved via the lay life also – in which case the choice comes in the realm of instrumental rationality as understood here.

[70] For medieval asceticism as instrumental rationality see Ch. 4 below.

[71] Passage beginning 'Die indische Askese war technisch' and ending 'hineingesteigert worden' (*Die Wirtschaftsethik der Weltreligionen*, vol. 2, p. 149).

## Four kinds of rationality

*Value* (alias *conviction*) and *instrumental rationality* are central in this investigation, together with the concepts of *formal* and *substantive rationality*.[72] These twinned concepts are not understood in an antithetical mode: on the contrary (it will be argued) each pair represents two interdependent ways of reasoning. The slightly pretentious word *symbiosis* will be used to capture this interplay between the values and instrumental thinking, and also between formal and substantive rationality. A further semi-technical phrase which will be used above all in the later part of the book is that of *interface values*: these regulate, within a given world-view, the boundaries between the different sorts of rationality.

## Example: annulments and dispensations

To give a preliminary idea of how these concepts will be deployed it is useful to begin with the example of two contrasting trends in the history of medieval marriage which can be analysed in terms of the categories just listed. On the one hand, it became increasingly easy from the thirteenth century on to obtain a dispensation to marry within the forbidden degrees of relationship.[73] On the other hand, it became extremely hard to get a marriage annulled, except on the grounds that one of the parties was already married – an exception which proves the rule of indissolubility. At first sight this 'scissors' pattern makes no sense.

To understand it one must realise that behind the two trends are two different ways of reasoning. The increasingly hard line on annulments belongs to the realm of value rationality and is explained by a conviction that a consummated marriage between a baptised couple is absolutely indissoluble. This conviction derived strength from a whole series of

[72] Weber, *Wirtschaft und Gesellschaft*, vol. 1, pp. 12–13, for value and instrumental rationality; *ibid.* vol. 2, p. 396 for formal and substantive rationality. For full discussion, see d'Avray, *Rationalities in History*, 58–64, 67–9. It will be evident that I cannot endorse the judgement of Stephen Lukes (who has, it must be said, himself played a central role in the philosophical and sociological study of Rationality) that 'The use of the word "rational" and its cognates has caused untold confusion and obscurity, especially in the writings of sociological theorists'; he adds that 'I think Max Weber is largely responsible for this. His uses of these terms is irredeemably opaque and shifting' (Lukes, 'Some Problems about Rationality', 207).
[73] For the extensive bibliography on the the forbidden degrees see e.g. Melville and Staub (eds.), *Enzyklopädie des Mittelalters*, vol. 2, pp. 409–10 (note too the discussion of the question by B. Jussen *ibid.*, vol. 1, pp. 163–4); the footnotes of Ubl, *Inzestverbot und Gesetzgebung*; and, for the later period, d'Avray, 'Lay Kinship Solidarity and Papal Law'. On kinship and the later medieval papacy see now L. Schmugge, *Ehen vor Gericht*, e.g. 58–61.

bonds with other elements of the religious system. The principle was an integral part of a coherent whole, thus in its context rational. From the thirteenth century on the Church authorities had the power to make the principle stick, at least far more than ever before. So this was conviction rationality, also known as value rationality.

The increasing willingness to grant dispensations is explained by a developing feeling among the Church's rulers that marriage to cousins and the like was not intrinsically wrong. It was deemed bad on aggregate, admittedly, for a number of reasons, not least because marrying a relative meant losing the chance to forge new links with a different clan. Marriage enlarged charity by creating new social bonds. To marry where a strong social bond of kinship already existed was to waste an opportunity to increase general social harmony. This general but not absolute principle that exogamy was salutary did not, however, pre-empt calculation about individual cases, where there might, for instance, be enmity between different branches of the same extended family or even where the petitioner for a dispensation was an ally to be kept on side. Calculation of this sort is instrumental rationality, also known as Means–Ends rationality.

The distinction has explanatory power, so that fuller causal analysis displaces one-sided explanations. As an example of the latter it is worth quoting an attempt by a team of economists to explain the kinship rules of the medieval Church by the logic of an economic firm, as opposed to 'public interest':

From a public-interest perspective, one would expect the eligibility rules aimed at preventing incest to be absolute, or nearly so. Even in the absence of concrete genetic knowledge or scientific rigor, longtime historical experience should provide reasonable guidelines on how far down the blood line of relatives could safely proceed in marriage. Church regulations, however, followed a seemingly erratic pattern that is difficult to reconcile with absolute guidelines.[74]

For this group of economists, the logic behind the erratic pattern can be reduced to profit-seeking. But that leaves too much out: above all that the rules were an application of a value that was understood to apply to aggregates rather than every case, so that there was room for instrumental reasoning. The interplay of instrumental and value rationality accounts for the apparent inconsistency more completely than does the 'rent seeking' explanation, which it can incorporate where necessary.

[74] Ekelund *et al.*, *Sacred Trust*, 93.

## Instrumental and value rationality

Instrumental rationality is be understood here[75] as the calculation of practical and of logical consequences, whether in the market or the monastery. The economists' research group probably regarded this as 'rationality' *tout court* and doubtless did not even contemplate the possibility of an instrumental rationality of asceticism. Here, on the contrary, the focus will be on limits set to instrumental rationality by value systems. It will also be understood that instrumental reasoning comes into play when the value system allows for more than one option and does not pre-empt the 'right' decision.

Value[76] rationalities are understood here as world-views and systems of conviction, secular and sacred: e.g. Communism, Liberalism, Catholicism, or Hinduism. Examples of individual values might be 'men and women are equal', 'souls are reborn in different bodies', 'there is a God', 'there is no God'. It will be noted that I use the word broadly, to include some 'is' convictions as well as 'ought' convictions. This is because the phenomenology of convictions about, say, the reality or non-existence of human souls is very much like the phenomenology of beliefs in, say, the rightness or wrongness of polygamy. Thus 'conviction' and 'value' will be used interchangeably in this book. As for the indissolubility of marriage, it was a value tied in to the whole religious world-view, based as it was on a much more than allegorical correspondence with the unity of Christ and the Church and within Christ of his divine and human natures.[77]

---

[75] For an interesting analysis by a modern philosopher, see Papineau, 'The Evolution of Means–Ends Reasoning'.

[76] This is not the place for a sociological analysis of 'value', for which see *Rationalities in History*, chs. 2 and 3. For other approaches, from which I have derived stimulus, see Satris, 'The Theory of Value and the Rise of Ethical Emotivism' (for a different perspective see Joas, *The Genesis of Values* – remarkably little overlap). On fact and value see notably Williams, *Morality: An Introduction to Ethics*; Davidson, 'The Objectivity of Values', 49: 'we should expect people who are enlightened *and fully understand one another* to agree on their basic values. An appreciation of what makes for such convergence or agreement also shows that value judgements are true or false in much the way our factual judgments are'; it should be added that Davidson is very optimistic about the possibility of consensus, and also that the argument about 'fact and value' continues: see e.g. Smart, 'Ruth Anna Putnam and the Fact–Value Distinction'. See also the issue of *Revue française de sociologie*, 47/4 (2006) devoted to the sociology of values (with special reference to Europe), and, for an original approach, Graeber, *Toward an Anthropological Theory of Value*. For remarks by Weber which clarify his own idea of value – 'that problem child of our discipline' ('jenes Schmerzenskindes unserer Disciplin') as he called it – 'Die "Objektivität" sozialwissenschaftlicher und sozialpolitischer Erkenntnis', in *Gesammelte Aufsätze zur Wissenschaftslehre*, 209–10, see *ibid.*, 210–12.

[77] d'Avray, *Medieval Marriage: Symbolism and Society, passim.*

People do not readily give up values once they are committed to them, but this study follows Weber in allowing that such convictions can be rational.[78] The reasons that justify them come from other elements of the world-views to which they belong, and the concrete experiences or simulacra of experiences which reinforce them. Thus an orthodox Jew may take a certain view of the State of Israel's boundaries because of his reading of biblical history, reinforced by empathetic awareness of the astonishing survival of his people through centuries of suffering and per-secution, and by experience of the power of the rituals which structure his family life. Concrete experiences and strong mental images give extra force and powers of resistance to value systems. Such experiences are rational arguments, in their way, though of course people with contra-dictory value systems can each feel that their convictions are born out by their personal experiences, as also by the way that observance of rituals or principles make them feel. Per se, there is an element of irrationality in the tendency of people to extrapolate too far from personal experi-ences and the like. On the other hand, a conviction reinforced in this way often does not depend only on experiences or strong mental images. Its coherence with other elements in the person's world view may seem to provide independent verification of the message sent by the strong mental images. Thus coherence provides the skeleton[79] but experiences and the like put flesh on the bones.

Convictions can be highly durable in the face of attack because they form a whole in which each part supports the rest intellectually, so that the antecedent probability of an argument against any one element is diminished by that argument's incongruity with all the other elements that it has not contested and – since it is hard to argue about more than one thing simultaneously – cannot easily confront at the same time. Empirical evidence for a miracle will cut little ice with people in whose world-view such occurrences have no place. For them, an overwhelming anterior probability weighing against what the empirical evidence may

---

[78] For a different view see Gavin Langmuir, who uses the phrase 'nonrational thinking' to mean what Weber calls 'value rational': see above, p. 4 n. 11, Max Weber, *Wirtschaft und Gesellschaft*, vol. 1, p. 12, and Langmuir, *History, Religion and Antisemitism*, 152 n. 18. They are clearly talking about the same thing but Langmuir does not regard it as rational. But on this line of thinking, convictions about, say, the equal rights of men and women must also be denied the designation of rational, as they are not easily demonstrable by simple logic or empirical testing, but, rather, convince us because of their coherence with our general *Weltanschauung*.

[79] Cf. Davidson, 'The Objectivity of Values', 50, and Walker, *The Coherence Theory of Truth*.

seem to demonstrate leaves their world-view unshaken.[80] The interdependence of different elements within value systems tends to give each of the latter a distinctive 'holistic' character. Though any two value systems are likely to have many individual elements in common – the Soviet Union and the USA accepted monogamy and material well-being as values, and Moslems, Jews and Christians share beliefs about Old Testament prophets – they tend to be quite distinctive in their overall 'Gestalt'. This distinctiveness is what anthropologists often mean when they talk of 'cultures' in the plural; which does not mean that all anthropologists deny the possibility of a common instrumental rationality.[81]

In one obvious sense, medieval instrumental rationality per se was the same as that of 'Modernity', in that people could put two and two together in causal calculations of the kind required to get through life. (They also used the same kind of logic, even at an academic level, which is a reason why it is not unusual for scholars trained in modern philosophy to develop an interest in medieval philosophy.) On the other hand, even the instrumental reasoning of the Middle Ages can look strange to modern observers, on account of the value-rational ends, premises and side-constraints which were often the context of these calculations. It should be stressed here, incidentally, that side-constraints (e.g. negative commandments) and premises, as well as 'ends', are values, to prevent the 'value–instrumental' distinction being collapsed into the 'ends–means' antithesis – an intellectual groove into which is easy to slip.[82]

### Formal and substantive rationality

A secondary distinction between formal and substantive (or 'material') rationalities can also be illuminating, especially in the examination of legal systems – defined in the broadest possible sense. This distinction also has a Weberian pedigree,[83] though its use in the present work owes

---

[80] Cf. Israel, *Radical Enlightenment*; Fogelin, *A Defence of Hume on Miracles*, 20, 34; compare the similar powers of resistence to empirical refutation of the the Azande system of poison oracles as studied by Evans-Pritchard when it was still in operation: Evans-Pritchard, *Witchcraft, Oracles and Magic under the Azande*, 141–2.

[81] Obeyesekere, *The Apotheosis of Captain Cook*; he was attacked by Sahlins, in *How 'Natives' Think*. For a good overall sense of the debate see Borofsky, Kane, Obeyesekere and Sahlins, 'CA Forum on Theory in Anthropology'. Cf. d'Avray, *Rationalities in History*, pp. 46–7.

[82] As with Runciman, *A Critique of Max Weber's Philosophy of Social Science*, 14. Conversely, not all ends are values: one can chose an objective by inclination without attaching any special worth to it.

[83] See e.g. Weber, *Wirtschaft und Gesellschaft*, vol. 2, p. 396, cited above at n. 71.

more to a later study.[84] Formal rationality delimits a sector of action or thought and makes rules for it that are protected by a firewall from extraneous considerations, however rational in themselves. Thus American courts disregard evidence, however damning, if it is 'the fruit of the poisoned tree' – say if it would not have been found but for an illegal search which set the investigation in the right direction. Again, the final examinations of a university language department may pay no attention to the disadvantaged pre-university schooling of some candidates.

Unhelpfully – in my view – formal rationality is sometimes treated as an antithesis of value rationality or associated particularly with modernity.[85] Studying the formal rationalities generated by medieval religious values is a good corrective to any such assumption. Canon law and the rules of religious orders, including liturgical regulations, are cases in point. There is nothing specifically medieval about this shaping of formal rationality by values. 'A formal reason usually incorporates or reflects substantive reasoning'[86] and this substantive reasoning can obviously include values.[87] Consistency, the fairness of eliminating uncertainty about what the law actually demands and the uneven application of it are common justifications for formal legality, and these reasons can certainly be held as values.

Substantive rationality is a 'parasite concept' in that it is only really useful in conjunction with 'formal rationality'. (When it is not being used in contradistinction to legal formality or other forms of formal rationality, substantive reasoning as the phrase is used in this book becomes indistinguishable from reasoning *tout court*.) Chairs of Examination Boards in British universities are used to administering rules about suspensions of rules. Thus there may be a rule that if a candidate scores over 70 per cent for a majority of his courses, he will be awarded a First Class Degree (roughly the same as 'Summa cum laude'). If, however, a candidate came down with influenza on the day of the last examination, and scored only 68 per cent instead of the 70 per cent that would have pushed him into the First Class overall, the Chairman or the Exam Board are likely to suspend the normal rule of classification, provided that there is a doctor's note. That is substantive rationality.

---

[84] Atiyah and Summers, *Form and Substance in Anglo-American Law*, 2. For an important older, (rather critical) account of legal formality see Kennedy, 'Legal Formality'.

[85] Kronman, *Max Weber*, 72; Brubaker, *The Limits of Rationality*, 16, 30; Mommsen, *The Age of Bureaucracy*, 21; Boucock, *In the Grip of Freedom*, 6, 65, 183; Breuer, *Bürokratie und Charisma*, 51–6.

[86] Atiyah and Summers, *Form and Substance*, 2.

[87] Atiyah and Summers define a substantive reason as 'a moral, economic, political, institutional, or other social consideration' (*ibid.*, 5).

Since it is necessary to estimate the degree of disadvantage suffered, some judgements may be specific to a given case. If a candidate has an epileptic fit during the exam, the decision to be merciful will be easy. If the candidate is unwell on account of a massive hangover, the decision will equally easily go the other way. On the spectrum of cases in between, judgement will have to be used by the board of examiners. When juries acquit in the face of the evidence and the law, because they think that the result would be unfair, they are giving substantive reasoning the upper hand over legal formality: examples being the acquittal of the Civil Servant Clive Ponting in his trial for revealing illegally that the British Government had been lying; or the habit of French juries of Weber's day of acquitting a man of murder if he had caught his wife and the victim *in flagrante*.[88]

Substantive reasoning may or may not be value rational. It is worth stressing that in the conceptual scheme used here, 'substantive' and 'value' rationality are by no means equated, though they overlap. An authoritative study of formal and substantive rationality in the common law tradition gives the example of a man who breaks a law about driving in a park because he wants to get to a meeting.[89] Values may have nothing to do with his decision to ignore the formal rule. In fact legal formality is often overridden by political considerations or the hope of a return favour, or simply by common sense where no ethical issue is at stake.

The distinctions between value and instrumental rationality, on the one hand, and formal and substantive rationality, on the other, are cross-cutting: one can have instrumental formal rationality, since systems of rules often serve pragmatic purposes; value-driven formal rationality, since formal rules can be saturated with values; substantive value rationality; and even formality as value rationality, in cases where the rule book is elevated to a value in its own right, a not uncommon case with minor bureaucrats. Nonetheless, within this wider matrix of possibilities, a simpler and less static schema is more useful for the present purposes, viz., that *the border between formal and substantive rationality is commonly defined and policed by instrumental reasoning operating within a framework of values*.

It must be emphasised again that this schema is not a theoretical procrustean bed into which data should be forced, or a law of society at

---

[88] Ponting, '*R. v. Ponting*'. Cf. Weber, *Wirtschaft und Gesellschaft*, vol. 2, p. 471, on the refusal of French juries of his day to convict for *crime passionel*.
[89] Atiyah and R. Summers, *Form and Substance*, 8.

least in anything but the weakest sense. This pattern of causal relations is worth looking for, as being common enough in history. Whether it obtains in a given society or situation is a matter of evidence. It is a good example of Weberian ideal-type: a simple schema to bring to the infinite complexity of the past in the hope that corresponding patterns will leap out once one asks the right questions.

### Symbiosis

As indicated at the start of this section, in framing and answering these questions two further concepts will be added to the Weberian quaternary: symbiosis and 'interface values'. The concept of symbiosis is an antidote to a natural tendency to treat the value–instrumental and formal–substantive distinctions as dichotomies. One must distinguish the types of thinking these pairs of concepts represent only to bring out the intimacy of their interactions.

It must be stressed once more: instrumental rationality need not be an alternative to value rationality: it can be an extension and application of it. The passage quoted earlier in which Weber suggested that Indian asceticism was technically probably the rationally most highly developed in world history is one that sociologically minded historians should bear constantly in mind. The rational technique takes its premises and parameters from a religious world-view in which renunciation of the flesh was a key value. Hindu value rationality creates and shapes instrumentally rational techniques of self-mortification. This is just one example of a general pattern.

The medieval Church's later medieval marriage policies once again provide a useful illustration. In the last medieval centuries the value of indissolubility, as an analogue of Christ's union with the Church, was propagated and enforced by technique: propagated by the mass communication system of preaching,[90] and enforced by a professionalised system of Church courts, which paradoxically drew attention to the value even when they granted annulments, since these were mostly on the grounds of a prior clandestine contract.[91] This was reciprocal. Furthermore, the relation between formal and substantive rationality was also symbiotic, as formal rules for suspending formal rules developed. This was the dispensation system: a development within the medieval Church quite distinctive in its self-conscious coherence, and dependent on a certain idea of ecclesiastical authority.

---

[90]  d'Avray, *Medieval Marriage*, ch. 1, 'Mass Communication'.
[91]  *Ibid.*, ch. 2, 'Indissolubility'.

## Interface values

The symbiosis of the aforementioned types of rationality is not a constant from one culture or value system to another. These systems include values that police the border between value and instrumental rationality, and, within the latter, between formal and substantive rationality. Here such values will be called 'interface values'.[92] The concept of 'equity' is a good example of an 'interface value', when it is understood as the right or duty of a court to suspend the formal law when it would do an injustice in a particular case.[93] So far as the medieval period is concerned the history of dispensations is an especially fertile field for investigation of this type of values. To return again to the example of later medieval marriage law (adumbrating points to be made more fully in the final chapter): the interface value was the medieval Church's view that the rules about 'forbidden degrees' would usually but not always increase charity by forcing people to marry outside their own extended families. This left much room for manoeuvre. It was obvious that the consanguinity and affinity rules could defeat their own purpose in cases of conflict between people related within the forbidden degrees, as happened on a grand scale in the late thirteenth-century struggle between the Angevin dynasty of Naples and the house of Aragon. Substantive considerations,

---

[92] One could also speak of 'interface theories', which give an account of the relation between ethical absolutes and pragmatic considerations in the more bloodless setting of academic discussion, without the existential pressure that rests on the answers to such questions when deep convictions and practical experiences or decisions are involved.

[93] The natural starting point for the history of Equity is Aristotle's concept of *epieikeia*, on which see Triantaphyllopoulos, *Das Rechtsdenken der Griechen*,; for an older treatment, see Jones, *The Law and Legal Theory of the Greeks*, ch. 3 on 'Law and Nature'; for more recent work on law in the *polis*, Foxhall and Lewis (eds.), *Greek Law in its Political Setting*; for a debatable but stimulating attempt to set Aristotle's ethical theory in its political and social context, see MacIntyre, *After Virtue*, chs. 11 and 12. The late medieval Court of Chancery developed into a court of Equity in the sense defined above (not to be confused with 'Equity' as a branch of modern common law): see Baker, *An Introduction to English Legal History*, 102–3; cf. Haskett, 'The Medieval Court of Chancery', notably 267–8. For something like Aristotelian *epieikeia* in the common law system of the USA, see Atiyah and Summers, *Form and Substance in Anglo-American Law*, 178–85. Equity is far from being a constant value in legal systems. In theory at least the civil law tradition emphasises certainty and predictability (Merryman, *The Civil Law Tradition*, 49–50 and ch. 8 *passim*), though equity can be built into the law for carefully specified circumstances (p. 52), and in practice the abstract character of the legal rules leaves judges much room for discretion (pp. 52–3.) Again in principle, Islamic jurisprudence is not friendly to anything really resembling this value: J. Makdisi, 'Legal Logic and Equity in Islamic Law'. A modern controversy between Herbert Hart and Ronald Dworkin implicitly assumes that *epieikeia* in an Aristotelian sense is a non-starter: Hart, *The Concept of Law*, 272. For discussion of the role of something quite close to the Western concept of Equity in classical Chinese jurisprudence see Langlois, '"Living Law" in Sung and Yüan Jurisprudence'.

even of a pragmatic kind, such as need to grant favours to friends in a Church-State conflict, could suffice for the formal rules to be overridden by dispensation in individual cases. There is more to such motivations than the simple analytical instruments used by the team of economists can detect, with their assumption that decision-making of all kinds can be analysed as an extension of economic decision-making.[94] The problem with that approach, as with rational choice theory generally – for this seems to be the framework within which they are working – is the elimination of value rationality from the equation.[95]

### Values and methodology

Weber's concept of value, which is the key to a broader view of rationality than the economists' team deploys, had another dimension: it plays a large role in his theory of how historians and social scientists should work: their 'methodology'. In brief, his view was that personal values necessarily affect what the historian or sociologist finds interesting and important, but need not shape the findings of research, if they try hard enough to prevent it from doing so. Weber himself tried hard in later life and to good effect. A reader of his later academic works – as opposed to some of his earlier research oeuvre or to his political and polemical writings and his correspondence – would be hard put to it to guess

---

[94] 'In its expanded form as the "science of choice," economics models the human decision nexus as a kind of economy, regardless of scientific domain. It matters little whether the problem is perceived as inherently economic or as anthropological, psychological, sociological, political, legal, or religious' (Ekelund *et al.*, *Sacred Trust*, 4).

[95] Though a distorting schema when applied on its own, without reference to value-rational constraints, Rational Choice Theory deserves more attention than most historians have given it so far, if only because it has been a massive movement in the Social Sciences. An 'exact phrase' keyword search in the British Library catalogue in January 2009 revealed 234 items – this in a field where articles rather than monographs are probably the dominant mode of publication. For orientation within this mass of scholarship see, for instance, Coleman, *The Foundations of Social Theory*; Favereau, 'The Missing Piece in Rational Choice Theory' (engages with Coleman); Shepsle and Bonchek, *Analyzing Politics* (very clear and lively presentation for undergraduates); Friedman (ed.), *The Rational Choice Controversy*; Rubinstein, *Modeling Bounded Rationality* (part of a movement to bring rational choice theory nearer to real-world decisions without abandoning the framework); Binmore, *Playing for Real* and *Just Playing*; Binmore, *Natural Justice* (trying to synthesise rational choice with evolutionary models and ethics); Stark and Bainbridge, *A Theory of Religion* (application to religion in a geometric spirit); Jerolmack and Porpora, 'Religion, Rationality and Experience'. For criticism and controversy e.g. Bruce, *Choice and Religion*; Green and Shapiro, *Pathologies of Rational Choice Theory*; Friedman (ed.), *The Rational Choice Controversy*; Sen, *Rationality and Freedom*, 26–37; Peter and Schmid (eds.), *Rationality and Commitment*. I explain its main features and some of the objections to it in *Rationalities in History*, ch. 1.

whether he was right wing or left wing, religious or not[96] (though he makes it clear that he holds empirical academic truth to be a value and that he knows it is not a universal one[97]). A topic can seem interesting from a variety of value positions. Leopold von Ranke's Protestantism did not prevent him from being interested in the history of the early modern papacy.

The distinction between value (or conviction) rationality and instrumental rationality can be applied to the methodology of research as well as to the objects of research. Empirical research is instrumentally rational. It is shaped by values, notably by a conviction that truth (though never the whole truth) is attainable, but these values may be shared by scholars of different sides of the major scholarly divides between left and right, religious and agnostic.

The fact that academics must accept the impossibility of refuting all the values and convictions with which they disagree need not mean that intellectual progress is impossible. Within any given academic community, even within the general academic *respublica litterarum* in our own time, there are large areas of overlap between convictions, creating a common arena in which research can progress and win assent from nearly all intellectual workers in the field. In the medieval field, the class analysis of later medieval English rural society by Rodney Hilton[98] has a solid empirical grounding. A rather old-school Marxist, he wisely picked as his field a time and place torn with class antagonism. Marxist categories may not work for history in general but they work well in Hilton's chosen field.

---

[96] Scholars sometimes read into Weber's academic work what they know about him from other sources: an example is Carroll, *Protestant Modernity*, who thinks Weber's sociology has a Protestant 'architecture', or Mommsen, *Max Weber and German Politics, 1890–1920*, who sees a nationalist idealogy as shaping Weber's work. Especially so far as *Wirtschaft und Gesellschaft* is concerned these interpretations seem quite mistaken to me. It was a *felix culpa* on my part that I read a good deal of Weber's oeuvre before knowing much about his life or views. Normally a good guesser of implicit ideologies, I was unable to work out what his own world view was. To a remarkable degree he stuck to his own principle of *Wertfreiheit* in later life, and when writing as a scholar.

[97] 'The objective validity of all empirical scholarship depends, and exclusively so, on belief in an objective reality structured by categories which . . . are inseparable from the assumption of the value of the kind of truth that empirical scholarship alone can give us. If a person attaches no value to this truth – and the belief in the value of scholarly truth is the product of particular cultures and not naturally innate – we have nothing to offer that person with the means that our scholarship puts at our disposal' (passage beginning 'Die objektive Gültigkeit' and ending 'nichts zu bieten') ('Die "Objektivität" sozialwissenschaftlicher und sozialpolitischer Erkenntnis', in *Gesammelte Aufsätze zur Wissenschaftslehre*, 212–13).

[98] E.g. *Bond Men Made Free* and *Class Conflict and the Crisis of Feudalism*.

Again, behind the cacophony of different historiographical voices interpreting Francis of Assisi it is possible to discern a remarkable amount
of consensus. Historiography of St Francis has certainly been a battle-
ground of conflicting values. For one thing, the interpretation of his life
and intentions had implications for how modern Franciscans should live,
so it was not easy for Franciscan scholars to write about their founder in
an entirely value-free way. But the story of St Francis mattered in an 'ide-
ological' way to scholars outside the Order and the Catholic Church, at
least after the publication of the classic biography by Paul Sabatier. This
presented Francis of Assisi as a saint and prophet whose method had
been smothered by the official Church's protection.[99] Naturally Franciscan and Catholic historians generally tended to take a different view.
Furthermore, analogies between the Franciscan Order's history and the
institutionalisation of Christianity itself were surely not far from the
minds of some of the scholars discussing Francis of Assisi around the turn
of the nineteenth and twentieth centuries. The upshot was a maelstrom
of conflicting interpretations. It was therefore reassuring when the great
Italian medievalist Raoul Manselli pointed out that virtually all historians
of Francis of Assisi shared a good deal of common ground: Francis was
the son of a rich merchant, near the border between bourgeois and nobil-
ity; he underwent a conversion in which his values were turned upside
down; he believed he had been inspired by God and that his rule should
be 'according to the form of the holy Gospel'; a small brotherhood gathered around him; he felt a profound devotion to priests, because they
consecrated the Body of Christ; there was widespread disquiet at the way
of life of the clergy of his day which provided a context for his conversion;
Pope Innocent III approved the rule written 'in few words and simply';
Clare of Assisi was inspired by him; he preached to the Sultan Al-Kamil
in Egypt; he underwent physical sufferings; he combined pliability and
inflexibility in his attitude to the rule; and he was dedicated to the poor
and suffering.[100] This non-trivial quantum of consensus offers hope of
writing in such a way as to convince historians with a wide range of
personal values of their own about the content of medieval values.

[99]  Sabatier, *Vie de S. François*, pp. vii–viii.
[100]  Manselli, 'Chi era Francesco d'Assisi?', 354–7.

# 2    Medieval values: structures

## Method

The following account of medieval values or convictions (as defined in the previous chapter[1]) has to be selective if it is not to turn into a *summa* on medieval religion.[2] The method will be to concentrate on a few examples of medieval convictions or values, and to analyse them via specific passages from sources. (The 'methodology' is thus none other than the 'gobbet' commentary technique familiar to university teachers and students of history in the British Isles.) For each of the extracts, thousands of others could have been substituted. This is in fact the point: one can take a source sample which bears on a given theme but which is otherwise selected more or less arbitrarily, and find that it leads out in all directions to other key beliefs within the medieval world-view.

Each of the themes selected fitted into a network of interrelated convictions. The ways in which each of these convictions or values was embodied in strong mental images, whether created by experience or in other ways, should also emerge from these analyses. So with each passage the commentary will aim to bring out the two features of conviction rationality: their interconnectedness in a network, and their concreteness.

## Spiritual 'gift economy'

Belief in what we might call a spiritual 'gift economy' was an underlying religious conviction which could not have been put concisely into words

---

[1] For fuller discussion of the conceptual framework, and comparative analysis of the structure of values and convictions, see d'Avray, *Rationalities in History*, ch. 2.

[2] For a *summa* on medieval religion see Angenendt, *Geschichte der Religiosität im Mittelalter*. The present study does not even attempt properly to explore the conviction rationalities of unorthodox Christian world-views, concentrating for the most part on mainstream official religion, without regarding other kinds as unimportant.

31

in the medieval period itself.[3] The monastic practice of confraternity was a characteristic institution of this spiritual economy, which was not so much a discrete belief as a whole network of related ideas: community of the absent living and dead with the community present, helping the dead, purgatory, charity towards the poor, the mass, the eucharist, the power of prayer, and the Psalm-drenched character of the monastic liturgy. The document translated below is connected with many of them.

To the reverend father and lord in Christ lord Ulrich, abbot,[4] by the grace of God, and to the whole convent of the Benedictine monastery of the blessed Virgin and Saint John the Evangelist in Plankstetten in the diocese of Eichstätt, Johannes, by the grace of God and the apostolic see abbot,[5] Conrad, prior, and the whole convent of the venerable monastery of St Emmeram in Regensburg of the same order, pertaining to the Roman Church with no intermediary, bound together in charity, sends wishes for eternal salvation in the Lord, and, after the course of the present struggle, for attainment of the prize of the heavenly kingdom. For the work of establishing a pure and devout spiritual brotherhood, in respect of which, in graciously granting your love, you have anticipated us, we come forward respectfully to give the thanks that are due, and, since faith has claims on faith, gracious favour brings a corresponding response, and charity calls for love, we give to you in return the same spiritual brotherhood both in life and in death, but also a sharing and communion in everything good that results from our prayers, our vigils and fasts, our alms and our masses, adding furthermore with reverent devotion that, when it should please the Lord of all things to call away any one of your community to the heavenly homeland from the prison of this world, and when we have been informed of death of this man, to whom may the same Lord grant happiness, we will, together with the vigils and the Mass for the Dead which will have taken place,[6] faithfully and reverently maintain the *memoria* of such men,[7] on a day which we can suitably manage, in accordance with the devout and long-established custom of our monastery; in addition to these things each priest should say a mass, those below the rank of priest should keep one vigil of the accustomed kind with the *Placebo*,[8] while *conversi* should say thirty *Pater noster*s, specially fulfilling these obligations for the salvation of the dead man, and one brother's portion of food and drink should be given on that day to the poor. Also, the man's name should be added to our martyrology, and

---

[3] This is a further illustration of the practical reliance of historians on concepts about concepts: analytical terms designed by the historian to elucidate medieval thoughts and draw out the connections between them.

[4] On Abbot Ulrich V. Dürner see Bauer, *Die Benediktinerabtei Plankstetten*, 25–7; on Plankstetten in this period see also Buchner, *Das Bistum Eichstätt*, vol. 2 (1938), 381.

[5] On Abbot Johannes Tegernpeck, see Bischoff, 'Studien zur Geschichte des Klosters St. Emmeram', 133–4.

[6] 'cum' here seems to be a preposition governing 'vigiliis...peractis' rather than a conjunction.

[7] The Latin moves from singular to plural.

[8] *Placebo*: Vespers for the Dead. See Du Cange *et al.*, *Glossarium*.

every year on that same day, with a gracious everlasting commemoration,[9] in the Chapter we will commend him to God through the help of devout prayers. And if the death of several men is communicated to us at the same time, we will do as much for them in the plural as we have determined to do in the singular for one alone.[10] Also, we wish to be bound to each of the things noted above if you too in each and every one of the aforesaid things make every effort to do the same reciprocally for us and our successors. As evidence of each and every one of these things and as a most firm guarantee of them we hand over these letters to you, strengthened by the attachment of our seals. Given and done in Regensburg in our aforesaid monastery, in the year of the Lord, etc., 1474, on Palm Sunday.[11]

[9] More literally: 'with the grace of a perpetual memorial', taking *gratia* as ablative and *memorialis* as genitive of *memoriale* as a neuter substantive – but the phrase is tricky.

[10] It is unclear to me whether in this case each dead monk will get a mass, etc., or whether all who die on the same day be remembered at the same mass, etc.

[11] 'Reverendo in Christo patri ac domino domino Ulrico dei gratia abbati totique conventui monasterii beate virginis ac sancti Iohannis /1// ewangeliste in Plancksteten ordinis sancti Benedicti Eystetensis dyocesis, Iohannes dei et apostolice sedis gratia abbas, Conradus /2// prior, totusque conventus venerabilis monasterii sancti Emmerami Ratisponensis dicti ordinis ad Romanam ecclesiam nullo medio /3// pertinentis cum caritatis nexu salutem in Domino sempiternam, et post presentis cursum certaminis regni celestis bravium suscipere. /4// Pro labore super sincere ac devote fraternitatis contractione, qua nos in favore vestre dilectionis prevenistis, vobis reverenter /5// assurgimus ad gratiarum actiones debitas [actiones debitas *corr. from* debitas actiones] et, quia fides fidem advocat, gratia gratiam conciliat, et amorem karitas interpellat, /6// vobis viceversa confraternitatem damus in vita pariter et in morte, se*d* et participationem ac communionem omnium bonorum /7// que aput nos fiunt in orationibus, in vigiliis et ieiuniis, in elemosinis et in missis, adicientes insuper pietate /8// devota, ut cum Domino universorum placuerit que*m*piam de vestris ex huius ergastulo seculi evocare ad patriam, obitusque /9// ipsius aput nos insinuatus fuerit, quem idem Dominus felicem faciat, cum vigiliis ac defunctorum missa peractis, iuxta /10// piam et usitatam nostri monasterii consuetudinem, die nobis convenienti, talium memoriam fideliter et devote peragemus, /11// insuper quilibet sacerdos unam missam, sub sacerdotio constituti unam vigiliam consuetam cum *Placebo*, conversi autem triginta /12// *Pater* specialiter persolvere debent pro defuncti salute, ac prebenda unius fratris illa die pauperibus erogari. Nomen etiam /13// ipsius nostro martyrilogio anotabitur et singulis annis iugis memorialis gratia eodem die in capitulo per devotarum orationum /14// suffragia deo habebimus recommendatum. Et si obitus plurimorum uno tempore nobis intimatus fuerit, tantum faciemus /15// pro eis in plurali quantum pro uno solo facere decrevimus in singulari. Astringi quoque volumus ad singula prenotata /16// si et vos in omnibus et singulis premissis parem nobis et nostris successoribus vicissitudinem reddere studueritis adimplere. /17// In quorum omnium et singulorum evidentiam ac robur firmissimum has presentes litteras vobis tradimus, sigillorum nostrorum /18// appensione communitas. Data et acta sunt hec Ratispone in prefato nostro [nostra *could be* read] monasterio, anno Domini etc. lxxiiii^to /19// dominica Palmarum./20//' (Clm. 14194, fol. 224^r [II], bound into the book). The scholarly modern catalogue describes the document thus: '(224^r) Ehemaliger Hinterspiegel, 2 zusammengeklebte Briefe, 1:...2.: Brief von Abt JOHANNES II. TEGERNPECK (1471–1493) und Prior CONRADUS von St. Emmeran an Abt Ulrich V. Dürner (1461–1494) von St. Maria und Johannes in Plankstetten vom Palmsonntag (3. April) 1474 betr. Erweiterung der Gebetsverbrüderung auf gegenseitige Aufnahme von verstorbenen Konventualen in die eigene Totenliste etc.' (Neske, *Katalog der lateinischen Handschriften*, vol. 2, p. 143).

This is just one of a series of such agreements made by the Abbot of St Emmeram around this time.[12] It was an old tradition at St Emmeram: to get an idea of what was meant by 'the man's name should be added to our martyrology' one can look at the facsimile of an eleventh-century martyrology, with necrology, i.e. with the names of dead monks, at the end of the scholarly modern edition.[13]

Martyrologies and necrologies are related. Martyrologies are organised according to the calendar, so once a name had been written beside the martyrology entry for that day it would be there as a reminder every year on that date. The saintly dead, remembered in martyrologies, were not so sharply separated originally from the other good dead, remembered in necrologies. Necrologies are part of the general phenomenon known to scholarship as *Memoria*, the liturgical making present of the absent dead and also the absent living.[14] Here it is only the dead who are in question.

---

[12] Bischoff, 'Studien . . . St. Emmeram im Spätmittelalter', 134: 'Between 1474 and 1493 confraternities with eighteen Benedictine monasteries were established or renewed with St Emmeram. Even the Provincial of the upper-German Franciscan province, Fr. Heinrich, accepted confederation with Sankt Emmeram' ('Zwischen 1474 und 1493 wurden mit 18 Benediktinerklöstern Verbrüderungen geschlossen oder erneuert. Auch der Provinzial der oberdeutschen Franziskanerprovinz, Fr. Heinrich, nahm die Konföderation mit St. Emmeram auf'); cf. Braunmüller, 'Conföderationsbriefe des Klosters St. Emmeram in Regensburg'. (The agreement edited here is mentioned briefly, p. 117: '32. 1474, 18. V, A. Ulrich in Planngksteten, Eist. Dioec.' Braunmüller's article was based on Clm. 14892. As he says, this MS 'was far from uniform in its contents, and was written between 1514 and 1519 by the then Prior and Librarian of St Emmeram, the learned and zealous Fr. Dionysius Menger (†1530), apparently for the purpose of providing the then Prior and Novice Master of that Abbey with a handbook for his office' ('hat einen gar mannigfachen Inhalt und wurde zwischen 1514 und 1519 von dem damaligen Prior und Bibliothekar zu St. Emmeram, dem gelehrten und eifrigen P. Dionys Menger (†1530), zu dem augenscheinlichen Zwecke geschrieben, dem jeweiligen Prior und Novizenmeister jenes Klosters als Handbuch für sein Officium zu dienen') (*ibid.*, 114). In the manuscript, fols. 110ᵛ–111ʳ (newer foliation), there is a copy of what looks like the corresponding letter of the Abbot of Plankstetten to the Abbot of St Emmeram about the same brotherhood of prayer. On the tradition of 'Gebetsverbrüderungen' in Plankstetten see Bauer, *Die Benediktinerabtei Plankstetten*, 19–20.

[13] Freise, Geuenich and Wollasch, *Das Martyrolog-Necrolog von St. Emmeram zu Regensburg*.

[14] For a seminal essay drawing together the results of much previous collective research and shaping them with some powerful insights see Oexle, 'Memoria und Memorialüberlieferung im früheren Mittelalter'; see also his article on 'Memoria, Memorialüberlieferung'. *Memoria* research continues, notably in the Berlin team under Michael Borgolte, in the context of a study of foundations. See for instance Lusiardi, 'Stiftung und Seelenheil'. More general bibliography on remembering the dead is too large to be given systematically. Note for instance Swanson, *Church and Society in Late Medieval England*, 296–9; Swanson, *Religion and Devotion in Europe*, 296–9; Jamroziak and Burton (eds.), *Religious and Laity in Western Europe*, notably Jamroziak, 'How Rievaulx Abbey Remembered its Benefactors'; Bijsterveld, 'Looking for Common Ground'; and J. G. Clark, 'Monastic Confraternity in Medieval England'.

What we have here is gift exchange – of spiritual goods (prayers and masses). The whole point of the gift exchange concept, rightly popular among historians, is that it is different from commerce, which tends to be impersonal *per se*. The exchange of spiritual gifts establishes community between the two monasteries of Plankstetten and St Emmeram.

It is not just a two-way agreement. Both help each other's dead by feeding the poor: a monk's ration. The association of feeding the poor with commemoration of the dead is standard.[15] The implications of this help to third parties are considerable: behind the idea is a wider notion of community, that of the Church as a whole, in which spiritual gift exchange is not simply bilateral, and charity helps not only the recipient but the other whom one originally wanted to commemorate.

Monks in the fifteenth century must have thought that purgatory was likely to face them when they died before they went to heaven, even if the document speaks at the beginning as if the dead monks go straight to their 'homeland'. This would probably be understood as optimism that they would be all right in the end, without an assumption that dead monks would all be saints who would go directly to heaven. They must have believed that the masses, prayers and charity to the poor would smooth the path to the heavenly homeland.

These sorts of agreements, though, go back before the great clarification and concretisation of ideas about purification which Jacques Le Goff emphasised,[16] and have their roots in the conviction that it was possible to establish a community of the living and the dead. Commemorations of the dead are not just an instrumental means of securing their release from purgatory: they are almost an end in themselves because they maintain community between the dead monks as well as the two monasteries. The feeding of the poor in connection with commemoration also goes back before the twelfth-century developments of ideas about purgatory, and probably has more to do with community.

*Memoria* is the creation of community by making the absent present in a non-physical way. In medieval Catholicism the idea of presence through liturgy was strongly developed, above all in the belief that the mass made Christ's sacrifice truly present, and enabled one really to receive his body and blood. The liturgy of the mass brought the living closer to the centre of the Church, including its members who had died.

---

[15] For some astonishing data see Dixon-Smith, 'Feeding the Poor to Commemorate the Dead'.

[16] Le Goff, *Naissance du Purgatoire*. Le Goff was too honest a scholar to deny the precedents for purgatory, but these antecedents do not seem to be central in early medieval *Memoria*.

The reference to the martyrology reminds us of the connection between the saints and the other dead. In early medieval *memoria*, the distinction between the ordinary dead and saints is not very sharp: the point is union with the dead, making them present, rather than a distinction between the suffering dead in purgatory and the saintly dead. The habit of writing the names of dead monks in the martyrology, beside the saints of the day, may have kept that habit of thought alive. It would certainly have created mental associations between dead monks and dead saints.

Different kinds of monks help with *memoria* in different ways: and thus the text reminds us that this community was highly structured, 'high grid' in Mary Douglas's terms,[17] and that this structuring was itself a part of the system of convictions. Only priests can say mass. At the other end of the scale are the *conversi*, the lay brothers, whose contribution to *memoria* is to say the Lord's Prayer a number of times. Between the two are the monks 'below the priesthood'. Presumably these are literate choir monks who were deacons, subdeacons, or in minor orders. They are committed to chanting the Vespers of the Dead, known by the opening word *Placebo*.

The Vespers of the Dead, like most of the monastic office, is dominated by the Psalms. This reminds us how far medieval religious values were permeated by Old Testament spirituality, the emotions of the Psalms. The spirituality of the Psalms is one more element in the set of convictions connected with commemoration, and ultimately with the whole system of medieval religious rationality, in its orthodox form. These convictions interlocked, as further examples illustrate.

### Miracles in a network of ideas

It was an age when the possibility of providing spiritual help at a distance through prayer, liturgy and charity was taken for granted, and embodied in foundations. Thus the supernatural order was accepted by the elite just as in 'popular religion'.[18] Even during the 'scientific revolution' which followed on the discovery of new works of Aristotle, whose system left no place for miracles (on this more in Chapter 3), the social and intellectual milieu gave support to the intellectual pioneers who set out to integrate Aristotle with a Christian scheme which included miracles. In the age of Aquinas the question of miracles would not be segregated from ideas about the Incarnation and redemption, and about the insertion of the supernatural into the natural order. In this intellectual context the

---

[17] Douglas, *Natural Symbols*, index s.v. 'grid', and especially clearly in *A Feeling for Hierarchy*, *passim*.
[18] Cf. above, Ch. 1, p. 15.

miraculous made sense. Awareness of the new critical approach to miracles in canonisation processes would put them in the realm of empirical experience and rationality.

A comparison between Aquinas and Hume shows how their different views of the matter are each rational within a wider structure of thought. Juxtaposition of their respective views illuminates both. Hume tacitly chose a 'divide and rule' approach to belief in miracles. He asks in separate contexts and separate writings whether there is a God interested in the affairs of men,[19] and whether miracles are credible.[20] This segregation was psychological as well as logical. Naturally enough, at the psychological level Aquinas considered all the issues simultaneously, even though his thoughts were laid out sequentially. On the logical level, equally unsurprisingly, he does not adopt Hume's 'divide and rule' approach: that is, his exploration of the idea of God at least allows for the possibility of miracles, and his explanation of miracles allows for the possibility of a God interested in the human race. Furthermore the experiences (with concomitant mental images) of Aquinas and Hume gave power and tenacity to their respective attitudes to miracles.

To focus discussion one may start with a passage from the *Compendium theologiae* of Aquinas.[21] This work differs from his famous *Summae* in that it does not progress by posing and solving problems, but sticks to simple exposition. It was unfinished but there are still scores of surviving manuscripts of the part from which the sections quoted come.[22]

*Chapter 136. That it is fitting that God alone performs miracles*

Since the whole order of secondary causes and their power comes from God, and he does not produce their effects through necessity, but by free will . . . it is evident that he can act outside the order of secondary causes, as by healing those who cannot be healed by the working of nature, or by doing certain things of this kind which are not in accordance with the order of natural causes: they are, however, in accordance with the order of divine providence, because the very fact that sometimes something should be done by God outside the order of natural causes is part of God's plan for the sake of some purpose. But when certain things of this kind are done by God outside the order of secondary causes, such deeds are called miracles, because it is a matter for wonder when an effect is seen but the cause is unknown. Since, therefore, God is a cause which for us is unknown, without qualification, when something is done by him outside the order of secondary

---

[19] Hume, *An Enquiry Concerning Human Understanding*, section 11, para. 27, ed. Beauchamp, pp. 109–10.

[20] Clear summary in Fogelin, *A Defence of Hume on Miracles*. Cf. d'Avray, *Rationalities in History*, 13, 24, 27, 83–9.

[21] Thomas Aquinas, *Compendium theologiae*. For a general study, see Pouliot, *La Doctrine du miracle chez Thomas d'Aquin*.

[22] Thomas Aquinas, *Compendium*, 8.

causes known to us they are called miracles without qualification; if, however, something is done by some other hidden cause to this or that, it is not a miracle without qualification, but in respect of the one who does not know the cause; so it happens that something appears to be a wonder to one person when it is not wonderful to another person who knows the cause of it.

Thus, however, to operate outside the order of secondary causes belongs only to God, who instituted this order and is not bound by it, whereas all other things are subject to this order; therefore it is for God alone to work miracles . . . Therefore when miracles seem to be done by some created being, either they are not true miracles, because they are worked by certain powers of natural things, even though those powers are unknown to us, as with the miracles of demons which are worked by magic arts; or, if they are true miracles, they are obtained as result of someone's petition to God, namely that he should make such things happen. Therefore since such miracles are only done by God, they can be fittingly taken up as an argument for faith which relies on God alone; for that something uttered by man is said with divine authority is never more fittingly shown than through the works that God alone can do.

Such miracles, although they are worked outside the order of secondary causes, should not be described without qualification as against nature, for the natural order itself has the characteristic that lower things are subject to higher things. Therefore the things which in lower bodies derive from the impression of heavenly bodies are not said without qualification to be against nature; although it may sometimes be against the particular nature of this or that thing, as is clear from the movement of water when the tides come in and out, which is an effect of the moon's action. Thus consequently even those things which happen by God's agency among creatures, although they may seem to be against a particular order of secondary causes, it is [sic][23] nevertheless in accordance with the universal order of nature; therefore miracles are not contrary to nature.[24]

The secondary causes are what we would call natural laws. Aquinas believes that only God, who instituted them, can suspend them. To indicate when humans speak with divine authority may be a reason for doing so.

The same train of thought is presented in a more academic form in the *Summa theologiae* (or *theologica*). The constant conjunctions observed in nature would not have appeared to Aquinas as evidence contrary to the evidence for a miracle; indeed his concept of miracle presupposed a regular causal order such as natural observation reveals. He was far from thinking that the workings of nature were micro-managed by divine interventions. The model of the universe in the mind of Thomas Aquinas is not unlike that of the Enlightenment thinkers – certainly the similarity is much greater than is often realised by specialists in Renaissance and

---

[23] The change of syntax from plural to singular is in the Latin.
[24] *Ibid.*, 1.136, *Sancti Thomae . . . Opera*, vol. 42, p. 133.

Enlightenment history. Aquinas assumed it was governed by an order of causes and effects, ultimately underpinned by God but not in an interventionist way.[25] God could, however, suspend this order for some special reason.[26] Hume does not worry about this possibility and we need to ask why.

Since both Hume and Aquinas were off the normal scale of intelligence it is unlikely that either had failed to see a logically obvious point. This makes the problem more interesting for the sociologically minded historian since it means that the answer is more likely to lie in more general features of the respective intellectual climates in which they were writing.

Hume's debate with Christianity was conducted in his mind rather like a knock-out competition. The hypothesis of a God interested in the fate of humans is eliminated early on in the logical sequence, before the debate about miracles even begins. For Aquinas and his contemporaries it was different. The various intellectual positions were more like pieces of a puzzle. All the parts of the problem remained on the table until they could be fitted together. The medieval scholastic approach piled syllogism on syllogism but ultimately it was a *Gestalt*, so to speak, a system held before the mind as a whole rather than a successive sequence of parts. The intellectuals' task was to find how they fitted together. To change the metaphor, they set about their task like someone trying to construe a long and complex sentence in a syntactic language: the essence of the exercise being to hold all the parts in the head together in

---

[25] Cf. Thomas Aquinas, *Summa theologiae, Prima Pars*, 1.105.5, in *Opera omnia*, vol. 5 (Rome, 1889), p. 475: 'Respondeo...' section, rejecting the idea that God made everything happen directly because, among other reasons, 'in this way the order of cause and effect would be taken away from created things' ('sic subtraheretur ordo causae et causati a rebus creatis'). Aquinas's notion of natural causation arguably has more in common with the one often found among practising scientists (in and since the Enlightenment) than Hume's 'constant conjunction' theory. For Hume, a law is 'A is always followed by B' rather than 'A causes B'.

[26] Cf. *Summa theologiae*, 1.105.6, especially 'ad 3': 'The reply is that God imparted a certain order to things in such a way as nonetheless to reserve to himself what he would do in a different way at some points in the future, for a reason. So when he acts outside this order, it is not changed' ('dicendum quod Deus sic rebus certum ordinem indidit, ut tamen sibi reservaret quid ipse aliquando aliter ex causa esset facturus. Unde cum praeter hunc ordinem agit, non mutatur'). Aquinas seems to imply that observation of natural causation is an appropriate means to a certain knowledge of God but that for a supernatural knowledge of God observation of miracles is an appropriate means: see *ibid.*, 2.2.178.1, Respondeo section, in *Opera omnia*, vol. 10 (Rome, 1899), p. 417: 'And this is a rational process. For it is natural for man to understand intelligible truth through effects perceived by the senses. And just as man, guided by natural reason, can come to a degree of knowledge of God through the natural effects God produces, so too, through certain supernatural effects, which are called miracles, man is led to a degree of knowledge of the things which he needs to believe' (passage beginning 'Et hoc rationabiliter. Naturale' and ending 'homo adducitur').

such a way that their relation to each other is transparent. If the approach to religion in the Enlightenment was essentially sequential, the medieval scholastic scheme, in a sense, was simultaneous.

Aquinas and medieval intellectuals generally could hardly eliminate in advance any thoughts about God's *modus operandi*, nor would it have been rational for them to do so. The Incarnation and all that leads to and from it would be vivid to them all the time, kept before the mind by prayer and liturgy. Some (like Aquinas) were good enough logicians to avoid assuming what they had not yet philosophically proved. They did not assume Christ's Incarnation and redemption to prove miracles and use miracles to prove Christ's incarnation and redemption. To say that their approach was holistic is not to say it was circular. It is simply to say they did not and could not exclude from their reasoning the Incarnation and redemption, at least as vivid hypotheses. Since these thoughts were before their mind they could not but affect the attempt to make sense of miracles. One could say that these salvation history hypotheses made a difference to the antecedent possibility of miracles.

To summarise: it may be possible to pin down with some precision why Aquinas and Hume differed about miracles – to go beyond the truism that one was religious and the other was not. They ordered their reasoning in different ways. Hume took problems separately and successively. His analysis of evidence for miracles excluded consideration of hypotheses about divine intentions on the grounds that even if there was such a thing as God its thought processes would be unguessable. Human analogies would be meaningless or misleading. So miracles get knocked out as a viable hypothesis before he gets to Christian ideas of God and redemption. Psychologically speaking it was natural for Aquinas to take the problem of miracles and of theodicy simultaneously: with the latter in mind he had a hypothesis at hand to explain why a normally inviolable law of nature might be suspended for a special purpose. This is a special case of a common occurrence with systems of values and convictions: answers to potential objections to one element of the system are forthcoming from other elements of the system.

Hume's approach to miracles is the photo-negative of this. In his publications he operates an implicit exclusion principle which keeps the question of whether there is a personal God and the question of miracles separate; discussion of the history of redemption does not enter either. This exclusion principle means that antecedent probabilities are stacked against the individual positions.[27] When Aquinas holds the question of miracles and the idea of a God redeeming the human race in the course

27 See d'Avray, *Rationalities in History*, pp. 86–8.

of history together before the mind, the two lines of thought complement one another and the objections to each individually cancel out. The difference in systems has much to do with different approaches to logical sequence. Each, though, in their different ways illustrates the holistic character of value rationalities and their strength against outside attack.

### Miracles and concrete thought

So far the argument has focused on the relationship of Aquinas's thinking on miracles to a network of ideas which left the possibility of them open, whereas Hume for practical purposes excluded the possibility. The holistic scheme into which miracles fitted in the age of Aquinas included not only abstract concepts but also vivid concrete representations, emotions and the experience of a whole form of life. Thoughts about the Incarnation and redemption permeated the emotional and social fabric of their lives. Men like Aquinas approached the problem of miracles with a hypothesis to make them plausible already vividly in mind. His whole form of life was built around familiarity with the history of God's progressive interventions in history, an order of grace and salvation superimposed on the order of nature. This was more than a theory. It was a way of life, embodied in the structuring of time through the liturgy and in the central ritual of the mass. The liturgy again and again represented God's instruction of the people of Israel, then the nascent Church, with supernatural revelations and healing miracles. The beliefs around the mass ran directly against natural common sense. The liturgy was a central recurrent experience in the life of Aquinas and his contemporaries. If Aquinas was the author of the powerfully emotional Office of Corpus Christi attributed to him[28] the point is reinforced, but it hardly needs to be. For Aquinas and his contemporaries, the idea that God might send

---

[28]  The tradition that Aquinas composed the Office of Corpus Christi may have something in it. In a remarkable article, L.-J. Bataillon drew attention to parallels in the choice of citations between the office and a sermon of Aquinas and commented that 'besides, it is not surprising that Thomas should have known a liturgy composed at Orvieto, considering that he spent time there, but one can no doubt go further and consider that these correspondences are in harmony with the tradition, however shakily attested, that attributes the Office to St Thomas; I would not be disinclined to suppose that he took some part in it, notably in the selection – which is a very remarkable one incidentally – of biblical passages for the responsories' ('il n'est d'ailleurs pas étonnant que Thomas ait connu une liturgie composée à Orvieto alors qu'il y séjournait, mais on peut sans doute aller plus loin et penser que ces correspondances vont dans le sens de la tradition, si mal attestée qu'elle soit, qui attribue l'Office à S. Thomas; je serais assez enclin à supposer qu'il aura pris une certaine part, notamment dans le choix, très remarquable d'ailleurs, des passages bibliques utilisés dans les répons') ('Un sermon de S. Thomas d'Aquin', 454).

a message through a miracle was not a far-fetched idea. For them, the antecedent probability that there would be miracles from time to time rested not just on the plausibility of the testimony but on a whole view of the world which was a way of life that they lived; a set of practices and experiences the context of which made such occasional divine interventions not just possible but likely: not normal or frequent (leaving aside the sacramentally miraculous), but to be expected, even, at special rare moments in the life of the Church, when the context was right – say when God wanted to draw attention to the sanctity of some individual.

The history of medieval attitudes to miracles is quite closely bound up with the next on our inevitably selective and so rather arbitrary list of medieval convictions: belief in the papacy. In the last medieval centuries official recognition as a saint depended on the successful outcome of a papal canonisation process, and that involved critical scrutiny of alleged miracles. The papacy now demanded detailed depositions from witnesses, then a critical scrutiny of them. Relatively few candidates emerged as saints from this process, which is a remarkable example of papal interaction with popular piety in the later Middle Ages. Popes could not prevent popular 'canonisation', notably of people who suffered violent deaths, deemed undeserved, whether or not their lives had been unusually virtuous.[29] Still, such cults were strictly unofficial. So far as papally recognised saints were concerned the criteria for verification of miracles were stiff.[30] They were signs confirming other evidence of the saint's virtuous life.[31] There is an elective affinity between this policy and the attitude to miracles found in Thomas Aquinas, for whom they are by definition exceptions, interventions by God to make a point.

## Papacy

Canonisation procedure ties miracles in with the papacy. Other interconnections could be illustrated by innumerable texts. Again the point is that one can fan out from almost randomly chosen texts to a wide variety of points on the map of medieval religious belief. A passage is selected here from a sort of register of privileges granted by the Pope to the Observant branch of the Dominican Order in the mid-fifteenth century. It illustrates the connection between the papacy and other structures of the medieval Church: the distinction between religious and secular clergy,

[29]  Vauchez, *La Sainteté en Occident*, 174–83.
[30]  See Goodich, 'Reason or Revelation?', 184–8. See now Goodich, *Miracles and Wonders*. For fuller discussion see below, Ch. 3, pp. 77–80.
[31]  Vauchez, *La Sainteté*, 583.

and the hierarchy within the latter; excommunication; belief in the cor-
porate unity of the Church; and indulgences. The passage also draws
attention to the way the conflict between the papacy and the Council of
Basel reinforced the former by making belief in papal office a practical
conscious choice. Many of the other beliefs selected for special attention
are bound up with the papacy in one way or another.

The passage is in a Munich manuscript (Clm. 28673) whose potential
to interest historians will be apparent to readers of the recently produced
scholarly catalogue.[32] To judge by the way in which the first special privilege is introduced, these were oral grants.[33] The Observant Dominicans
were a reformed branch of the order.[34] As these passages show, they for
their part supported the Pope in his conflict with the Council of Basel.
A legacy of the Great Schism, in which two and then three claimants to
the papal office had divided the Western Church for a generation, was
'Conciliarism'. One solution proposed to the problem of the schism had
been that general councils should run the Church. The revived papacy
resisted the idea but found after calling a council that it had spun out of
control: so there was a new schism, though this time it was a case of a
council against a pope rather than a conflict between two claimants to
the papal throne (eventually the council did appoint its own pope).

The passage took for granted certain basic convictions. To understand
these extracts one needs to know how popes dealt with the internal and
external relations of religious orders, how confession was fitted into the
structures of church government, how excommunication worked, and
how schism had cemented papal authority.

I brother Antony of San Germano of Vercelli, Vicar General, etc., as above,
obtained in 1440 [i.e. 1441[35]] on the... [*a space is left blank*] of January towards
the end,[36] from our lord pope Eugenius the following, which I wrote down thus.
First, our lord pope granted to all our friars who are or will be confessors in the

---

[32] Neske, *Katalog der lateinischen Handschriften... Clm 28615a–28786*, 107–11.

[33] 'Let everyone who reads this list note that our lord Pope Eugenius IV, at the request
of Brother Leonard of Rome, granted orally...' ('Notum sit omnibus hanc cedulam
legentibus quod dominus noster Eugenius papa quartus, supplicante fratre Leonardo de
Roma, concessit vive vocis oraculo...'] (MS Munich, Staatsbibliothek, Clm. 28673, fol.
106ʳ; 4ᵘˢ *is written in the margin beside* quartus); Cf. Neske, *Katalog... 28615a–28786*,
110.

[34] Cf. Walz, *Compendium historiae Ordinis Praedicatorum*, 65–75. The history of Dominican
Observants seems to need more research, but see now Beebe, 'Felix Fabri and his
Audiences'.

[35] Assuming that the start of the year was being reckoned as the feast of the Annunciation,
25 March, *after* Christmas; see Cheney and Jones, *A Handbook of Dates for Students of
British History*, 12–13.

[36] This could mean 'towards the end of the day', or it could mean that there was uncertainty
about the date but that it was near the end of the month.

convents under our authority [*regulatis*], the grace that they may absolve people whose confessions they hear from all cases reserved to the bishop, throughout these two provinces, namely those of St Dominic and of Lombardy, for as long as the Schism shall last. I mean also the cases retained by the same bishops and their vicars. Secondly, that in places where there is schism and where it will be, the man who is or will be at that time the Vicar of the reformed convents, and, in his absence, all those in charge of the convents now and in the future, may, with the authority aforesaid, choose at their own discretion brothers to hear confessions. This is saying[37] that often the bishops of those provinces[38] are schismatic; therefore, since they are excommunicated, our brothers cannot legally be presented to them [for approval]. Thirdly, that all such confessors may absolve all schismatics, past, present or future, whether they are clerics, or in a religious order, or seculars,[39] from any excommunication which has fallen on them by reason of the schism or because they have adhered, or adhere, or in the future adhere to the devil's council of Basel, acting against the sentence of our lord pope.[40]

---

[37] An interpretative translation of 'In hoc dicitur'.

[38] 'provinces': 'illarum' might also conceivably mean 'dioceses'; or be a scribal error for 'illorum' – but that would be the *facilior lectio*.

[39] In this context, 'seculars' would seem to mean 'laypeople', rather than members of the secular clergy.

[40] 'Ego frater Antonius de sancto Germano Vercellensis, vicarius generalis etc., ut supra, obtinui 1440 die [*space follows*] Ianuarii circa finem a domino nostro papa Eugenio infrascripta que sic scripsi. Primo dominus noster papa gratiam concedit omnibus fratribus confessoribus nostris qui sunt et erunt in conventibus nostris regulatis quod possint absolvere sibi confitentes ab omnibus casibus episcopalibus ubicumque in his duabus provinciis, scilicet beati Dominici et Lombardie, quousque schisma durabit. Intendo etiam de retentis per eosdem episcopos et eorum vicarios. Secundo quod in locis ubi est et erit scisma vicarius conventuum reformatorum qui est vel erit pro tempore, et presidentes quicumque conventuum in absentia sua, presentes et futuri, possint ad audientiam confessionum elligere [*sic*] fratres prout eis melius videbitur cum auctoritate prefata. In hoc dicitur quod sepe episcopi illarum et eorum vicarii scismatici sunt, ideo secundum iura fratres nostri eis presentari non possunt [pn't], cum sint excommunicati. Tertio quod omnes tales confessores possint absolvere omnes scismaticos tam clericos quam religiosos et seculares, qui fuerunt vel sunt vel erunt schismatici ab omni excommunicatione ratione scismatis acquisita seu quia diaboli concilio Basilee adheserunt vel adherent vel adherebunt, contrafacientes sententie domini nostri pape' (Clm. 28673, fol. 106$^v$). The passage continues: 'Again, that all who may have fallen into a state of irregularity [a technical term meaning something forbidden for a cleric without necessarily being sinful] by reason of such excommunications, by conducting services in the aforesaid [places], or doing other things through which someone is made irregular, may receive dispensations for these things from the said friars, so long as they now wish to adhere to our lord Pope. Thus too they may be absolved from the aforesaid excommunications so long as they wish to adhere to our lord Pope and not to contravene any further. Fourthly that our brothers in places which are in schism can administer the sacrament of the eucharist to all penitents without distinction in our churches, and even to the sick who are housebound in the houses and places where they are sick: namely by celebrating mass in such houses, not carrying the sacrament throught the streets' ('Item quod omnes qui ratione talium excommunicationum laqueum irregularitatis incurrissent [*sic*] celebrando in predictis vel alia faciendo per que efficitur quis irregularis, possint a predictis fratribus dispensari in eisdem, dummodo amodo velint domino nostro pape

The passage presupposes two types of institution, each embodying fundamental values of the Western Church. On the one hand there was the 'secular' clergy, above all bishops and priests. Christ had created this status group, so it was believed. According to the standard theological textbook of the later Middle Ages priests were successors of the seventy-two disciples mentioned in Luke 6:13; the 'greater pontiffs', i.e. the bishops, were successors of the apostles; and the Pope was the successor of St Peter.[41] On the other hand, there were 'the regulars', members of religious orders like the Dominican Order, who also saw themselves as continuing the work of the apostles.[42] So in both cases we have a theological conviction bound up with the central doctrines of the religion and embodied in institutions and ways of life: the kind of combination that our ideal-type of values and convictions tries to capture.

Also embodied in practice was the assumption and conviction that the papacy regulated relations between these two kinds of religious elite. The extract takes for granted a system by which Franciscan and Dominican superiors put forward to the bishop friars deemed suitable to hear confessions, a pastoral function which came under episcopal oversight. The rules governing the licensing of confessors had been laid down by the papacy: to simplify a little, the Dominican and Franciscan superiors would propose appropriate friars from cities or dioceses where their orders had communities, in such a way as to make it clear that they were asking for a privilege, though it was one that the bishop could not deny: he could reject particular candidates but if he tried to turn down all proposals papal authority overrode his.[43] Such regulation was typical of the ways in which the idea of papal authority was embodied in the practices of the later medieval Church.

The passage deals with absolution from excommunication. Another passage from the same manuscript reminds us not to assume that everyone was blasé about excommunication by the fifteenth century. It shows that people with an anxious and scrupulous disposition were worried

---

adherere. Sic et ab excommunicationibus supradictis absolvi possint dum velint domino nostro pape adherere et ultra non contravenire. Quarto quod fratres nostri in locis scismaticis possint indifferenter omnibus penitentibus sacramentum Eukaristie in ecclesiis nostris conferre, etiam infirmis, domum exire non valentibus, in domis et locis ubi infirmantur: scilicet in domibus talium celebrando, non portando sacramentum per vias' (*ibid.*). This set of privileges is among a number of such interesting lists in Clm. 28673.

[41] Peter Lombard, *Sententiae*, Lib. 4. Dist. 24. cap. 11, in *Magistri Petri Lombardi... Sententiae*, vol. 2, p. 404.

[42] d'Avray, *The Preaching of the Friars*, 43–54.

[43] See *Corpus iuris canonici, Clement.* 3.7.2 and *Extravagantes communes* 3.6.2; Friedberg, *Corpus*, vol. 2, pp. 1161–4 and 1273); the relevant decree was passed by Boniface VIII, revoked by his successor Benedict XI, and reinstated by Clement V. See too Le Bras, 'Boniface VIII, symphoniste et modérateur', 391–2.

about their contacts with the excommunicate, which might be hard to avoid in cities and other places where a lot of people (especially among the more powerful) were likely to be excommunicate.[44]

Both excommunication and absolution presuppose a network of ideas. Excommunication meant different things at different times:

> by the turn of the twelfth and thirteenth centuries excommunication had been divided into two essentially different sanctions. The penitential forum . . . retained only the penalty of exclusion from the eucharist and the other sacraments, soon to be called 'minor excommunication'. Major excommunication, entailing the full social exclusion of the biblical tradition, belonged to the ecclesiastical courts.[45]

Both sorts would come within the scope of the privilege recorded here. Exclusion from the eucharist and other sacraments was not such a minor thing in terms of religious meaning. Once the eucharist and the mass are involved, the whole Christian theodicy, with Christ's incarnation and his redemption of humanity, is also drawn in. None of this is said but it is all presupposed. Conversely, 'major' excommunication's religious meaning should not be exaggerated. It did not imply damnation.[46] 'Major' excommunication became the routine enforcement mechanism in later medieval ecclesiastical jurisdiction, as imprisonment is of the modern state's jurisdiction.[47] It was known that an excommunication could be

---

[44] 'it may often happen that many people who are under some sentence of excommunication, and especially the more powerful of them, will be in cities and [other] places and impossible for the people to avoid, either at services or outside them, which is often a source of dangers and scandals and many scruples to anxious persons. In fact such people should be given absolution – unless they are people who have been denounced by name – even if they did not seek to avoid those people over and above what was done to avoid them by the clergy and people in common' ('sepe occurrat in civitatibus et locis nonnullos et precipue potentiores aliqua excommunicationis sententia innodatos fore nec tamen a populo vel a clero in divinis vel extra vitari, ex quo timorativis pericula et scandala et multe scrupulositates [scrupulositatis *MS?*] frequenter occurrunt. Est quod tales absolvantur, etiam si non velint eos vitare nisi prout in communi a clero et populo vitantur, nisi fuerint illi nominati denunciati') (Clm. 28673, fol. 107ᵛ, from 'Concessiones facte per dominum Eugenium papam 4ᵐ 1439 die 23 Novembris, in civitate Florentie ad petitionem quorumdam fratrum Minorum', *ibid.*).

[45] Vodola, *Excommunication in the Middle Ages*, 36. Cf. pp. 41–2: 'By the end of the [twelfth] century, papal decretals confirmed the decretist doctrine that contact with excommunicates was punished by exclusion from the sacraments rather than by full social exclusion. Given the name "minor excommunication", the new sanction was made a function of the penitential forum.' I am not clear from Vodola whether this was the only way to incur 'minor excommunication'.

[46] *Ibid.*, 42–3. Cf., however, Murray, *Excommunication and Conscience in the Middle Ages*, 21, for some 'practical churchmen' (contrasted with theologians) who took a harder line.

[47] Vodola, *Excommunication*, 38–40 and chs. 4–7.

based on a mistake.[48] In modern states no one thinks that a 'guilty' verdict actually makes someone guilty: it is a judgement that they are guilty, with corresponding consequences. One needs to note that the medieval Church officially recognised the possibility of erroneous excommunications. In its application, 'major' excommunication belongs to the world of instrumental rationality. Still, it too involved exclusion from the sacraments. It also made one ineligible to act as a godparent at a baptism. It connects with the whole system of religious meaning behind the sacraments. It too presupposes the idea of the Church as a unity.

Then there is the personal and emotional aspect of absolution. In the religious culture of Catholicism, which was already well in place by this time so far as confession was concerned, absolution will often have been a strong personal experience for the penitent who has sought it out, and where excommunication was involved it would be more than perfunctory for the confessor too. The passage brings out both aspects of the ideal-type of convictions proposed above: their interconnectedness, and their character as a concrete mode of thought.

The passage discussed here deals especially with people excommunicated for schism. As noted above, the earlier 'Great Schism' from 1348 to 1417 had fostered an alternative ecclesiology by which popes were subordinate to general councils. The subsequent Council of Basel spun out of papal control and declared the Pope deposed, shortly before the Observant Vicar General obtained the privileges in question here. A certain passion comes through the Observant Dominican list: they speak of the 'devil's council'. Dominicans who obtained these privileges from the Pope were evidently committed papalists.

Paradoxically, it may be that commitment to the papacy was strengthened by the trauma of the Great Schism and the challenge of Conciliarism. In the thirteenth century, belief in the papacy must for the majority have been an assumption taken for granted rather than a choice in the face of a challenge. Two significant facts about preaching: first, a model sermon of the great thirteenth-century Franciscan revivalist Berthold of Regensburg has the following thought-provoking passage, where he is arguing that one ought to accept what St Paul says:

Again, the [resurrection of the dead] is proved by apostolic writings. If the pope commanded something or even taught anything, people would give him their assent. Far more should one assent to apostles. [1 Cor. 15:51]: 'Indeed we will all be resurrected . . .'[49]

---

[48] Murray, *Excommunication*, 39–42, with an interesting discussion of X.2.13.13.
[49] 'Item [resurrectio mortuorum] probatur per scripta apostolica. Si papa quid mandaret aut etiam doceret, crederetur ei. Multo magis credendum est apostolis. [1 Cor. 15:51]:

Papal authority is taken for granted as an axiom. On the other hand – this is the second significant fact – relatively little about the papal office has been found so far, at least in routine model sermons designed for preaching in the thirteenth century.[50] (The same probably holds good for the fourteenth century, though it has not been investigated from this point of view.) The two facts together suggest that papal authority must have been for many a sort of latent belief before the Schism, accepted but not very intense because not much challenged. There were of course very many challenges to papal authority in the pre-Great Schism period, but they were mostly to do with the limits of papal power in relation to that of secular rulers and seldom[51] challenged papal supremacy within the religious sphere, however that might be defined.

In the mid-fifteenth century belief in the religious sovereignty of the Pope had become a conscious decision. For two or three generations, the period of the Great Schism and the subsequent challenge from Conciliarism and the Council of Basel, an alternative model of a 'constitutional monarch' had become a real option, for many clerics and intellectuals, at least. The converse would also have been true for the same sort of people. Commitment to the papacy would be a stronger choice than before.

This may be why there is so much preaching about papal authority at the end of the Middle Ages.[52] It becomes a well-developed topic in model sermons that would have reached large numbers of laypeople, because they were preached on feast days that had become holy days of obligation, when people were supposed to go to church and not to work. Feast days of St Peter in Chains and the Chair of St Peter had been promoted to holy days of obligation by this time (in addition to the Feast of Sts Peter and Paul, which had ranked as a day off work from an earlier time). Preaching on St Peter links the idea of the papacy with the wider religious system, including indulgences and the mystical body, which the Dominican Leonardus de Utino brings together in his very papalist sermon on St Peter:

For since the souls in purgatory are members of this our mystical body, because of the charity in which they passed away, they are able to receive (*capaces*) all the good things which are done and have been done; and just as the stomach

---

"Omnes quidem resurgemus . . .''' (BL MS Harley 3215, fol. 32[va], from a sermon on the text 'Noli esse incredulus sed fidelis' (John 20: 27); Schneyer, *Repertorium der lateinischen Sermones*, vol. 1, p. 474, Bertholdus de Ratisbona no. 25).

[50] d'Avray, 'Papal Authority and Religious Sentiment in the Late Middle Ages', 407 and n. 47 (citing studies by Phyllis Roberts and J.-G. Bougerol).

[51] For an exception, see Garnett, *Marsilius of Padua and the 'Truth of History'*.

[52] For what follows, see d'Avray, 'Papal Authority'.

distributes the substance of food to all the members of the body, so does the Church distribute all the merits, both present and past, to its members.[53]

This was the period in which indulgences were being increasingly abused as a source of money, and the reaction would be part of the origins of the Reformation. These passages show us another side of the indulgence system, in which its religious meaning was drawn out in connection with unsolicited propaganda for the papacy.

Regular preaching on the papacy and its place in the theological scheme of things, on a day in the year when many people got off work and went to church, will have strengthened belief in papal authority as a religious conviction in many minds, precisely in the period immediately before the Reformation.

## Penance

For penance, the document selected is a petition to the papal Penitentiary.[54] The institution itself links penance to the papacy. Behind the document lies a premise about the human role in redemption that was central in the network of convictions, embodied in rituals and other actions, that made medieval Christianity a coherent value rationality. The imitation of Christ by penance was embodied in the liturgical year, connected with purgatory and indulgences, and so again with papal authority. The document also gives a glimpse of the human emotions bound up with penance: above all, release from guilt.

The case is recorded in a medieval formulary from the late fourteenth or earlier fifteenth century:

This account is presented to your Holiness on behalf of Katherine of Baldesheim, a woman of the diocese of Mainz, that when one day, which was a feast day, she wanted to go to church, to say her[55] prayer to God, she left her two infant children, who were less than three years old, at home, it happened that one of those children got to the fire and caught fire and was burned and died; the said Katherine, seeing this and being filled with grief because of it, went to a certain priest who was her confessor and confessed it to him of her own accord, for which crime the aforesaid confessor enjoined to that woman that for seven years she should be bound and obliged to fast on bread and water on each and every Friday;[56] which penance was afterwards reduced to five years in such a way that she would only

---

[53] d'Avray, 'Papal Authority', 398. The sermon is 'In festo beato Petri apostoli'.
[54] For bibliography on penance in the Middle Ages, in addition to the works cited below, see Angenendt, *Grundformen der Frömmigkeit im Mittelalter*, 130–1.
[55] 'eius' – note 'eius pueros' just after.
[56] 'omnibus et singulis diebus veneris seu feriis sextis'.

have to carry out the penance for five years as she was bound;[57] but since, Holy Father, the woman giving this account, who has performed the penance up until now, cannot do so any longer because of her bodily and constitutional weakness, for this reason the petition is made on the part of the aforesaid Katherine to your Holiness that you may mercifully deign to order that the aforesaid penance be commuted into other works of piety . . .[58]

Once again one can trace a network of ideas radiating out from the passage. It describes a small event that is part of a system. The system allowed for private confession and penance, non-solemn public penance, and solemn public penance for very public crimes.[59] The confession was probably a private one, to judge by the words 'a certain priest who was her confessor'. Whether or not the penance was public it is hard to say with certainty, but more probably not.[60]

What is implied here? There is an embedded assumption in medieval Christianity that Christ's self-denial and then ultimate sacrifice enabled other humans to perform meaningful sacrifices that could play a role in their redemption. Everyone did penance in Lent or at other times, imitating Christ by giving things up. Lenten penance was appropriate before Easter just as sacramental confession was appropriate before receiving communion. Fasting and celibacy fitted within this framework, as did monasticism in its many forms and the more extreme forms of individual asceticism. Ultimately they were all imitations of Christ's human suffering. Still, penance had a special role after confession and absolution from sin.

Even when a sin has been forgiven in confession, there is still an assigned penance to perform. One could not just walk away after absolution. Christ's sufferings atoned for sins, but the sinner's voluntary suffering should be added to it. This penance is expressed in years, which

---

[57] 'deberet, ut teneretur'.

[58] Göller, *Die Päpstliche Pönitentiarie*, i/2: *Quellen*, 156 no. 17. For a discussion of the formulary see Goeller, *Die Päpstliche Pönitentiarie*, i/1: *Darstellung*, 55–7; Göller thinks the manuscript could belong to the early fifteenth century though it could be even earlier: *ibid.*, 55.

[59] Mansfield, *The Humiliation of Sinners*, index, s.v. 'penance' and *passim*.

[60] Cf. *ibid.*, 125–6: 'During the late twelfth century and the early thirteenth century, when theologians were rereading the old books of tariffs and trying to classify what they found according to the tripartite system, it was easy to identify all the *carenae* and seven-year penances with the solemn rite and all the pilgrimages with the nonsolemn rite. This intellectual exercise did not describe the practice. Not only pilgrimages but many other types of satisfactions came to be imposed in all public penances.' This might imply that seven-year penances and the like tended to go with some kind of public penance, though not necessarily the solemn sort. See, however, Payer, 'The Humanism of the Penitentials', 352–3: this suggests that any confessor might impose penances sounding like the early medieval tariff sort.

is reminiscent of indulgences. Officially, indulgences were expressed in years because they corresponded to penance on earth (not to 'real' years in purgatory). Both penance on earth and indulgences correlated inversely with suffering in purgatory, which is how indulgences could be expressed in days or years – the quantification of indulgences referred to penance they replaced.

Many authors, however, thought that one should carry out the penance imposed in confession even if an indulgence covered the time; Aquinas said that the penance imposed by the priest is a means of salvation or healing. Evil tendencies survive as a legacy of the sins forgiven and the penance could combat these.[61]

These happenings presuppose two structures: easily available confession, and the papal Penitentiary. Both have roots stretching far back into the past but took a stable form in the thirteenth century. By that time penance or confession was recognised as one of the seven sacraments – a list that was the creation of twelfth-century thinkers, who also came up with clear definitions of a sacrament. Annual confession was made a general obligation by the Fourth Lateran Council in 1215, and the result was a proliferation of handbooks to help confessors guide penitents. These were maps to the world of wrongdoing, but they dealt with the central doctrines of medieval Catholic belief as well as with sins, since confessors had to make sure that penitents knew the basics. Katherine of Baldesheim was presumably used to going to confession at regular if not frequent intervals and it is likely that she knew something of the central beliefs of her religion through that practice as well as in other ways. Confession was not only a key component of the value rationality of medieval Christendom, but also a channel for inculcating the main lines of the system as a whole.

The story, which must be true in its main lines, shows us how confession and penance were a way of dealing with a tragedy. Quite possibly after the accident a harsh penance was what the mother wanted. When it was too much for her later on, she did not simply discontinue it – who could have stopped her or known whether she was fasting? She went to what must have been some trouble to ask the papal Penitentiary to release her.

The papal Penitentiary dealt with cases like this and also with sins for which only the pope could grant absolution (except at point of death) and with dispensations of all kinds.[62] Most of its work with penitents is

---

[61] Paulus, *Geschichte des Ablasses im Mittelalter*, vol. 1, p. 292.
[62] On the Penitentiary see Salonen and Krötzl (eds.), *The Roman Curia*, and further references below, Ch. 6, p. 155 n. 24.

hidden from us, though the survival of late medieval registers gives us much detail about the dispensations it granted. Quantitatively speaking, only a tiny proportion of penitents would have dealt with it in the kind of way that Katherine of Baldesheim did, but the connection between the papacy and penance seems to have had strong roots in the medieval imagination. It is a motif in Icelandic sagas, for instance.[63] It also seems to have had quite deep roots chronologically. In the second or third decade of the eleventh century, so before the Gregorian Reform, Pope John XIX wrote to an Archbishop of Canterbury about a man from England who had come to Rome and sought forgiveness in tears because he had accidentally killed his own child.[64] The Pope gave him a severe penance of twice the habitual seven-year unit, to save him from desperation.[65]

Penance was part of the religious experience of many people long before the reforms of Gregory VII and Innocent III: some would undergo it, and probably more would observe it, as public penance of one sort or another was an established institution.[66] After 1215, when the Fourth

---

[63] 'Rome was the favourite destination of the penitential journeys of the Icelanders, above all for confession at the papal court of reserved cases, endorsing in this respect a tendency characteristic of medieval Scandinavia as a whole, for it had been evangelised late though missionary activity stemming directly from Rome. It may be added that to visit the apostolic see remained the aim which is most frequently mentioned in the sagas even where devotional pilgrimages are concerned, and we have seen that . . . the pilgrimage to the see of Peter always had an at least implicitly sacramental character, because of the pope's supreme authority where the remission of sins was concerned' (passage beginning 'Roma risulta la mèta privilegiata' and ending 'in materia di remissione dei peccati') (Cucina, 'Il pellegrinaggio nelle saghe dell'Islanda medievale', 154; Chris Abrams drew my attention to this important study).

[64] 'We found the bearer of the present letter after he had come to the papal court and in our presence sought penance with tearful prayers, saying that he had by accident killed his own child' ('Visis apostolorum liminibus presentium latorem litterarum illic repperimus, qui ante nostram presentiam lacrimabiliter fusis precibus penitentiam petiit, dicens casu accidente ei evenisse, ut proprie sobolis vitam extingueret') (Zimmermann (ed.), *Papsturkunden 896–1046*, no. 550, p. 1044). Cf. also *ibid.*, nos. 408–10, pp. 777–9, and for background Aronstam, 'Penitential Pilgrimages to Rome'.

[65] 'Therefore, lest he become a prisoner of desperation, we gave him fourteen years of penance, namely, in such a way that in each year he would live on bread and water only for three lenten periods' ('Nos vero, ne in desperationis vinculum incurrisset, indiximus ei penitentiam XIIII annorum, ea videlicet ratione, ut per unum quodque annum III quadragesimas in pane et aqua perficiat') (Zimmermann, *Papsturkunden*, no. 550, p. 1004). The Pope goes on to say that he told the man that he could be allowed back into church after a year, and to ask the Archbishop to intercede with the King to get the man's property restored: presumably it had been confiscated because of the death of his child.

[66] Hamilton, *The Practice of Penance*. Note that her study 'revealed a much greater diversity than had hitherto been suspected by historians', and that 'this variety . . . suggests that penance, far from being a relatively rare practice, confined to members of the elite, may have been more widely practised, not only by the clergy, but by the laity, than is often supposed' (*ibid.*, 207).

Lateran Council made annual confession obligatory, the experience of personal private penance must have become increasingly general. It was also in the thirteenth century that preaching became a powerful system of mass communication,[67] and penance was a recurrent theme in one form or another – not only in penitential seasons.[68] It comes up, for instance, in the sermons about marriage, literal and symbolic, preached on the Sunday when the Gospel of the Marriage feast of Cana was read.

### Marriage as signifier

The place of marriage in a network of mutually supporting religious ideas and the ways in which the ideas and connections were made concrete and vivid can be analysed more succinctly because it has already been done elsewhere.[69] The model sermon for the marriage feast of Cana reading by Peter of Reims, an early Dominican of the French province,[70] is as good an example as any and is edited and translated.[71]

The sermon uses human marriage as a symbolic way into a range of different points in the medieval religious scheme of things. Marriage stands for unbreakable union, and this was a period in which social practice would have reinforced the medium, since indissolubility was being enforced as never before.[72] Thus the practical workings of the law tended to converge with the message of symbolism. Being married would in any case have been an experience common to most and for many a strong basis for symbolism.

Supplementary imagery builds on the core symbolism: for instance, the sinning soul is vividly compared to a girl of servile status who was engaged or married to the son of a King but who dishonours her bridegroom and loses him. The list of things she loses includes inheritance, moveables, and personal freedom, and again it would have made the message more concrete to a substantial proportion of those to whom the sermon was preached, who could draw on knowledge of the social conditions around them.

The sermon branches out from marriage to many central themes in the medieval religious scheme of things. The characteristic structure of sermons from the thirteenth century on facilitates this way of thinking:

---

[67] d'Avray, *Medieval Marriage Sermons*, 15–30, and d'Avray, *Medieval Marriage*, 37–58.

[68] This is so well known to anyone who has worked on the genre that references would be otiose, and could not convey the generality, if not ubiquity, of the theme of penance.

[69] d'Avray, *Medieval Marriage Sermons*, 'Postill' sections.    [70] *Ibid.*, 5.

[71] *Ibid.*, 100–17; see also the 'Postill', 50–63.    [72] d'Avray, *Medieval Marriage*, ch. 2.

the sermons of the friars start from a single text, but fan out from it. Although the whole sermon may be based on one sentence or phrase of Scripture, or often on one word or image, we seem, in many cases at least, to be taken far afield and in many directions from this point of departure. The text is in fact not so much an idea as a matrix of ideas.[73]

That style of thought is evident in this sermon, which fans out from the marriage feast of Cana to sin and penance, baptism, the ages of salvation history, Christ's union with the Church and the individual soul, religious orders, the active and contemplative life, Mary, the marriage in the Virgin's womb of the divinity and humanity of Christ. It was a way of thinking characteristic of the preaching of the time. The allusions to some of the themes just mentioned are brief but the preacher could have expanded on them *ad libitum* when actually preaching the sermon.

Moving beyond this particular sermon, this is the point to draw attention to a nexus around the idea of marriage which exemplifies both the key features of values or convictions as defined in this book: interconnectedness and concreteness. Three medieval sacraments, marriage, holy orders, and baptism, were all connected together through the marriage symbolism representing Christ's union with the Church.

Marriage was connected to holy orders by the rules about 'bigamy', defined not in the modern sense but as remarriage after the first wife's death or marriage to a widow. In the medieval Church 'bigamy' in this sense barred the way to the higher orders of the priesthood.[74] Peter Damian laid out the rationale:

just as Christ, who is the 'high priest of future goods' ... is the husband of one bride, that is of the whole holy Church, which is without doubt a virgin, since it keeps the integrity of the faith inviolably: so too each and every priest is commanded to be the husband of one wife, so that he may seem to present the image of that supreme spouse.[75]

As for baptism, it too was tied in with the theology of marriage. Only a marriage between a baptised couple was absolutely indissoluble. If the couple had not been baptised, and one converted to Christianity, he or she could divorce and remarry a Christian if the first spouse opposed the practice of the new religion.[76] It was baptism that made the difference: a marriage between one of the faithful and a baptised heretic was as

---

[73] d'Avray, *The Preaching of the Friars*, 246.     [74] d'Avray, *Medieval Marriage*, ch. 3 (a).
[75] Peter Damian, Letter 28, to the Hermit Leo of Sitria, in *Die Briefe des Petrus Damiani*, 248–78 at 264; translation from d'Avray, *Medieval Marriage*, 135 (note there the error '464' for '264').
[76] Peter Lombard, *Sentences*, Lib. IV, Dist. XXXIX, CAP. 5 (221), *Determinatio*, in *Magistri Petri Lombardi ... Sententiae*, vol. 2, pp. 489–90; Gratian, *Decretum*, PARS II, C. 28, q. 2 c. 2, Friedberg, *Corpus Iuris Canonici*, vol. 1, p. 1090.

indissoluble as a marriage between two faithful believers.[77] Since all three sacraments were decisive rites of passage, and since they are so closely bound up together, the resulting nexus fits the ideal-type of conviction rationality closely.

The other component of our ideal-type of value rationality – strong mental images – should also be mentioned here. Indirectly, or no doubt in the majority of cases directly, marriage was a part of everyone's life. It was not only a junction of many different ideas and components of the medieval system of values and convictions, therefore, but also a concrete experience. In our own time, historians have found it easy to interest students and readers in marriage because it is a vivid and interesting subject for most people: everyone can relate to it in some way or another. It would have been the same in the Middle Ages *mutatis mutandis*: convictions about marriage would seldom be purely abstract and propositional, even for priests and clerics. Even monks whose lives were set far from the secular world would in most cases have memories of the marriage of their parents. So ideas about marriage were 'value rational' in both senses: because they were concrete as well as on account of their place in a coherent system.

### Humanity of Christ

Much more central even than marriage in the value rationality of medieval Christianity was the Humanity of Christ. One way in which this was made concrete and vivid to the imagination is encapsulated in a Good Friday address by an Italian Franciscan (*c.* 1300) about the ways in which the 'best painters' represent him suffering on the cross – one instance among endless possible examples, though it is an interesting one for art historians:[78]

so that when he was dying he did not even have the earth nor a piece of wood on which he could rest his head as he was dying[79] – which beasts and worms have – since the cross of Christ was like a.T. Tau, without a piece of wood on top, but only a branch below and two crosswise. Nor did he even have a piece of

---

[77] 'marriage is a sacrament: and therefore, with respect to what the sacrament necessarily involves, it requires equality with respect to the sacrament of faith, namely baptism, more than with respect to interior faith' ('matrimonium est sacramentum: et ideo, quantum pertinet ad necessitatem sacramenti, requirit paritatem quantum ad sacramentum fidei, scilicet baptismum, magis quam quantum ad interiorem fidem') ('Thomas Aquinas', *Summa theologiae*, *Supplementum*, q. 59, art. 1, Ad 5, in *Opera omnia*, vol. 12, p. 120).

[78] For a good, select, but recent bibliography on 'Bild- und Passionsfrömmigkeit' see Angenendt, *Grundformen*, 135. Add, for the early medieval period, Chazelle, *The Crucified God in the Carolingian Era*.

[79] The repetition is in the Latin.

wood on which he could lean his body when he was dying, nor a place where he might rest or sleep the sleep of death, as others, sinners, have: but his body was bent, and strained to fall down, had it not been prevented by the nailing down of hands and feet; therefore the best painters paint him all broken in pieces in the middle, and separated from the wood of the cross as if he were falling, and with his limbs as it were completely pulled apart, in such a way that all his bones could have been counted; and then was fulfilled the prophecy: '. . . they counted all my bones [Ps. 21:18] . . .'[80]

This kind of devotion assumes that Christ's sufferings on the cross were not affected in their essential character or intensity by his divinity. It shows one of the ways in which his Passion was made concrete and vivid to the imagination. The devotional emphasis is characteristic of the period from the eleventh century on, but its dogmatic roots lie back in the fifth century, with the decision of the Council of Chalcedon that Jesus Christ was one person in two natures, divine and human, so that his human nature was not in any way transformed by the union into something different from that of other humans.[81] If the alternative view had been adopted, it would probably have prevented the appearance of empathetic and emotional attempts to imagine Christ's bodily sufferings, which met with no dogmatic obstacles when they appeared centuries later in the West. When they did, they affected the whole manner in which the two most crucial times of the liturgical year were experienced by both clergy and laity. At Christmas, Christ's helplessness as a human baby was brought home by cribs and nativity scenes. In the week before Easter, the sufferings of the Passion were imagined as vividly as possible. The doctrine of two natures in one person which this kind of religious sentiment tacitly assumed won the day at the Council of Chalcedon in part as a result of a letter sent by Pope Leo I to the clergy and people of Constantinople.[82] This letter brings out the connections between his idea

---

[80] 'ut, cum moreretur, non habuit etiam terram nec lignum ubi caput cum mo|reretur [fol. lxxxiiii^va] reclinaret, quam habent bestie et vermes, quoniam crux Christi erat ad modum.t. Thau, non habens lignum superius, sed solum bracchium inferius et duo transversalia. Nec etiam habuit lignum ubi corpus suum apodiaret cum moreretur, nec locum ubi requiesceret vel sompno mortis dormiret, sicut habent ceteri peccatores, sed corpus flectebatur, cadere nitebatur, nisi conclavatione manuum ac pedum detineretur; et ideo optimi pictores depingunt eum totum confractum in medio, et a ligno crucis tanquam si caderet separatum, et quasi totaliter dismembratum, ita ut omnia eius ossa possent numerari; et tunc adimpleta est prophetya (Ps. 21: 18): "Dinumeraverunt omnia ossa mea"' (MS Birmingham University 6/iii/19, fol. lxxxiiii^rb/^va). On the writer see d'Avray, 'A Franciscan and History', esp. 259–60.

[81] Denzinger and Schönmetzer, *Enchiridion symbolorum*, no. 293, p. 103 and no, 301, p. 108.

[82] Leo the Great, Epistola 59, in *PL* 54, cols. 865–72; *The Letters and Sermons of Leo the Great*, 58–61 (an old but good translation).

of Christ's human nature and his vision of Christ's true humanity with the Passion and Resurrection;[83] baptism;[84] original sin;[85] grace;[86] the mystical marriage;[87] the Virgin;[88] and the eucharist.[89] Words about the

[83] 'Nor do they perceive that their blindness leads them into such an abyss that they have no sure footing in the reality either of the Lord's Passion or His Resurrection: because both are discredited in the Saviour, if our fleshly nature is not believed in Him' (*The Letters*, 59); 'Nec sentiunt se in hoc praeruptum sua obcaecatione deduci, ut nec in passionis Dominicae, nec in resurrectionis veritate consistant: quia utrumque in Salvatore vacuatur, si in eo nostri generis caro non creditur' (*PL* 54, cap. 2, col. 868).

[84] 'For the very condition of a new creature which at baptism puts off not the covering of true flesh but the taint of the old condemnation, is this, that a man is made the body of Christ, because Christ is also the body of a man' (*The Letters*, 60); 'Ipsa est enim novae conditio naturae, quae in baptismate non indumento verae carnis, sed contagio damnatae vetustatis exuitur, ut efficiatur homo corpus Christi, quia et Christus corpus est hominis' (*PL* 54, cap. 4, col. 871).

[85] 'For such was the state of all mortals resulting from our first ancestors that, after the transmission of original sin to their descendants, no one would have escaped the punishment of condemnation, had not the Word become flesh and dwelt in us, that is to say, in that nature which belonged to our blood and race' (*The Letters*, 60); 'Talis enim erat omnium a primis ducta genitoribus causa mortalium, ut originali peccato transeunte per posteros, nullus poenam damnationis evaderet, nisi Verbum caro fieret, et habitaret in nobis (*Joan*. 1, 14), in ea scilicet natura quae nostri et sanguinis esset et generis' (*PL* 54, cap. 4, col. 870).

[86] 'All they to wit who though they be born in Adam, yet are found reborn in Christ, having a sure testimony both to their justification by grace, and to Christ's sharing in their nature' (*The Letters*, 60); 'Hi utique omnes, qui licet in Adam sint nati, in Christo tamen inveniuntur renati, habentes fidei testimonium, et de justificatione gratiae, et de communione naturae' (*PL* 54, cap. 4, col. 870).

[87] 'For he who does not believe that God's only-begotten Son did assume our nature in the womb of the Virgin-daughter of David, is without share in the Mystery of the Christian religion, and, as he neither recognizes the Bridegroom nor knows the Bride, can have no place at the wedding banquet' (*The Letters*, 60); 'quam qui susceptam ab unigenito Dei Filio in utero Davidicae virginis diffitetur, ab omni sacramento Christianae religionis alienus est; et nec sponsum agnoscens, nec sponsam intelligens, nuptiali non potest interesse convivio' (*PL* 54, cap. 4, col. 870).

[88] 'Nor do we say that the blessed Virgin Mary conceived a Man without Godhead, Who was created by the Holy Ghost and afterwards assumed by the Word, which we deservedly and properly condemned Nestorius for preaching: but we call Christ the Son of God, true God...born of a human Mother, at the ordained fullness of time' (*The Letters*, 60); 'Nec dicimus quod beata Virgo Maria hominem sine Deitate conceperit, qui creatus a Spiritu sancto postea sit susceptus a Verbo, quod Nestorium praedicantem merito justeque damnavimus; sed dicimus Christum Dei Filium, Deum verum...natum de matre homine certa plenitudine temporis' (*PL* 54, cap. 5, col. 872).

[89] 'In what density of ignorance, in what utter sloth must they hitherto have lain, not to have learnt from hearing, nor understood from reading, that which in God's Church is so constantly in men's mouths, that even the tongues of infants do not keep silence upon the truth of Christ's Body and Blood at the rite of Holy Communion? For in that mystic distribution of spiritual nourishment, that which is given and taken is of such a kind that receiving the virtue of the celestial food we pass into the flesh of Him, Who became our flesh' (*The Letters*, Feltoe, 59); 'In quibus isti ignorantiae tenebris, in quo hactenus desidiae torpore jacuere? ut nec auditu discerent, vel lectione cognoscerent, quod in Ecclesia Dei in omnium ore tam consonum est, ut nec ab infantium linguis veritas corporis et sanguinis Christi inter communionis sacramenta taceatur. Quia in

eucharist from this letter were incorporated into the *Decretum* of Gratian, though which they were guaranteed a massive diffusion.[90] Reading it in that context, one might not immediately realise how closely it was linked with Leo's beliefs about Christ's human nature: but in fact his thought is a seamless web in the original letter.

## Trinity

Though the medieval theology of the Trinity has received its share of attention,[91] and the special case of Joachim of Fiore and his influence has attracted high-quality scholarship,[92] there is much more to be done on the Trinity as a religious conviction outside the context of intellectual history. Private prayers should be a privileged source for the history of religious beliefs, including belief in the Trinity.[93] Normally no one is obliged to say them. If they do so it is an act of choice often combined with emotion. The following anonymous prayer comes from a manuscript of the mid-fifteenth century full of material relevant to the history of religious sentiment, including other interesting prayers.[94]

Prayer to the Holy Trinity

Praise to the unbegotten Father, glory to the only begotten one, and honour and jubilant praise to the holy Spirit. You, almighty Father, through your only son, strengthen the work of eternal redemption in me. You, Jesus Christ, only begotten of the supreme father, protect in me the grace which you have given us, reconciling [us] to God with your blood. You, holy Spirit, the Paraclete, preserve in me the illumination of faith with which you sanctified me in baptism. O God threefold and one, give me temporal joy as it pleases you and insofar as it is for my good, and grant too the eternal reward which remains wonderful for everyone. Hear me, O holy Father. Have mercy, kind Son. Save us, gracious holy Spirit. You holy and undivided Trinity, help me, wretched as I am, rule and govern me,

---

illa mystica distributione spiritalis alimoniae hoc impartitur, hoc sumitur: ut accipientes virtutem coelestis cibi, in carnem ipsius qui caro nostra facta est transeamus' (*PL* 54, cap. 2, col. 868).

[90] The passage quoted in the previous note: see Gratian, *Decretum*, PARS III D. 2 De cons. c. 38, Friedberg, *Corpus Iuris Canonici*, vol. 1, p. 1327.

[91] Random examples: Davis, 'Hincmar of Reims as a Theologian of the Trinity'; Wetter, *Die Trinitätslehre des Johannes Duns Scotus*; Robb, 'The Fourth Lateran Council's Definition of Trinitarian Orthodoxy'; Courth, 'Trinität'.

[92] E.g. Patschovsky, 'Die Trinitätsdiagramme Joachims von Fiore'.

[93] For background and prayers on the Trinity generally see Haimerl, *Mittelalterliche Frömmigkeit*, index of 'Sachen' s.v. 'Dreifaltigkeitsgebet'. Note his comment on p. 24, in a section on 'Zisterziensische Frömmigkeit', that 'Mystik ruht dogmatisch auf der Lehre von der heiligmachenden Gnade, den drei göttlichen Tugenden, den Gaben des Heiligen Geistes, und der Einwohnung der Dreifaltigkeit in die Seele' (p. 24).

[94] For a modern scholarly description see Glauche, *Katalog der lateinischen Handschriften*, 28–82.

save and preserve me, for I glorify and exalt you, not that you might gain status from my most unworthy prayers, but that one whom you have created should not strive against you. Holy Trinity and true Unity, almighty God, who made heaven and earth and everything in them, into your holy and special care I commit my body and soul, thoughts, words, and all my acts, that you may defend me from evil spirits and never deliver me over into their power, but that your grace may always shine out in me; and in the books of life write my name yourself, so that it is indelible. O merciful and holy Trinity, who does not despise anyone who comes to you for refuge, hear me and free me from all my sins and the punishment due. Make me happy and give me consolation in all things and lead me to eternal life, you who are threefold and one. O awesome and holy Trinity, in your mercy defend all who put their faith in you, and hear my prayer. Increase in me my fear and love of you, my faith in you and understanding of you. Put into my heart what is pleasing to you, and take what you hate in me right away from me. Who lives and reigns for ever and ever Amen.[95]

The prayer is not an example of 'concrete thought' when read in the context of an academic book, but when prayed with conviction it must have been quite different. Even outside its real setting in life one can see at a glance how it meshes with a range of distinct convictions: about creation, grace, redemption by Christ, baptism and the Holy Spirit, evil spirits, temporal happiness (not despised as such), and heaven.

Prayer evidence shows that Trinitarian belief fits the ideal type of a rational conviction set out above: concrete as opposed to purely abstract thinking, and strong connections with other convictions within the

---

[95] 'Oratio ad sanctam Trinitatem. Laus deo patri ingenito, gloria unigenito, et spiritui sancto honor et iubilatio. Tu pater omnipotens per unicum filium tuum confirma in me opus redemptionis eterne. Tu unigenite summi patris Iesu Christe custodi in me gratiam quam dedisti nobis, reconcilians deo patri in sanguine tuo. Tu sancte spiritus paraclite, illuminationem fidei qua me in baptismo sanctificasti conserva in me. Trinus et unus deus da gaudium temporale ut placitum et michi profuturum, tribue et premium perenne quod omnibus manet laudabile. Exaudi pater sancte me. Miserere fili benigne. Salvos nos fac spiritus alme. Tu sancta et individua trinitas, me miserum adiuva, rege et guberna, salva et conserva, quia te glorifico et magnifico, non ut meis in|dignissimis [fol. 83ʳ] laudibus extollatur, sed ut creatura tua non resistat. Sancta trinitas et vera unitas omnipotens deus, que fecisti celum et terram et omnia que in eis sunt, in tuam sanctam ac singularem custodiam committo corpus meum et animam, cogitationes [cogitato's MS], verba et omnes actus meos, ut me a malignis spiritibus defendas, et numquam [umquam MS] in eorum potestatem me tradas, sed tua semper in me clareat gratia; et in libris vite nomen meum ipse [read ipsa?] scribe ut non deleatur. O pia et sancta trinitas, que nullum ad te confugientem despicis, exaudi me et ab omnibus peccatis et penis libera me. Letifica et consolare me per omnia et perduc me in vitam eternam, que es trinus et unus. O veneranda [vereranda MS] et sancta trinitas, clementer defende omnes in te credentes et exaudi orationem meam. Auge in [me] timorem et amorem tuum, fidem et intelligentiam tuam. In [In with otiose stroke?] cor meum hoc insere quod te delectat, et quod odis in me, longe fac a me. Qui [Quod could be read] vi <vis et regnas per omnia secula seculorum, Amen> [passage in angle brackets supplied from sense]' (Clm. 4649, fols. 82ᵛ–83ʳ).

world-view. This combination can also be found in the preaching and the vernacular poetry of the same period.

German vernacular poetry about the Trinity has been studied by Peter Kern. One of his main arguments is that the poets repeatedly weave the idea of the Trinity together with ideas about the Virgin Mary and the Incarnation.[96] In a sense this is unsurprising or even logically predictable, but that is the point: the three themes really were logically connected within the medieval scheme of things, so that ideas about each reinforced ideas about the others. The same study shows poets trying to bring home the idea of the Trinity with the help of an analogy deemed crude by academic theology: water, ice, and snow are all the same thing; and it draws attention to the use of the same analogy in a sermon on the Trinity;[97] more on preaching below.

Both prayers and vernacular poetry take us beyond intellectual connections into the realm of affect. Both genres aim to express feelings and help others feel them. The poetry aims at the imagination and prayers are a vehicle for acts of the will. In both cases we are dealing with concrete rather than just abstract thought.

[96] 'I limit... the range of my investigations to the subset of thirteenth- and fourteenth-century poems in which the idea of the Trinity is linked to the idea of the Incarnation, a combination of themes which occurs frequently enough and in which the Mother of God naturally also becomes a central figure, bound up in many different ways with the mysteries of the Trinity and the Incarnation' (passage beginning: 'Ich grenze' and ending 'Trinität und Inkarnation' (Kern, *Trinität, Maria, Inkarnation*, 9). This leaves open the possibility that combinations with other doctrines could be found.

[97] 'The analogy between the Trinity and Water-Ice-Snow, which are all a single element, is used in the *sermones populares* of Peregrinus (d. post 1335) as one of the many examples with the help of which the preacher sought to clarify the dogma of the Trinity for the people. Furthermore, this analogy is found in a late medieval commentary on the Sentences of Peter Lombard. Significantly, this analogy for the Trinity is introduced as a "rough and ready illustration of the Trinity and Unity of God" that is presented only to "common people or peasants". In fact so far as I can see the Ice-Water-Snow analogy is not to be found in specialised theological writings; on the other hand it was often employed in vernacular poetry' ('Die Trinitätsanalogie von Wasser, Eis und Schnee, die alle ein Element sind, ist in die Sammlung von *sermones populares* des Peregrinus (gest. nach 1335) aufgenommen worden, als eines von vielen Beispielen, mit denen der Prediger dem Volk das Dreifaltigkeitsdogma erläutern wollte: ... Außerdem findet sich diese Analogie innerhalb einer spätmittelalterlichen Sentenzenerklärung: ... Bezeichnenderweise wird dieser Trinitätsvergleich als *grossum exemplum de trinitate et vnitate dei* eingeführt, das nur *vulgaribus seu rusticis* vorgelegt werde. Tatsächlich läßt sich m. W. die Eis-Wasser-Schnee-Analogie in der theologischen Fachliteratur nicht nachweisen; dagegen hat sie ist in der volkssprachigen Dichtung häufige Verwendung gefunden' (Kern, *Trinität*, 152). In the next chapter I will discuss in a different context ('Propaganda') a widely diffused model sermon on the Trinity in which the doctrine is made vivid to the imagination by analogies, and linked with a range of other topics: death as the result of original sin, man's relation to the whole created world, the powers of the soul, expulsion of demons, simony, God the Father's mercy and love, prayer, the redemption, heaven, purgatory, hell, the world, and mercy.

## Structures: conclusion

The ramifications of each of these medieval religious beliefs into other parts of the world-view to which they belonged have been briefly explored, and it is clear that most of the values and convictions discussed above are bound up in one way or another with each of the others. It is unnecessary to recap the connections in detail: it will be clear already that we are dealing with a network of mutually dependent ideas, where the antecedent probability of each was enhanced by assent to the rest. Miracles were authenticated by papal canonisation processes. They recalled the healing miracles of Christ, which were linked to forgiveness of sins, making the link with penance. The scene of Christ's first miracle, the marriage feast of Cana, was a classic starting point for preaching on marriage as a religious signifier. The miracle of the Resurrection presupposed his suffering humanity, which was in turn bound up with the doctrine of the Trinity. The second person of the Trinity, not only as God but as man, was made present in the eucharist, which was central to the 'spiritual gift economy' of the living and the dead. The Apostolic Penitentiary linked the system of penance with the papacy, which was also the supreme judge of cases involving the validity of marriage, indissoluble because of its signification of Christ's union with the Church. A papal defence of the doctrine of the humanity of Christ was transmitted to the innumerable users of Gratian's *Decretum*, which quoted his dictum that 'receiving the power of the heavenly food, we pass into the flesh of Him who was made our flesh'.[98] The papacy provided ritual reinforcement to the doctrine of the Trinity by making Trinity Sunday a major feast (below, p. 97), and the papacy was the linchpin of the indulgences system, which was increasingly important in the spiritual gift-exchange system linking the living and the dead. One of the *signifiés* in sermons on the marriage feast of Cana was penitence.[99] Trinitarian formulae play a prominent role in marriage-ring ritual.[100] Penance was connected with the 'spiritual gift economy' because suffering in purgatory varied inversely with penance already done on earth, except that the mutual prayers of communities joined in confraternity could diminish the former and speed the soul towards the beatific vision. All these interconnections, and the others explored under the individual themes, contributed to strengthening the structure of the whole system.

---

[98] See above, pp. 57–8 n. 89.
[99] See d'Avray, *Medieval Marriage Sermons*, index, s.v. 'penance'.
[100] Molin and Mutembe, *Le Rituel du mariage*, 160–1, 163–7.

One could extend the analysis to other convictions, such as belief in the eucharist and sacrifice (closely connected ideas themselves), which have not been selected for particular analysis here, partly because they have received concentrated treatment elsewhere.[101] The interconnections gave the system strength. The medieval religious world-view does indeed show the powers of resistance that are sociologically characteristic of complex nets of interlocking values cemented in social practice and by emotional experience.

Nevertheless, it lost control over a large part of Europe at the Reformation. Moreover, one could argue that similar breakaway movements (if with different doctrinal contents) could have taken place much earlier but for the protection afforded to the Catholic system by the states of Europe. When that support was shaky, as happened for a while in the Languedoc in the thirteenth century, in the England of Wyclif, and in Bohemia when the Hussite movement was getting under way, then dissent flourished proportionately. This should not surprise us. Value systems have great powers of survival but they are seldom able to retain an absolute monopoly without the help of force. Furthermore, force certainly facilitated the original conversion to Christianity: notably in the seventh and eighth centuries. Nevertheless, force was seldom the sole factor. To explain the dynamics of the flows and ebbs of the medieval Church's hold on the population of Europe, and of the rise and fall of dissident religious movements, we need to look at other types of explanation as well.

---

[101]  Rubin, *Corpus Christi*; Bynum, *Wonderful Blood*.

# 3  Medieval values: dynamics

## Loss and gain

Where do values come from and what becomes of them in the end?[1] The loss and gain of beliefs can be two sides of the same coin. The point here is simply the almost tautologous one that the conversion, insofar as it was successful, can mean losing values and beliefs as well as gaining them. Conversion in the strongest sense involves abandoning one set of convictions and forms of life to embrace a different one. In such cases questions about loss and gain are almost the same. This chapter deals with both, the emphasis being sometimes on one side, sometimes on the other.

## Individuals and systems

Belief systems relatively rarely disappear, and more often merely retreat. What this must mean in practice is that they lose some adherents and fail to recruit or to reproduce themselves up to full strength. This would have been the case with Conciliarism, a movement in full retreat by the end of the fifteenth century, though it never disappeared and was able to reassert itself in the context of Gallicanism. Conversely, papalism seems to have expanded its appeal in the second half of the fifteenth century, despite historiographical stereotypes to the contrary.

## Experience and changing convictions

The shift of values in the fifteenth century back to a papalist world-view deserves more attention, and we have a privileged vantage point from which to observe the process in an autobiographical letter by Aeneas Silvius Piccolomini. This is an attempt to explain his shift from

---

[1] The same question is treated in a more general and comparative framework in *Rationalities in History*, ch. 3.

Conciliarism to acceptance of papal monarchy over the Church: it shows how the course of events as well as discussions with friends changed his point of view.

The letter in question was a 'Bull of Retraction' sent by Aeneas Silvius Piccolomini to Cologne University in 1463, several years after he had become Pope, and when he was in his late 50s, giving an account of his own changing views.[2]

We do not have to read this absolutely literally to treat it as a valuable source – one for which there are few parallels in the medieval period. Of course public figures' memories of their past actions and attitudes are unreliable, and Piccolomini was not an exception.[3] It is possible, for instance, that he compressed the timing of his change of views. Perhaps experiences and discussions worked unconsciously on his attitudes over a longer period of time, and he read the process back into something more like a conversion experience. If so, we can probably still learn from the letter as an unconsciously fictionalised account of an internal change that really took place; and Piccolomini's curiosity about himself and his habit of self-revelation[4] are further reasons for taking his history of his own opinions seriously.

Perhaps some may say that we acquired this [anti-Conciliarist] opinion with the papal[5] office; and that we changed our view with our status. Not at all; by no means. Hear, my children, how we behaved. A brief account will make clear to you the truth so far as this matter is concerned, and will answer any objection. In 1431 we went to Basel together with Dominic Capranica, whom Martin V had created cardinal in a secret consistory, and whom Eugenius IV had spurned. There we found that the council had begun. It had indeed been revoked by Eugenius, although those who had come to it did not want to obey, and asserted that a council which had begun could in no way be dissolved without the consent

---

[2] Pius II, 'Bulla Retractationis', paras. 4–7, pp. 152–60. (The bull is directed to the 'rectori, et universitati scholae Coloniensis' (p. 148). On earlier editions, see Praefatio, at p. xii. For an introduction to Pius II's life and work see Worstbrock, 'Piccolomini, Aeneas Silvius (Papst Pius II.).

[3] Worstbrock, 'Piccolomini', col. 639, passage beginning 'Die kirchenpolitische Wende' and ending 'den Schriftsteller nicht'. Similarly, Prof. Claudia Märtl stresses (in a personal communication) that this curious 'Bulla' represents a late retrospect on his changing views. My thanks to Prof. Märtl for making available to me while still in press two papers by S. Iaria which reconstruct his changing attitudes from, mainly, his own writings before the Bulla Retractationis: 'Silvio Piccolomini und das Basler Konzil' and 'Enea Silvio Piccolomini und Pius II'.

[4] Cf. again Worstbrock: 'the transformation of 1445 left unaffected his ingrained Humanism, his openness to all human life, his need to express himself as a descriptive writer and narrator' ('seine humanistische Grundprägung, seinen alles Leben aufnehmenden Sinn, seinen Drang zu schildern und zu erzählen, ließ die Wende von 1445 unberührt') ('Piccolomini, Aeneas Silvius (Papst Pius II.), p. 639).

[5] 'pontificatu' here probably 'papal' rather than 'episcopal'.

of the Fathers who had gathered for it. Julian, cardinal of Sant'Angelo,[6] was there, a Roman, outstanding for his life and learning,[7] superior to the rest in eloquence. When he heard that Eugenius had revoked the council, he gave up the presidency, as if out of obedience to the Roman Pontiff. Since, however, against Eugenius' will, the council grew larger every day, and many bishops from different regions and royal ambassadors arrived; and since not a few cardinals too came there, after fleeing the Roman Curia, he resumed his presidency. He extolled in a remarkable way the authority of the council, and began to play down the eminence of the first see [i.e. Rome]. When the legates of Eugenius came, and asserted the greatness of the bishops of Rome, he seemed to confute them...[8]

Piccolomini was carried along with the flow of opinion around him, and when the tide began to turn he did not want to change his views automatically:

Nor could we love Eugenius, whom so many and such great witnesses declared to be unworthy of the pontifical authority. The legates of Paris University, whose fame is so great, were there. At times[9] speakers from your university [Cologne] and from other universities of the German nation were present; and all with one voice exalted to the skies the authority of General Councils. There were few who dared to speak of the power of the Roman Pontiff... In addition, came the consent of Eugenius himself, who revoked his own dissolution of the council, and approved its continuance... Pupils normally turn out to resemble their masters.... The disciple is not above his master, says the Lord, nor were we able to conquer our master. Julian... and many others were masters to us; the school was the gathering at Basel, at which it was rare for anyone to defend

---

[6] I.e. Cardinal Giuliano Cesarini. See Strnad and Walsh, 'Cesarini, Giuliano', and Christianson, *Cesarini: The Conciliar Cardinal*. Christianson suggests that Piccolomini is unreliable on the subject of Cesarini: see pp. 66–7 and 183.

[7] 'doctrina'.

[8] 'Dicent fortasse aliqui, cum pontificatu hanc nobis opinionem advenisse; et cum dignitate mutatam esse sententiam. Haud ita est; longe aliter actum. Audite filii conversationem nostram; brevis narratio erit, quae vobis, quantum ad rem attinet, veritatem aperiet, et obiectioni faciet satis. Anno salutis primo, et trigesimo supra mille quadringentos cum Dominico Capranica, quem Martinus quintus in secreto consistorio cardinalem creaverat, Eugenius quartus spreverat, Basileam petivimus; ibique concilium inchoatum invenimus; verum ab Eugenio revocatum, quamvis congregati noluerant obedire; asserentes jam coeptum concilium sine consensu patrum, qui convenissent, haudquaquam potuisse dissolvi. Julianus aderat s. Angeli cardinalis, natione Romanus, moribus et doctrina conspicuus, et qui eloquentia praestaret ceteris. Is, audita Eugenii revocatione, praesidentiam dimisit, tamquam summo pontifici vellet obedire. Sed, cum augesceret in dies, Eugenio vel invito, concilium, et multi ex diversis regionibus episcopi, et regum legati adventarent; cardinales quoque ex Romana curia profugi in dies nonnulli concurrerent, praesidentiam resumpsit; et auctoritatem concilii mirum in modum exstollens eminentiam primae sedis supprimere coepit. Venientes Eugenii legatos, et potestatem Romanorum praesulum magnificantes, apparenter confutavit' (Pius II, 'Bulla Retractationis', para. 4, pp. 152–3).

[9] 'aliquando'.

the cause of Eugenius. To mutter anything against the dignity of the council was to commit the crime of heresy. Public opinion was on the council's side, not that of Eugenius. As for the supremacy of the Roman see, there was either silence, or contempt. 'the council, the council' – the words were everywhere in the air . . . and although Eugenius afterwards transferred the council to Italy, and came together with the Greeks at Ferrara, and finally went to Florence; although cardinals Julian of Sant'Angelo and John of St Peter, in whom we had great faith, went over to him; although very few remained in the faith of Basel, yet we did not want to yield . . . So we remained at Basel, until Eugenius was, as we believed, deposed by just judgement, and Amadeus of Savoy put in his place, and called Felix V . . . But when Frederick the King of the Romans [i.e. Holy Roman Emperor-elect] stopped at Basel and, being asked to go to Felix, who was there, he could in no way be persuaded to honour him as if he were the Roman Pontiff, or to speak with him in public, then we first considered it possible that we had followed the wrong side, when the King of the Romans, the future Emperor, was doubtful in so great a matter, and was more inclined to the side of Eugenius. We pondered much and often about how to find the truth, for we never erred willingly. When we were asked to join Frederick's household, we did not refuse. For at that time he was neutral, together with almost the whole of Germany . . .[10]

Little by little Piccolomini began to change his mind:

We learned many things from the neutrals of which we had been unaware before. We found that Eugenius had been falsely accused of many things, and that the

[10] 'Nec Eugenium diligere poteramus, quem tot, tantique testes indignum pontificio dicerent. Aderant legati Parisiensis scholae, cujus est fama percelebris. Affuerunt et aliquando vestri, et aliorum studiorum Germanicae nationis oratores; et uno cuncti ore, concilii generalis auctoritatem ad caelum efferebant. De potestate Romani pontificis pauci erant, qui loqui praesumerent; . . . Accessit et ipsius Eugenii consensus, qui dissolutionem concilii, a se factam, revocavit; et progressum ejus approbavit. . . . Quales magistri sunt, tales evadere discipuli solent. . . . Non est discipulus super magistrum, inquit dominus; nec nos magistrum potuimus superare. Julianus nobis . . . et alii complures fuere magistri; schola, Basiliensis conventus, in quo raro aliquis Eugenii causam defendit. Adversus concilii dignitatem mutire aliquid, crimen haeresis fuit. Una omnium vox concilium Eugenio praeferebat. De sedis apostolicae praecellentia aut silentium erat, aut contemptus. Concilium, concilium cuncta sonabant. . . . Et quamquam postea Eugenius concilium in Italiam transtulerit, et cum Graecis Ferrariae, ac demum Florentiae convenerit; quamquam Julianus sancti Angeli, et Johannes s. Petri cardinales, quibus plurimum credebamus, ad Eugenium defecissent; quamquam paucissimi in fide Basiliensium remansissent; noluimus tamen cedere . . . Mansimus igitur Basileae, quoad Eugenio, ut credidimus, justo judicio deposito, Amedeus Sabaudiensis suffectus est, et Felix quintus appellatus . . . At cum Fredericus Romanorum rex, apud Aquasgrani coronatus, domum repetens, Basilea transitum fecisset, rogatusque Felicem illic praesentem accedere, nullo pacto persuaderi potuisset, ut honorem ei, tamquam Romano pontifici exhiberet, aut publice verba cum eo misceret, tum primum consideravimus possibile esse, quod partem erroneam sequeremur, quando rex Romanorum, imperator futurus, in tanto negotio dubius esset, et ad Eugenium inclinaret magis. Multum, et saepe intra nos ipsos cogitavimus, quis esset modus inveniendi verum; nunquam enim volentes erravimus. Rogati in familiam Federici transire, non renuimus. Erat tunc ille cum tota fere Germania neutralis' (Pius II, 'Bulla Retractationis', para. 4, pp. 154–6).

cardinals who had come to Basel had wanted to brand with infamy a good and holy man, because of private enmities.[11]

This turns into the description of a mild conversion experience, if the phrase is not too incongruous for a careerist like Piccolomini:

By chance at this time Cardinal Julian of Sant'Angelo, whom we mentioned above, ... came to Flavianum, which today is called Vienna ... Out of old habit we talked with him often; we often disputed about Basel; we held to our old opinion, he had adopted a new one. We extolled the authority of a General council, he greatly praised the authority of the Apostolic See ... In the end, when we convicted the cardinal with his own writings and sayings ... He laughed, and said: 'Aeneas, you are proceeding against me with documents [an allusion to Cicero[12]] ... Why is it not permitted at any time to leave what is false and embrace what is true ... The Lord took the veil from my eyes and I saw the marvels of his law: I recognized my earlier errors, and understood fully how far those at Basel had departed from the truth ...' The words of the man, which he often repeated to us with burning charity ... embedded themselves in our heart. [He describes his eagerness to discuss these problems with other learned men who came to Basel.] And when the Emperor, to procure the union of the Church, initiated an assembly of his own nation in Nuremberg, and resolved that the supreme pontiff Eugenius should be urged to proclaim a new council at Constance, and to send a legate; and also to induce those at Basel to move there, so that peace might be restored to the Church, those at Basel were the first to refuse. When Thomas Asselbachius [i.e. Thomas Ebendorfer[13]], a distinguished German theologian, heard this, he said: 'Now I know that those at Basel are not led by the Holy Spirit, when they flee from so just a law of the Emperor.' Many other learned men ... said the same thing. Considering these things, the darkness at last fell from our eyes ... We recognized our error; we came to Rome, we rejected the dogma of those at Basel ...[14]

---

[11] 'Multa inter neutrales didicimus, quae nos antea latebant. Eugenium falso de multis accusatum invenimus; cardinalesque, qui Basileam venerant, ob privatas inimicitias bono et sancto viro notam inurere voluisse ...' (*ibid.*, para. 4, p. 157).

[12] *Tusc.* 5. 11. 33.

[13] See Lhotsky, *Thomas Ebendorfer*. As a corrective to the impression of Ebendorfer's views left by the passage quoted here, note Lhotsky's comment, p. 43, passage beginning 'in eine vorbehaltlose Anerkennung des Papalsystems' and ending 'wenn nicht Eugen IV. alles zunichte gemacht hätte'.

[14] 'Forte per id temporis Julianus sancti Angeli cardinalis, cujus supra meminimus ... Flavianum venit, quae hodie Vienna dicitur ... Saepe cum eo sermonem pro veteri consuetudine miscuimus; saepe de rebus Basiliensibus disputavimus; tuebamur antiquam sententiam, ille novam defendebat. Extollebamus generalis concilii auctoritatem, ille apostolicae Sedis potestatem magnopere collaudabat. ... Ad extremum cum suis scriptis, dictisque cardinalem revinceremus ... subridens ille, tu, inquit, Aeneas tabellis obsignatis agis mecum ... Cur enim non liceat omni tempore, relicto falso, verum complecti? ... Revelavit dominus oculos meos, et consideravi mirabilia de lege sua: cognovi priores errores, et quantum a vero procul abiissent Basilienses, plane intellexi. ... 6. Haeserunt pectori nostro verba viri, quae saepe ad nos repetiit non sine charitate ardenti, et amore singulari. ... Cumque caesar ad unionem ecclesiae

Aeneas Silvius Piccolomini was very interested in himself and did not have to write this account, so it probably gives us a good idea of this history of his convictions as he perceived it later. Even on the rather extreme hypothesis that he is being consciously insincere, it would be an excellent analysis of the movements of opinion by an acute observer of human nature and his own times. He was born in 1405, so his early years were spent before the Great Schism was ended. A precocious boy would have been well aware of the situation. While the schism continued, Conciliarism looked the answer to a lot of people (even if it had produced a third claimant to the papacy). Piccolomini was still a young man when he went to the council of Basel in 1432, as Cardinal Capranica's secretary. In the hothouse atmosphere of the council he could be excused for thinking that the future of the Church lay with Conciliar sovereignty, and that his own personal career would benefit very directly from this development: the council elected its own 'antipope' and Piccolomini got the job as his secretary. In short, he probably never had much occasion to develop papalist convictions in his youth.

Then, as things developed, it would have seemed less certain whether he had thrown in his lot with the winning ideology. As he describes in his letter, he began to get the sense of a wind of change blowing in a papalist direction. The attitude of the Emperor and the influence of important ecclesiastics whom he respected played their part.

Perhaps the influence of Cardinal Julian of Sant'Angelo was especially important. Now a convert to the papalist view would not be short of reasons. Papal supremacy was woven into the very fabric of medieval theology and canon law. Conciliarism too had some pre-Schism roots,[15] but it took some clever modern scholarly detective work to discover them. Before the schism an acceptance of papal supremacy at least in spiritual things had been so to speak the default setting of most believers, and the old simple arguments could reassert themselves whenever it looked as though papal government was working again.

The influence of arguments should not be underestimated. In this history of his religious opinions Aeneas Silvius early on gives a simple

procurandum in Norimberga suae nationis conventum instituisset, decrevissetque summum pontificem Eugenium adhortari, ut Constantiae novum concilium indiceret, legatumque mitteret, ac Basilienses pariter inducere, ut eo se transferrent, ibi ut pax ecclesiae redderetur, primi Basilienses recusavere. Quod audiens Thomas Asselbachius ex Germanis insignis theologus, nunc, inquit, scio Basilienses, Spiritum Sanctum non habere ductorem, quando tam aequam imperatoris legem effugiunt. Idem multi alii dixere viri doctissimi... 7. Quibus consideratis, caligo tandem ab oculis nostris cecidit... Recognovimus errorem nostrum; venimus Romam, Basiliensium dogma rejecimus' (Pius II, 'Bulla Retractationis', paras. 5–7, pp. 157–9.
[15]  Tierney, *Foundations of the Conciliar Theory*.

justification of papal supremacy. On the one hand, there are a priori considerations: God would not have left his Church without order, which implies hierarchy, which implies a head.[16] These are linked up with familiar arguments for papal primacy from the New Testament.[17] Perhaps Cardinal Julian of Sant'Angelo put such considerations before him, and the changing situation did the rest.

Which does not mean Piccolomini was a turncoat. He was certainly a man interested in his success, but that might have applied to institutions as well as his own career. In his 20s and early 30s, he might well have thought that the papacy would never recover its old form. It had survived the schism but there it was, looking distinctly shaky again less than two generations later. When the papal cause gathered strength again, as he describes in this bull, the whole pattern began to look different. Instead of a deadly crisis, a brief revival, then another crisis producing a new form of government, he saw an institution that had weathered storm after storm. Granted the papal ideas familiar even to their opponents, the experience of his own times could explain how 'the darkness fell from our eyes', as he dramatically put it.

Aeneas Silvius Piccolomini's penchant for self-revelation and explanation gives us only one man's view of his internal life. No one experiences crises in quite the same way. Still, his case gives us some insight into the kind of individual histories that make up the advances and retreats of conviction rationalities.

### Tendencies and counter-tendencies

Piccolomini was experiencing the undertow of a reaction against Conciliarism. Thanks to his interest in his own inner evolution we can feel the pull along with him, through his writings. If we then move from the

---

[16] Pius II, 'Bulla Retractationis', para. 3, p. 151: passage beginning 'Nec putetis divinam providentiam' and ending 'in ipsum influit'.

[17] 'Nor, to be sure, did Christ channel the supreme authority, as if of the leader of his army, to anyone other than to his vicar, the first being St Peter, to whom we know that the care of the Lord's flock was entrusted. Nor do the evangelists preserve the memory of two or more Peters; nor did the Lord establish two or more men to take his place like equal heads; but he set up one, Simon Peter, at the summit and as the leader and shepherd of the whole flock, saying: "Thou art Peter [etc.]"' ('Nec profecto in alium, tamquam sui exercitus ducem, supremam auctoritatem Christus principaliter derivasset, quam ei suum vicarium, qui primus fuit Petrus, cui commissam novimus dominici gregis curam. Nec duos, pluresve Petros evangelistae commemorant; nec duos, aut plures instituit dominus, qui suum locum tamquam capita tenerent, aequalia; sed unum constituit, ut verticem, ac ducem, et pastorem universi gregis Simonem Petrum, dicens, tu es Petrus [etc.]' (Pius II, 'Bulla Retractationis', para. 3, pp. 151–2). There are more arguments for papal primacy in para. 10, pp. 160–4 – with an excursus into papal history.

individual to the collective level, the ebb of the conciliarist tide fits a more general pattern memorably expressed in the Hegelian idiom of his day by Leopold von Ranke, in whom there is more grand theory than his modern positivist reputation recognises:

In this Europe of ours, no power, and no doctrine either, least of all a political one, has ever succeeded to the point of complete supremacy. . . . Still, always even those ideas that were striving to achieve exclusive domination have met with a contradiction growing out of the inexhaustible soil of ordinary life and bringing forth fresh forces.

If we see that no power can arise which does not at the same time rest on the basis of the idea [sic], we can add that it finds in the idea the force that contains it; the great life-generating struggles are also consummated at the same time in the regions of conviction and thought.[18]

In the previous chapter we saw how the idea of papal authority was intertwined with many threads of medieval thought. In Chapters 5 and 6 its routine interactions with ordinary life will be exemplified. It was unsurprising that a reaction against Conciliarism should gather force. Then, as the council at Basel turned into a talking shop full of academics, it was natural for doubts to arise about its efficacy as a sovereign organ of government. The counter-tendency which pulled Piccolomini with it was both a reaction and a revival of convictions temporarily in abeyance.

### Dynamic equilibrium: thirteenth-century Paris

The fifteenth-century advance of ecclesiological constitutionalism and its subsequent retreat are overlapping but distinguishable phases. Sometimes, however, the trend and counter-trend are practically simultaneous, with the result that the interplay of forces can be underestimated. What looks like secure solidity is actually a dynamic equilibrium. Arguably, this was what happened in thirteenth-century Paris, as the scholastic method grappled with the implications of Aristotle's works about man and nature, which had recently been translated.

---

[18] 'Niemals jedoch ist in unserem Europa weder eine Macht noch eine Lehre, am wenigsten eine politische, zu vollkommener Alleinherrschaft gediehen. . . . Noch allezeit hat sich auch den zur ausschliessenden Herrschaft anstrebenden Meinungen ein Widerspruch entgegengesetzt, der, aus dem unerschöpflichen Grunde des allgemeinen Lebens entsprungen, frische Kräfte hervortrieb.

Nahmen wir wahr, dass keine Macht emporkommen wird, die nicht zugleich auf der Grundlage der Idee beruhe, so können wir hinzufügen, dass sie auch in der Idee ihre Beschränkung findet; die grossen, lebenerzeugenden Kämpfe vollziehen sich immer zugleich in den Regionen der Überzeugung, des Gedankens' (L. von Ranke, *Die Römischen Päpste in den letzten vier Jahrhunderten*, 2 vols. (Leopold von Ranke's historische Meisterwerke, 15–16; Vienna, n.d.), vol. 1, pp. 406–7.

To return to the Hegelian–Rankean idiom, thesis, antithesis and synthesis were almost simultaneous. Two sets of ideas held each other in check, or created a third one: like two currents meeting, their force was betrayed only by a troubled surface along the line where they met. The tension below the surface was revealed above all by the condemnation in 1277 by the Bishop of Paris Étienne Tempier of a long list of propositions deemed subversive and allegedly current in the Paris Faculty of Arts.[19] Some of these were certainly radical, such as that theological discourse was founded on fables – that it contained falsehoods like other religions.[20]

Now, the 1277 condemnation cannot be taken as an accurate account of attitudes in the Arts Faculty (though opinions differ about how far it was off the mark),[21] or as a map of battle-lines on either side of Aristotelian philosophy. To pursue this second point: one of the most apparently Aristotelian ideas was the belief that the world has existed from all eternity. While it probably is a genuinely Aristotelian idea, it became a subject of debate *before* the translation of Aristotle's works on the natural world, and the argument about it did not take a 'for or against Aristotle' form. The debate was started by Peter Lombard's Commentary on the Sentences, not by new Aristotelian texts; scholars like the Franciscan Bonaventure and Pecham, who were once seen seen as anti-Aristotelians, used Aristotle as an authority on the issue; personalities had much to do with the high feelings that developed during the debate; scholars disagreed about what Aristotle had actually taught about the eternity of the world and many thinkers denied that he had taught it as a demonstrable truth.[22] So things are not so simple: it was not a straightforward 'science versus religion' debate.

---

[19] For an edition with a good survey and discussion of the rich bibliography, see Piché with Lafleur, *La Condamnation parisienne de 1277*. Richard C. Dales's summative judgement is harsh: that a group of 'able and devout Christian philosophers and theologians' were 'attacked for largely non-doctrinal reasons, and condemned by a dishonest and vengeful committee of theologians (and we do not know that they were predominantly Franciscans) who had the ear of a fairly unintelligent, though fearful and conservative bishop' (*Medieval Discussions*, 176). He may be too confident that what survives on parchment represents all that people were saying, but of course this is impossible to prove.

[20] '152 (183). Quod sermones theologi fundati sunt in fabulis' (Piché with Lafleur, *La Condamnation*, 124); and '174 (181). Quod fabule et falsa sunt in lege christiana, sicut in aliis' (Piché with Lafleur, *La Condamnation*, 132). Cf. Hissette, *Enquête sur les 219 articles*, 274–5. Hissette says, p. 275, that we should distrust the testimony of the men behind the condemnation ('il faut se méfier du témoignage des censeurs').

[21] Cf. Piché with Lafleur, *La Condamnation*, 285; Bianchi, *Il vescovo e i filosofi*, 198–9. Pouliot, *La Doctrine du miracle chez Thomas d'Aquin*, ch. 1, is less inclined to dismiss the condemnation as unfair.

[22] Dales, *Medieval Discussions*, 259–60 (and 170–1 for Bonaventure's and Pecham's use of Aristotle).

Yet, even granted all that, the rediscovery of Aristotle's natural and social scientific writings could surely have posed a non-trivial threat to belief. Enlightenment historians, familiar with a 'tamed' Aristotelian tradition, do not always appreciate how subversive his writings could have been when first surveyed as a whole by Christendom's intellectual elite. They tend to see him as the old intellectual order and as integrated comfortably with orthodox Christianity. In the early Middle Ages Aristotle was indeed comfortably at home in the Christian thought world. From the Carolingian Renaissance to the twelfth century scholars became increasingly familiar with his logical writings, but most of his substantive writings on nature and man were not known in Latin; and as a logician he posed no threat. It was only in the twelfth and thirteenth centuries that the substantive writings became available in the West.[23] Even in the early thirteenth century the newly translated works of Aristotle were 'admired more than read, frequently referred to, sometimes quoted textually but rarely understood'.[24] In the third and fourth decades of the century scholars began to penetrate the thought of the Arabic Aristotelians, but understanding of Aristotle's own thought as a whole remained superficial.[25] It was only from around the 1240s that scholars in the Faculties of both Arts and Theology got to grips with this magnificent but foreign body of thought in a serious way.

This was the dangerous moment for medieval Catholic intellectuals. It was not so much any one Aristotelian teaching – say the eternity of the world – as the coherence and intellectual power of a whole massive self-contained system in which the supernatural might seem alien and superfluous. Aristotle offered a fairly comprehensive interpretation of the natural, social and ethical world. His works gave no hint of a God interested in intervening in history by working miracles or revealing truths. If anyone did have doubts about dogma, they had a satisfying secular synthesis to put in its place.

But did they have doubts? It is hard to find anything directly heretical in the writings of the scholars at whom the condemnation was principally aimed, Siger of Brabant and Boethius of Dacia.[26] There is little firm proof that belief was being undermined by debates in the Arts Faculty. On the other hand, one has to consider the bias of evidence, which is heavily

---

[23] See Luscombe, *Medieval Thought*, 62, for a convenient summary.
[24] Marenbon, *Later Medieval Philosophy*, 55.    [25] *Ibid.*, 56.
[26] Pouliot, *La Doctrine*, 33, following Hissette, gives statistics for the number of condemnations at least probably directed at each. Pouliot himself clearly thinks that Siger's views at least did pose a potential threat to orthodoxy: *La Doctrine*, 28–31, 39–40. Nonetheless, as Dales points out (*Medieval Discussions*, 175), 'all the published statements of these two men [Siger and Boethius of Dacia] affirm their personal Christian faith'.

against the survival of risky theories in written form. Furthermore, if a theory was known at all in a lively intellectual community like Paris, and if conservatives were afraid of it, it seems hard to believe that no one at all had played with the idea, even if the fears of the Bishop were disproportionate. Other evidence of scepticism in less elite environments has been collected by scholars, working skilfully against the bias of the evidence, so that there was almost certainly a lot more than they have found.[27] Why should we assume that students were immune to subversive ideas, especially when they had at hand the intellectual wherewithal to fit them into a this-worldly system that looked like the future of research?

As usual in such cases, one needs to find a middle way between the attitudes to inference such as that of the two Cambridge scientists walking in Scotland. When they passed a black cow in a field, the engineer said: 'All cows in Scotland are black'. 'No', said the pure mathematician, 'one cow in Scotland is black on one side'. As a rule of thumb for communities like the one in question the following may be proposed: intellectuals will take more risks in oral and informal discussion than they would commit to writing.[28] Even today, *mutatis mutandis*, it is highly likely that 'politically incorrect' remarks are more common in universities than a scrutiny of academic writings would reveal. Private oral utterances are naturally more daring than written texts in the public domain. There is a sort of *a fortiori* principle of oral dissent: it is always a step ahead of what writings reveal. What seems to be on balance the most probable hypothesis is that the leaders of the movement had no desire to rock the religious boat but that some of the students felt differently and expressed their views in informal discussion.

Let us at least call the Aristotelian corpus a potential threat to religious certitudes, one that might have grown rather than diminished as understanding of its coherence of gathered impetus. In the event, however, the shock-absorbers of scholastic theology were able to contain it. Here I understand scholastic theology as the systematic application of logic to authoritative religious texts, and the concentration on discrepancies between them, and on tough problems generally, particularly by use of the 'Quaestio' method, which forced practitioners to see opposite sides of

---

[27] Arnold, *Belief and Unbelief in Medieval Europe*, ch. 6, esp. 226–9; Reynolds, 'Social Mentalities and the Case of Medieval Scepticism'; Murray, 'Piety and Impiety in Thirteenth-Century Italy'.

[28] Cf. Piché with Lafleur, *La Condamnation*, 180. Hissette, *Enquête*, 275 endorses, as a reasonable guess, Mandonnet's speculation that certain propositions could be echoes of theories current among the students even if without the approval of the Masters of Arts ('certaines propositions pourraient être des échos de "propos qui circulaient parmi la population scolaire et que les maîtres se seraient empressés de désavouer"'); Libera, *Penser au Moyen Âge*, 197–8 and 376 n. 10.

arguments.[29] In the previous century Peter Abelard's *Sic et non* had flung this incipient tradition into the deep end by setting out problem topics and apparently contradictory topics without providing answers, a procedure which could have been subversive but which seems instead to have stimulated thought.[30] Abelard's own approach is an example of the role of contingency in the history of beliefs. He had an intellect comparable in power to the minds behind the Enlightenment, men like Spinoza, and a nonconformist personality, but in the end he did not want to subvert the belief system but to strengthen it by enhancing its rational coherence:

his rationalism can be seen, not as a critical effort directed at Christian doctrine from the outside, but rather as an audacious attempt to rethink many traditional positions in the light of what Abelard himself would have regarded as at once a rationally coherent and profoundly Christian moral theory.[31]

Though some of his views were very controversial and his affair with Héloïse made him notorious, Abelard's thought went into the mainstream of the tradition,[32] and scholastic theologians set about proposing solutions to the kind of problems he raised. Much of the most original philosophical thinking within the scholastic tradition was worked out in the course of tackling the paradoxes of core theological doctrines like the Trinity. Scholars were not always sufficiently aware of it. The Catholic historians who pioneered the history of scholasticism came from an educational curriculum which separated philosophy from theology more sharply than or differently from the medieval thinkers they were studying, so that they tended to separate out metaphysics and epistemology from the theological contexts in which they had been most acutely discussed. The more recent wave of scholars interested in the ancestors of modern logic and linguistic philosophy distilled and collected medieval innovations in those fields.[33] Only quite recently has the creative philosophical thought been put squarely back in its theological setting, above all by John Marenbon (as noted earlier in a different context[34]):

---

[29]  The bibliography is endless. One may single out R. W. Southern's incomplete masterpiece *Scholastic Humanism and the Unification of Europe*, vol. 1: *Foundations*, and vol. 2: *The Heroic Age*. Grabmann, *Die Geschichte der scholastischen Methode*, is still well worth reading. For what seems to me an extremely well-thought-through and usable ideal-type of Scholasticism generally (as opposed to just scholastic theology) see Quinto, *Scholastica*, 416–17. In the many books of Alain Boureau a highly original mind reflects on different aspects of scholasticism: see e.g. *L'Empire du livre*.

[30]  See e.g. Clanchy, *Abelard: A Medieval Life*, 87–8 (this is a classic scholarly biography).

[31]  Marenbon, *The Philosophy of Peter Abelard*, 338.

[32]  Luscombe, *The School of Peter Abelard*.

[33]  Marenbon, *Later Medieval Philosophy*, 85–7.    [34]  See Ch. 1, at n. 49.

Most of the important thinkers of the thirteenth and fourteenth centuries were theologians; most of their important works were treatises of theology. Not only did theologians like Aquinas, Henry of Ghent, Duns Scotus and Ockham presuppose the articles of faith: the main aim of their work was to understand them better and elaborate their consequences. . . . theologians did not merely take it for granted that God is triune – often their most complex explorations of the human soul were carried out simply in order to penetrate the mystery of the Trinity.[35]

If the most innovative and creative ideas about human psychology were being explored in connection with the doctrine of the Trinity, the whole belief system would be strengthened by the conjunction. This took place above all in the universities of Paris and Oxford, and/or within the Dominican and Franciscan Orders. These cutting-edge intellectual advances were embedded in ecclesiastical institutions which had from the beginning been closely associated with the papacy.[36] The sort of intellectual energy that operated outside the establishment in the radical Enlightenment was intimately bound up with the core values and institutions of the medieval Church, and helped to reproduce them. The scholastic method in theology as such is best understood as a form of instrumental rationality, so this is a case, and as we shall see below there are many, of the symbiosis of instrumental and conviction rationality.

The assimilation of Aristotle was at least partly a matter of timing. Two thinkers of exceptional talent came to grips with the new corpus almost before anyone was aware of the threat it might pose. The first was an outstanding interpreter of the newly translated works, and the second, his pupil, was endowed with a special gift for synthesis. The result was that solutions appeared almost as soon as anyone had begun to think about the problems. Both were Dominican friars, and both worked to integrate Aristotelianism into their system of values and beliefs. Albert the Great was an intellectual force in Paris from 1240, in the decade when Aristotle was properly understood. Albert understood his pagan predecessor exceptionally well.[37] From 1246 he had Thomas Aquinas among his pupils, so Aquinas was taken straight to the philosophical cutting edge by a teacher who saw Aristotle as an opportunity rather than a threat. Equipped with an excellent understanding of the new corpus, Aquinas set about synthesising it with Christian belief. So, for instance, he proposed arguments from causation for the existence of God

---

[35] Marenbon, *Later Medieval Philosophy*, 190–1.
[36] Verger, *Les Universités au Moyen Âge*, 34, 42, 79–91 *passim*, 111–12.
[37] Nevertheless, as an anonymous reader pointed out to me, he 'insisted – even when faced with evidence to the contrary – on taking the Liber de causis – really a translation based on Proclus – as the theology of Aristotle': so there were limits to his insight into ancient thought.

which were compatible with the eternity of the world in both directions, thus maximising compatibility with Aristotelian philosophy. Aquinas did believe that the world had been created in time (on the strength of the Bible, etc.), but did not think that reason could prove this on its own[38] or that a proof for God's existence as first cause depended on it.[39]

The philosophers in the Arts Faculty also played a part in absorbing the shock of Aristotle's thought into the Catholic system. The Masters of Arts in the sights of Bishop Tempier's condemnation, Boethius of Dacia and Siger of Brabant, were passionate Aristotelians – but they were also well integrated into ecclesiastical structures. These two were not obviously Voltairean. Siger took refuge at the papal court when he felt threatened at Paris, and Boethius was or later became a Dominican friar.[40] They too belonged to the religious establishment – an important difference from Enlightenment figures like Spinoza, Voltaire or Hume. Ideas do not exist in a vacuum. Scholasticism was not only an intellectual method but a social structure allowing innovation to coexist with orthodoxy.

### Convergence and miracles

For all their basic orthodoxy, it was not Siger of Brabant and Boethius of Dacia who synthesised an Aristotelian idea of nature with a Christian understanding of miracles as rational evidence in their own right, for they accepted miracles on faith, and did not regard them as proofs.[41] Around the same time, the status of miracles as hard rational evidence was being enhanced from an entirely different direction, by the methods adopted in papal canonisation processes. This exemplifies another ideal-type important for understanding the dynamics of convictions, viz., the effect of convergence. In the process of 'de-Christianisation' which gathered speed in the later nineteenth century, the convergence of two essentially independent developments, Darwinism and German biblical criticism, goes a long way towards explaining the loss of faith among late Victorian intellectuals.[42] But convergence and timing can work in the opposite direction as well: when independent intellectual developments both converge to reinforce a conviction. For the thirteenth century, this ideal-type should be combined with the one analysed in the previous section: for the convergence of these two independently rational supports for miracle must have helped to neutralise doubts that were in the air at

---

[38] Marenbon, *Later Medieval Philosophy*, 71–2.
[39] Cf. *Summa contra Gentiles* 1.13, p. 14: passage beginning 'Et ad hoc dicendum quod via efficacissima ad probandum Deum esse est ex suppositione aeternitatis mundi'.
[40] Dales, *Medieval Discussions*, 175–6.
[41] Cf. Pouliot, *La Doctrine, passim,* and esp. p. 64.
[42] Cf. d'Avray, *Rationalities in History*, p. 103.

that time. The Benedictine Engelbert of Admont (*c.* 1250–1331) wrote a treatise on miracles in which he complains about people who do not believe in the miracles of Christ; it has been suggested that he had educated people in mind.[43]

Aquinas's ideas about miracles were examined in the previous chapter. It was argued above that 'his concept of a miracle presupposed a regular causal order such as natural observation reveals'.[44] For him, this regular causal order would have been Aristotelian. It was, however, slotted neatly into his Christian world-view. In a particularly economical formula Aquinas argued that 'God imparted a certain order to things in such a way as nonetheless to reserve to himself what he would do in a different way at some points in the future, for a reason. So when he acts outside this order, it is not changed.'[45] There is no need to repeat the analysis developed above: the essential finding is that Aquinas saw the (Aristotelian) laws of nature as regulating the physical world rather as examination regulations govern the practices of sensible universities: the proviso 'normally' was always attached.

While Aquinas was developing his solution to the problem of miracles, the papal Curia was acquiring a name for treating miraculous claims unsympathetically, while ultimately remaining open to conviction.[46] Paradoxically, this must have reinforced belief in the supernatural[47] by showing that it could on occasion stand up to intense scrutiny and meet the criteria of legal proof. This was the period in which canonisation processes began to subject both the miracles and the virtues claimed for the putative saint to rigorous scrutiny of a quasi-legal character. Aquinas's contemporary, the canon lawyer Hostiensis (or Henry of Susa) 'saw the processes as a deliberate introduction of obstacles to causes in order to make sure that only the best would survive and to prevent inflation: "lest the number of saints be infinitely multiplied, with the result that charity and devotion grow cold and sanctity become worthless"'.[48] The canonists seem to have been on the same page as the Curia in favouring stringent criteria, not least in the assessment of miraculous claims.[49]

---

[43] Goodich, 'Reason or Revelation?', 183.    [44] See above, p. 38.
[45] *Summa theologica* 1.105.6, esp. 'ad 3', and see above, p. 39, n. 26.
[46] I am grateful to Robert Bartlett for scrutinising the section that follows.
[47] Cf. now Bartlett, *The Natural and the Supernatural*, 9–16.
[48] Kleinberg, 'Proving Saints', 190.
[49] *Ibid.*, 197–8, 200–1, 205. Kleinberg expresses some reservations, viz., that 'events are ambiguous and people's accounts of them are interpretative and subjective', that 'except for the possibility of self-interest or gain, a witness's motivation was never questioned', and that 'witnesses who claimed to have had a miracle happen to them' were 'allowed to attibute the miracle to the saint of their choice' (*ibid.*, 200); otherwise his emphasis is on critical rigour.

These developments were well under way before the Aristotelian system had been understood sufficiently for faith to be threatened seriously. The default setting of the papal Curia was to reject miraculous claims – or at least that was its reputation. Those who tried to get someone officially recognised as a saint faced a formidable hurdle near the end of the road: tough scrutiny by a small committee of cardinals.[50] Albert of Armagh, writing around the middle of the thirteenth century, reports a cardinal as treating the dossier of the miracles of Edmund of Abingdon almost cynically. He was not only unconvinced but also expressed personal scepticism about resurrections attributed to St Martin of Tours.[51]

The 'scepticism of members of the Sacred College was notorious throughout the whole of Christendom'.[52] Yet these cynical observers of popular religion also believed in miracles when the evidence seemed compelling.[53] It was rational for the wider intellectual community to accept the proofs for the few miracles that survived the rigorous scrutiny of a canonisation process. Canonisation processes had rarity value.[54] Between the pontificates of Innocent III (elected 1198) and Clement V (d. 1314) the Papacy ordered only twenty-three processes.[55] Actual canonisations were even rarer. The selectivity can only have strengthened the currency. The rarity of Nobel Prizes impresses on popular consciousness the stringency of the criteria that we assume must be applied. The classic study of later medieval sanctity by André Vauchez showed that only a tiny proportion of those who were thought by their admirers to be saints came even near to being canonised.[56] It is unlikely that hardheaded scholars at Paris or elsewhere would have been entirely unaware of this combination of conviction with critical rationality at the centre of their religion.

The rigour has been reaffirmed by a recent study by Michael Goodich.[57] He comments, for instance, in connection with the

[50] Vauchez, *La Sainteté*, 561.
[51] I paraphrase Vauchez and translate from his own translation of the Latin: Vauchez, *La Sainteté*, 561–2.
[52] 'le scepticisme des membres du Sacré Collège était notoire dans toute la chrétienté'. Vauchez, *La Sainteté*, 561.
[53] *Ibid.*, 581.
[54] Kleinberg, 'Canonization without a Canon', 13; Vauchez, 'Conclusion', 361.
[55] Vauchez, *La Sainteté*, 656–9.    [56] *Ibid., passim.*
[57] Goodich, 'Reason'. There is a certain dislocation between the substance of this important paper and its conclusion, which is that 'On the one hand, an increasingly refined judicial procedure was supported by philosophical arguments in the rational examination and confirmation of miracles.... On the other hand... cautious papal policy sometimes fell back on the demand for a further miracle... Such a miracle, however unreliable, had sometimes been experienced by the pope himself or by someone close to the Curia, in order to bolster the case for canonization. Thus, a private revelation

canonisation process of Thomas of Hereford (a politically *engagé* and high-minded thirteenth-century bishop who took the anti-royal side in the 'Barons Wars' against Henry III of England), that:

> The employment of historical precedent, contemporary scientific and medical evidence and common sense found in this document likewise reflects a determined effort to reduce the miracles confirmed by Rome only to those cases which provide irrefutable evidence of divine intervention contrary to the laws of nature.[58]

and, more generally, that:

> the putative saint's miracles in the thirteenth and early fourteenth centuries were scrupulously examined according to acceptable judicial procedures. The aim was to establish the exact circumstances in which the alleged miracle occurred, identify reputable and reliable witnesses, note the 'natural' means employed to cure an ailment prior to resort to the supernatural, and to demonstrate how this miracle either converted nonbelievers or strengthened the faith of Christians. This procedure entailed the deposition of expert witnesses such as physicians who could testify that the miracle had occurred contrary (*contra naturam*), beyond (*supra naturam*) or apart from (*praeter naturam*) the known laws of nature. Such reliable persons and notaries likewise appear not merely as officers of the court, but also as deponents who were either acquainted with the putative saint or were themselves aided by his curative powers.[59]

As Goodich implies, a method of investigation deriving from legal procedure is allied here with a sophisticated conception of the miraculous, one which assumes that laws of nature are the norm. He connects this attitude to the miraculous with academic discussions of the period.[60]

The rationality of these proofs is different from that of the scholastic method (though like the latter it would come under the rubric of instrumental rationality – in the service of values). It is in fact close to the method of modern historians, paradoxical though that may seem. It is worth looking more closely at a particular case, and the canonisation process of Yves Hélory is a good example of the scholarly approach

---

or a miracle that had not been fully tested according to the philosophical and judicial standards noted earlier was employed in order to clinch the putative saint's claim to sanctity' (p. 196). What this amounts to is that even after a subset of the miracles originally proposed for examination had passed the rigorous quasi-legal tests to which they were subjected, popes sometimes needed an extra push of a more personal if less rigorous sort. This is very different from showing that untested miracles or visions were trusted *against* the weight of the rigorous canonisation evidence.

[58] Goodich, 'Reason or Revelation?', 185–6. On this canonisation, see Bartlett, *The Hanged Man*. A critical edition of the remarkable canonisation process is being prepared by Susan Ridyard for the Oxford Medieval Texts series.

[59] Goodich, 'Reason or Revelation?', 181.      [60] *Ibid.*, 182–3.

employed.[61] The depositions of witnesses were only the starting point. The cardinals responsible composed

> in narrative form, two small treatises, one containing a short account of the life of the saint, the other of his miracles . . . [they] divided each of these two summaries into chapters, the chapters themselves into paragraphs, and at the end of each paragraph, they mentioned, by giving an extract or a reference, the proofs on which it was based, as contained in the depositions given during the enquiry.[62]

The cardinals gave precise references to the location in the register into which the depositions had been transcribed from the original roll.[63]

A historical method that provided apparently overwhelming evidence for a small hard core of genuine miracles was thus developed in the same cultural space as a science-compatible theory of the miraculous. The two roughly contemporary developments were entwined, as Goodich's analysis shows, but they were essentially independent in origin, and each could have developed without the other: indeed, they represent different types of reasoning, scholasticism being abstract and deductive, the canonisation processes empirical. They converged to neutralise the threat that the new science would surely otherwise have posed to belief in the miraculous by the intellectual elite.

## Charismatic leaders

The previous section dealt with what we might call the dynamics of stability: powerful forces interacting in ways that reproduced existing structures, while incorporating new elements of strength. We may now turn to the dynamics of more dramatically obvious changes. For Max Weber, new social structures can emerge under the influence of charismatic leaders, or rather of their followers, for his ideal-type is quite different from the modern usage of the word to mean 'magnetism'. Weber asks us to

> define 'Charisma' as a quality, deemed to be extraordinary . . . of a personality, on account of which this person is judged to be endowed with supernatural or superhuman or at least specifically extraordinary powers or properties, which are not accessible to everyone else, or as sent by God, or as an outstanding model and consequently a 'Leader'.[64]

The medieval period is not short of examples of movements started by 'charismatic' individuals, though they did not necessarily survive very

---

[61] La Borderie et al., Monuments originaux de l'histoire de Saint Yves.
[62] I translate from ibid., pp. xl–xli.    [63] Ibid., p. xlii.
[64] Weber, Wirtschaft und Gesellschaft, vol. 1, p. 140, passage beginning ' "Charisma" soll eine als außeralltäglich' and ending 'und deshalb als "Führer" gewertet wird'. For fuller discussion see Rationalities in History, ch. 3, pp. 104–6.

long. In the mid-eighth century the English missionary St Boniface gave a vivid description of a movement started by a man called Aldebert. He apparently claimed that 'an angel of the Lord had brought to him from the ends of the world relics of wonderful yet indefinite sanctity, and that from then on he had been able to obtain whatever he asked from God';[65] he got many peasants to believe that he was a man of apostolic sanctity and that he worked wonders; he had with him his own bishops,[66] men without education, and put himself on a level with the apostles of Christ; he drew multitudes to the services he held, distributed his nail-clippings and pieces of hair as relics, and claimed to know the secret sins of the people who came to him, so that they had no need to confess.[67] It did not come to anything.

The movement started in the twelfth century by the Lyons merchant Valdes, on the other hand, is still in existence today, though there are debates about how far it preserved the same identity over the centuries.[68] The movement did not break away from Catholic orthodoxy immediately, but when it did so one factor, 'to judge by later Waldensian writing, was the sense that Valdes had a direct mission from God' (so a leading historian of medieval heresy[69]) – which would put him squarely within Weber's definition of a charismatic leader.

A perhaps even more remarkable 'charismatic leader' than Valdes was Francis of Assisi. With his emphasis on poverty and preaching his values were in some ways similar: both represent the 'apostolic life' movement that transcended the divide between orthodoxy and heresy in the central Middle Ages.[70] Still, he may be said to have established a new value: the idea of a religious order owning nothing even in common – an idea whose extraordinary novelty – except of course that the apostles were regarded as a precedent – drew the following admiring comments.[71]

---

[65] St Boniface, *Die Briefe des heiligen Bonifatius und Lullus*, ed. Tangl, 111.
[66] 'conduxit episcopos . . . qui se contra precepta canonum absolute ordinarunt' (*ibid.*).
[67] *Ibid.*, 111–12.
[68] On the Waldensians see e.g. (out of a vast literature) Biller, 'The Waldenses in the Fourteenth and Fifteenth Centuries' and 'The Historiography of Medieval Heresy', and Cameron, *Waldenses: Rejections of Holy Church*. For a brilliant critique of a historiographical tendency (especially on the part of Cameron and Grado Merlo) to minimise the unity over time and space of the Waldensian movement, see P. Biller's remarkable 'Goodbye to Waldensianism?'.
[69] Lambert, *Medieval Heresy* (3rd edn.), 73.
[70] Grundmann, *Religiöse Bewegungen im Mittelalter* (1961), *passim*. There is an English translation with an important historiographical introduction by Robert Lerner: Grundmann, *Religious Movements in the Middle Ages*.
[71] They are from a sermon in Bnf. lat. 3736, incipit *Surrexit Elias* (Eccl. 48:1) 'Secundum Augustinum nova faciunt mirari' attributed to the early fourteenth-century Dominican Jacques de Lausanne by a scholarly BnF catalogue and by Johannes Baptist Schneyer:

When Blessed Francis started the new religious order[72] of his brothers this was a very new thing: to found so great an order upon poverty – upon nothing; it was new and unprecedented. St Benedict founded the order of monks, but not on nothing, indeed upon great revenues and possessions; in the same way Augustine [founded] his order of canons regular. Therefore, when St Francis started so great and holy an order without revenues, he did something so new that the whole world was and is amazed.[73]

It is a Weberian commonplace that charisma must be routinised to survive, but it can blend with the institutions that develop from it, as our preacher thought had happened with the Franciscan Order:

And therefore if you are amazed and ask how an order which has no foundation on earth endures, I reply: Christ placed the foundation there and rules it [the order] through his own self, and therefore it can indeed be shaken and buffeted, but cannot fail.[74]

Francis himself could write in the authentic tones of charismatic authority. He has given up his position at the head of the order, and says that: 'I am determined to obey the Minister General of the Order and the guardian whom he sees fit to give me. I want to be a captive in his hands so that I cannot travel about or do anything against his command or desire, because he is my superior.'[75] Yet just before he has written: 'In

---

see *Catalogue générale des manuscrits latins*, vol. 6, p. 677, and Schneyer, *Repertorium der lateinischen Sermones*, vol. 3 (1971), p. 98, no. 532; both link it to BnF lat. 18181, fol. 238[va] and I have cursorily examined this to correct MS lat. 3736, without time to check properly: but it suggested the emendations given below. On Jacques de Lausanne see d'Avray, *The Preaching of the Friars*, 108 and n. 3. In fact the content of the sermon makes me wonder if it can be by anyone except a Franciscan, but for present purposes it does not matter. Schneyer gives it the liturgical siglum *S37* which = 'in translatione s. Nicolai', and the BnF catalogue implies that the sermon is for the translation of St Dominic, but the content makes this problematic.

72  *Religio* can mean 'religious order'.

73  'Quando beatus Franciscus incepit novam religionem fratrum suorum hoc fuit novum valde: fundare tantum ordinem super paupertatem, super nichil: fuit novum et insolitum. Beatus Benedictus fundavit ordinem monachorum, sed non super nichil, *immo* super magnos redditus et possessiones. Similiter Augustinus ordinem canonichorum regularium. Unde quando beatus Franciscus incepit tantum et tam sanctum ordinem sine redditibus, fecit tantum novum quod miratus est totus mundus et miratur' (BnF lat. 3736, fol. 247[r], miratus . . . miratur] totus mundus est *MS, with the* 'est' *probably inserted in an attempt at correction*).

74  'Et ideo si miramini et queritis quomodo religio durat que fundamentum nullum in terra habet, respondeo: Christus posuit ibi fundamentum et regit eam per seipsum, et ideo bene potest concuti et pelli, sed non deficere.' BnF lat. 3736, fol. 247[v]: fundator et fundamentum] fundamentum *MS*). Cf. Weber, *Wirtschaft und Gesellschaft*, 661: 'untrennbar mit ihnen verbundene'.

75  'The Testament of St Francis', in *St Francis of Assisi: Writings and Early Biographies*, ed. Habig, 67–70 at 68–9. For background see e.g. Burr, *The Spiritual Franciscans*, 3–4; note his comment (*ibid.*, 3) that the *Testament* 'highlighted the tension between juridical and charismatic authority'.

virtue of obedience, I strictly forbid the friars, wherever they may be, to petition the Roman Curia . . . for a papal brief, whether it concerns a church or any other place, or even in order to preach, or because they are being persecuted.'[76] The document contains other assertions of charismatic authority – charismatic because Francis seems to expect to be obeyed even though he holds no office:

> this is a reminder, admonition, exhortation, and my testament which I, Brother Francis, worthless as I am, leave to you, my brothers, that we may observe in a more Catholic way the Rule we have promised to God. The Minister General and all the other ministers and custodes are bound in virtue of obedience not to add anything to these words or subtract from them.[77]

Or again: 'When God gave me some friars, there was no one to tell me what I should do; but the Most High himself made it clear to me that I must live the life of the Gospel' (ibid., 68).

Some thought Francis possessed the power to discern sometimes the secrets of people's souls[78] or to foretell future events.[79] He was sent by God 'to show men the way to salvation in a changing world'.[80] Again, companions of St Francis who came to feel that the order had departed from his intentions[81] firmly believed the views they rightly or wrongly attributed to him were divinely inspired. They tell a story about leading men in the order who were afraid that the rule Francis was composing would be too strict. When they came to him to make their point:

> St. Francis turned his face towards heaven and addressed Christ thus: 'Lord, did I not tell you that they would not believe you?' Then the voice of Christ was heard in the air replying: 'Francis, there is nothing of yours in the Rule, but all which is there is mine. I want the Rule to be observed as it is to the letter, to the letter, to the letter, and without gloss, and without gloss, and without gloss.' He continued: 'I know how much is possible to human frailty and how much I wish to help them. Let those who do not wish to observe it leave the Order.' Then St. Francis turned to the brothers and said to them: 'Do you hear? Do you hear? Would you like me to have it said to you again?[82]

---

[76] St. Francis, ed. Habig, 68.     [77] Ibid., 69.
[78] Bériou, 'Saint François, premier prophète de son ordre', 291–2.
[79] Ibid., 293-4.     [80] I cite Bériou, 'Saint François', 297.
[81] Their views are set down in the so-called Scripta Leonis, on which see Burr, The Spiritual Franciscans, index s.v. Scripta Leonis, and Scripta Leonis, Rufini et Angeli sociorum S. Francisci, ed. and trans. Brooke. This source or group of sources genuinely represents the views of friars who had been close to Francis himself, though it was written down late in their lives, when controversy in the order may have given a sharp edge to their memories.
[82] 'The Writings of Leo, Rufino and Angelo', para. 113, in Scripta Leonis, ed. and trans. Brooke, 287.

This kind of perception of St Francis legitimised a rigorist strand within the Franciscan Order.[83] The friar or friars whose view of St Francis is represented in the last quoted passage had been with him and known him, but time and controversy within the order had moulded their memories. Nevertheless, the conviction that Francis was inspired by God was almost certainly held in his lifetime, indeed he held it himself, as his Testament shows. That conviction, intensely felt and accepted as right by his followers, helps explain the enormous success of the order. Thus Francis's charismatic leadership may be said to explain two movements: the Franciscan movement generally, and the passionate subset of friars who felt that the original ideal had been compromised.

The influence of charismatic leaders is an unpredictable factor in history, since the movements they start can be powerful forces. Often the values embodied in these movements were not actually invented by the charismatic leader. Even St Francis was a man of his time. The 'apostolic' values he represented were widespread well before him.[84] He magnified and intensified the impact on history of ideas already in the air. That he echoed attitudes around him (if felt with less force) also helps to explain his influence.

### Overlapping values and conversion

This brings us to the next point about the internalisation of new belief systems, the rather obvious one that (*ceteris paribus*) people are more easily converted to systems which overlap significantly with their existing convictions.[85] In the early thirteenth century, around the time when the Franciscan movement was gaining momentum, groups broke away from two heretical movements, the Humiliati and the Waldensians, to submit to the papacy and rejoin the Church.[86] In the twelfth century the contrast between the 'apostolic' way of life of the early Waldensians or Humiliati,

---

[83] Writing of the period around 1300, Burr comments that 'Italian rigorists tended to be more critical [than French reformists] of thirteenth-century developments in the order, more insistent on returning to the original intention of Saint Francis as seen in extra-legal documents like the *Testament* and the Leo sources, and more willing to solve the problem by splitting the order' (Burr, *The Spiritual Franciscans*, 73).

[84] Cf. Grundmann, *Religiöse Bewegungen*, who famously argued that the same stream of religious sentiment flowed into the Franciscan Order and into heretical movements; cf. also Lapsanski, *Perfectio evangelica*.

[85] On conversion in the Middle Ages, see now Berend (ed.), *Christianisation and the Rise of Christian Monarchy*. Her 'Introduction' (*ibid.*, 1–46) includes an excellent list of references (pp. 39–46), which makes it otiose to give one here.

[86] Lambert, *Medieval Heresy* (2002 edn.), 100–3; on the Humiliati, Andrews, *The Early Humiliati*, chs. 2 and 3.

on the one hand, and the wealth of bishops, not to mention the mediocrity and sexual laxity of the lower clergy, would have been striking. In the thirteenth century Pope Innocent III offered the possibility of retaining core values of the these apostolic movements within the limits of the Church. That obviously smoothed the path to conversion, especially since many members of these movements had been more or less dogmatically orthodox anyway, and at odds with the authorities over practical matters such as the right to preach.[87] Moving backwards in time to quantitatively much more massive conversions, there is reason to think that Anglo-Saxon paganism had some beliefs that paved the way for Christianity. It is true that we do not know as much as we would like about the pagan religion that Christian missionaries found, since remarkably few identifiable traces of it survived.[88] There is, however, evidence for the following three things that could have made Catholic Christianity easier to accept. First, there were sacrifices, which would have made it easier to explain the idea of the mass, the eucharistic sacrifice.[89] (The evidence for this is the story in Bede about the backsliding king Raedwald, who had in the same temple a Christian altar and a 'small altar on which to offer victims to devils'.[90]) Secondly, the idea the death of the hero as an appropriate climax for a narrative seems to have been embedded in the Germanic ethos, unless Beowulf is a purely Christian creation, an implausible hypothesis. This would have been a better preparation for understanding the centrality of the Passion

---

[87] The 'heretical' Humiliati especially seem (so far as the evidence goes) to have been dogmatically conventional except in their attitude to preaching without permission and to oath taking: see Andrews, *Early Humiliati*, 62.

[88] The near-disappearance of paganism need not mean that populations abandoned their old beliefs en masse or that all acquired Christian values. Some no doubt underwent real conversions. The rest died without having the opportunity to pass on their core values to a new generation. Pre-Christian Germanic paganism and Catharism are rather unusual cases of religious systems which did not survive with a self-conscious identity.

[89] Cf. Bartlett, 'Reflections on Paganism and Christianity in Medieval Europe', esp. 64–7. Though Bartlett is more concerned to point out the contrasts between pagan and Christian sacrifice, he also makes it clear how much they had in common: 'Christians were rooted in a sacrificial tradition that left an imprint on their language and thought' (p. 64); 'The use of the language of sacrifice for the eucharist acquires a particular sharpness when we find it in the missionary field, where sacrifices of a literally bloody kind could also be encountered. When Wulfram of Sens was on board ship off the coast of Frisia "the hour arrived in which the sacrifice of a saving victim was to be offered to God". The wording . . . is precisely that used by missionary writers when describing pagan animal sacrifice; but here the meaning is the eucharist' (p. 65). For an update of Bartlett's presentation of paganism see his 'From Paganism to Christianity in Medieval Europe'.

[90] *Bede's Ecclesiastical History of the English People*, ii. 15, ed. Colgrave and Mynors, p. 191. Bede adds that 'Ealdwulf, who was ruler of the kingdom up to our time, used to declare that the temple lasted until his time and that he saw it when he was a boy' (*ibid.*).

than an ethos where the hero was always effortlessly victorious. Thirdly, they probably had a status group analogous to priests.[91] These three non-trivial features of pre-Christian belief would all have provided leverage for the preaching of the missionaries. At least some core convictions could have survived into the new religion in a transmuted form.

### Literacy and orality

Pre-Christian religions of the barbarian West were not fixed in written texts, so its values and beliefs were more fluid and could more easily slide into Christian categories. Those Anglo-Saxons who underwent a genuine conversion from pagan to Christian convictions in the seventh century no doubt had to give up some values to which they had been emotionally attached. The fact that these had not been crystallised in writing[92] probably helped that process.

### Externally caused crises of value

The fact that the pre-Christian pagan religions of Europe were non-literate makes it harder to analyse the stages of their defeat, which is a pity, because they are probably the clearest examples of crises of rationality caused from outside in the medieval period. For these pagan religions did crumble: even allowing for assimilation and survivals, the coherence of pre-Christian religions in Anglo-Saxon England and Scandinavia did not survive. It is thus impossible to do what has been done with notable success for imperial China: that is, analyse the stages of the retreat of one world-view before the onslaught of another.[93] It was not just a matter of force. Force was decisive once the kings and the elite had been convinced, but they were not convinced by force. One can only make educated guesses at how they were won over, because we can only see the process from the perspective of the victorious world-view.

A plausible story of loss and gain is reconstructed from archaeology and cautious analogy by John Blair.

Changes in ritual practice were normally led by kings and nobles, precisely the groups who had the strongest reasons, even after baptism, to retain traditional modes of burial. There is evidence from Ireland and (less clearly) Wales that ancestral graves were thought not merely to mark the boundaries of family lands, but to defend them against encroachers. From seventh-century England a group of rich barrow-burials, set high on frontier zones and sometimes with their feet

---

[91] See *ibid.*, ii. 13, pp. 183–7: the Coifi story.
[92] 'One thing that Christianity did offer . . . – a thing that, in the main, the older religions did not – was literacy' (Bartlett, 'Reflections on Paganism', 56).
[93] Cf. d'Avray, *Rationalities in History*, pp. 98–100.

pointing towards open country, so strongly recall Irish and British descriptions of 'sentinel' burials that it seems reasonable to interpret them in the same light. If so, the English kings and aristocrats who . . . accepted Christianity would have faced the problem defined, in an Irish context, by Thomas Charles-Edwards: 'relegated to graveyards of churches the dead lost their power to defend the land which they left to their heirs'. . . .

The Church did nonetheless offer believers an appealing alternative: to await the resurrection in ground sanctified by the proximity of holy relics (*ad sanctos*) or of an altar used for mass, where a stream of prayer and liturgy could pour out forever for their souls.[94]

After surveying the spread of this Christian form of burial in continental Europe and among the non-English insular peoples, Blair returns to the Christianisation of England:

These trends, which had barely penetrated the Christian English by *c.*650, would affect them deeply over the next century. Like their neighbours, the English needed churches around which they could reorientate family identities, shielding them from King Radbod's worrying sense of faithlessness to a larger kindred. As English Kings and nobles began their great phase of monastic endowment they created family shrines of a new kind, as expressive of worldly status as their parents' barrows and much more able to preserve it in permanent, coherent memory. In such contexts, the new ways of burial would run no risk of disempowerment.[95]

Thus it was possible to meet social and psychological needs with resources from the new system of values.


### Destruction of the social framework

The defeat of Anglo-Saxon paganism eventually had a huge impact on the social order, not least through the proliferation of minsters (the central theme of Blair's *opus magnum*), but the social transformation did not exactly precede and cause the religious transformation. Good medieval examples of a clear causal link between drastic social and economic transformation on the one hand and a real transformation of religious values on the other are not so easy to find.[96] The sophisticated Marxist recognises that a system of beliefs can survive the transformation of a society's substructure. Catholic Christianity's survival of the end of the

---

[94] Blair, *The Church in Anglo-Saxon Society*, 59–60.    [95] *Ibid.*, 65.

[96] In my *The Preaching of the Friars*, IV. ii–iii, pp. 216–39, I argued that urbanisation and the 'commercial revolution' of the central Middle Ages are not reflected in a straightforward and privileged way in mendicant preaching, as some good historians had suggested. This is just a single case and does not mean that I reject a substructure to superstructure causal link in principle.

Roman social and economic order is a remarkable case. To quote Perry Anderson:

Issued from a post-tribal ethnic minority, triumphant in late Antiquity, dominant in feudalism, decadent and renascent under capitalism, the Roman Church has survived every other institution – cultural, political, juridical or linguistic – historically coeval with it. Engels reflected briefly on its long odyssey . . . but limited himself to registering the dependence of its mutations on those of the general history of modes of production. Its own regional autonomy and adaptability – extraordinary by any comparative standards – have yet to be seriously explored. Lucács believed it to lie in a relative permanence of man's relation to nature, unseen substratum of the religious cosmos. But he never ventured more than asides on the question.[97]

By the time that the Empire in the West had gone into terminal decline, the clergy had its own social structure of bishops, lower clerics and monks. That social structure continued. If the clerical social structure had been destroyed, continuity of values could not easily have been maintained – it is almost a tautological point.

This suggests a less ambitious version of the base-to-superstructure ideal-type. Some systems of values and beliefs are heavily dependent on a particular social class or form of social organisation, which may be important in a society without necessarily constituting its whole 'substructure'. The elimination of such a class, status group, or social organisation could destroy the beliefs that go with it. The often cited thought-world system of the Azande[98] may be a case in point. Could the belief in magic and in poison oracles survive apart from the society in which Evans-Pritchard found it? Probably not, though in practice the system has been undermined ideologically as well as by social change.

That sort of combination is probably more usual than the transformation of beliefs by social change alone, so another element can be added to this ideal-type. Thus: destruction of a social class or organisation is more likely to destroy a world-view if this happens in conjunction with a threat on the rational level, say from a rival rationality. One should explain the destruction of Catharism as a religion along such lines.[99]

Catharism is one of the forms of dualism, the explanation of evil as the creation of an evil principle, with a tendency to identify matter, the

[97] Anderson, *Passages from Antiquity to Feudalism*, 131–2 n. 11.
[98] Discussed in d'Avray, *Rationalities in History*, ch. 2.
[99] The account of Catharism which follows is mainstream but different from the presentation in a brilliant but provocative recent study: Pegg, *A Most Holy War*. Pegg is unsympathetic to the idea that there was a coherent Cathar dualist value system – except perhaps in the late period of violent persecution. I do not think this interpretation can cope with sources like the 'Liber de duobus principiis': *Livre des deux principes*, ed. Thouzellier (admittedly from Italy), but he is preparing his case (personal communication) on which scholarship will doubtless eventually pronounce a verdict.

flesh, sex and procreation as this principle's creations. This movement is one of the best- and the worst-known phenomena in medieval studies, because it has attracted intense interest, in the same kind of way as do the Knights Templar, so that not all of the books on it are very professional. The attention itself is justified. Dualism is a serious and for many an intuitively attractive system: witness the success of Manichaeism in winning a large following in both the Roman empire and the Chinese empire,[100] as well as points in between. Catharism seems not to derive from Manichaeism 'genetically' but its success in the West has to be explained in part by the appeal of such intuitions. It also required, however, an infrastructure of *perfecti* who had received the sacrament of consolation, the *Consolamentum*; they gave the same sacrament in a different form to the dying, who thus became technically *perfecti* for the brief remainder of their life (if they happened to recover the situation was difficult as they were supposed to live the perfect life of chastity and abstinence from meat).[101]

The campaign against Catharism was effective: the famous Albigensian Crusade, increasingly sophisticated inquisitorial persecution, and also effective orthodox pastoral work by the friars. The destruction of the institutional organisation of the *perfecti* was thus one of several reasons for the demise of the movement, but any explanation that ignored it would be deficient. As James Given has written:

At the beginning of the thirteenth century, the Good Men and Good Women[102] had had a more elaborate set of religious institutions, complete with bishops and their assistants, a network of convents, and regular meetings. . . . In Languedoc . . . as a result of the Albigensian crusades, heresy was driven into hiding. It became impossible to support any but the simplest forms of organisation. During the thirteenth century what organisation the Languedocian branch of the Cathar church had crumbled away. Convents disappeared, as did the Cathar diocesan structure. The last Good Men who tried to revive the sect in the early fourteenth century were essentially independent entrepreneurs, who cooperated among themselves on only an ad hoc basis.[103]

As for the strong movement in Italy, some 200 Cathars, 'described as perfect', were burned in 1278:[104] a crippling blow. Without *perfecti* it was hard to maintain the faith, and losses on that scale must surely have had

---

[100] Lieu, *Manichaeism in the Later Roman Empire and Medieval China.*
[101] Arnold, *Inquisition and Power*, 124–30; Arnold notes that 'if the recipient survived their illness, they were supposed to receive another *consolamentum* to place them more firmly in the Cathar faith, making them a proper *perfectus*' and mentions a man who tried to live the life for a few days after recovering, then gave up (p. 127; cf. also 126 on the second *consolamentum* that those who recovered were supposed to receive). See too Borst, *Die Katharer*, 193–7, and Lambert, *The Cathars*, index *s.v.* 'consolamentum'.
[102] I.e. the *perfecti*.    [103] Given, *Inquisition and Medieval Society*, 120.
[104] Lambert, *The Cathars*, 283.

an impact,[105] quite apart from discouraging recruitment of new *perfecti* and making it harder for anyone who felt ready to risk his or her life to receive the *consolamentum*.

Even so, the decline and disappearance of Catharism had other causes. It was important for the inquisitors to get public opinion on their side as far as possible:

> Inquisitors could be on very thin ice, and really unpopular executions did provoke dangerous outbursts and attacks. From this perspective, the most important work of an inquisitorial tribunal was ideological: a matter of convincing the community to view their Cathar neighbours as heretics, with all that the word came to imply, and of defining for the community the orthodox Catholic alternative.[106]

The attack by preachers on Cathar ideas about sex, marriage and the body, and the corresponding emphasis on the essential goodness of marriage, no doubt had a cumulative effect on hearts and minds.[107] Propaganda combined with the persecution out of existence of the *perfecti* status group were more deadly to the movement than either would have been on their own, though the movement would probably have survived in some form but for the dismantling of its social infrastructure.

### Internally generated crises and resilient recoveries

Another movement which ended up being regarded as more or less heretical carried the seeds of a crisis within it. This was Joachimism, inspired by the writings of Joachim of Fiore.[108] This monk in the Cistercian tradition was loyal to the papacy[109] and against negotiating with

---

[105] A heretic caught in the inquisitor's net at Bologna 'recalled his mother's complaint that she no longer found good men who would maintain the faith' (*ibid.*, 285); 'the mass burnings at Verona are likely to have reduced the numbers of perfect coming to Bologna . . . it seems that in Bologna, as amongst the last remnants in Italy of the broken Churches of Languedoc, becoming a perfect had lost its attraction and that this more than anything else was taking the heart out of the Church' (*ibid.*).

[106] Lansing, *Power and Purity*, 149. On the Languedoc, Given, *Inquisition*, 219, makes a distinct but closely related point: 'Our examination of the work of the inquisitors should have made it clear that repression in the Middle Ages was not simply a matter of the drawing of boundaries and the infliction of punishment on those who went beyond them. . . . the great *sermones generales* were staged as impressive spectacles designed to teach the masses about the correct nature of orthodox belief and the dire fate that awaited those who opposed the church.'

[107] d'Avray, *Medieval Marriage*, 67–72.

[108] The bibliography is huge but for a good general study of the life and works see Potestà, *Il tempo dell'Apocalisse*.

[109] Potestà, *Il tempo*, 266: for all the dynamite his ideas contained, 'the full loyalty' of Joachim to the Papacy was not in question ('la piena fedeltà . . . non pare in discussione').

heretics,[110] Like Marx in the nineteenth century or Arnold Toynbee in the twentieth, Joachim thought he had grasped the overall structure of History with a capital *H*. The Bible was his key and especially the book of Revelation. A double-sevens pattern was one of his schemata: seven ages up to Christ and seven ages after him, with each age after Christ mirroring the corresponding age before him.[111] Insofar as writers influenced by Joachim of Fiore's prophecies of the end of history risked dating the future, they laid themselves open to refutation by events. This kind of refutation seems to have been less devastating than one might have thought. As Sir Richard Southern commented, 'each failed Antichrist gave an additional plausibility to the claims of his successor, just as in tossing a coin a long succession of "heads" arouses a strong expectation that the next toss will turn up "tails"'.[112] As Southern pointed out, 'it took nearly 500 years from the death of Joachim' for people to accept that it was a two-headed coin.[113] Thus Joachimism illustrates two contrasting though not incompatible points: the internal generation of crises within systems of convictions, and the surprising resilience of these systems in delaying them by fighting a stubborn rearguard action or in resolving them altogether.

As already discussed in another context, a successful resolution was the eventual outcome of the crisis caused in medieval intellectual life by reflection on Aristotle's substantive philosophy. At first sight this looks like an externally caused crisis. After all, Aristotle's substantive works (as opposed to his technical logic, long known in the West) were imported from outside Christendom, in the first instance from the Arabs. Nevertheless, the trouble taken to translate and assimilate these ideas was an impulse from within, deriving from the religious elite's existing interest in problem-solving through reason. This could have posed a grave threat – for instance, Aristotle believed that the world had never been created – but in the event it was contained for reasons already discussed.

Medieval Christianity also repeatedly generated heretical ideas from within its own religious belief-system, though the system was resilient and powerful enough to repress them, until Luther. Joachimism arose out of reflection on the Book of Revelation and History by an abbot with emphatically orthodox intentions. The Waldensian movement and the challenge to the Church of the Franciscan Spirituals arose in part out of the belief in the inspiration of the Bible and evangelical poverty shared with the orthodox.

---

[110] *Ibid.*, 364 on 'total closure' ('chiusura totale') towards heretics.
[111] Cf. d'Avray, 'A Franciscan and History', 267 n. 20, with further bibliography.
[112] Southern, 'Aspects of the European Tradition of Historical Writing: 3', 177.
[113] *Ibid.*

Paradoxically, the heretical movements generated from within Latin Christendom are a symptom of the hold of religion on minds: on the whole, people do not risk their lives for disagreements over something in which they are uninterested. Conversely, the persecution of heresies in the later medieval centuries owed much of its ferocity to the strength of the convictions whose dominance was threatened: rather as in modern times the phenomenon called 'the War against Terror' bears testimony to the deeply held belief in the secular nation state, whose safety was held to justify almost any expedients in the early twenty-first century. As with the more brutal methods used in the War against Terror by liberal democracies previously opposed to such methods as torture, it may be that some of the ferocity was caused by fear and did not grow organically out of the core convictions themselves.

### Repression and persuasion

Repression is a major aspect of the medieval Church's resilience in the face of dissent,[114] but repression works best when driven by passionate conviction and supported by majority opinion: so it is not an adequate explanation for its own success. To explain the strength of conviction with which orthodox Catholic beliefs were held throughout the Middle Ages – arguably more intensely than ever in the last half of the period – one must look elsewhere, to the methods for reproducing convictions from one generation to the next and of intensifying them through mass persuasion. Here we are in the realm of instrumental rationality. In the first part of this study it was repeatedly stressed that instrumental rationality is not antithetical to the rationality of convictions but complementary with it: techniques and instrumental calculation are consciously deployed (on oneself as well as on others) to strengthen values and convictions. This is one aspect of the symbiotic relationship of the two rationalities, the other being almost the same phenomenon seen from a different angle: the colouring and shaping of instrumental rationalities by the values they serve. The next chapter discusses this reciprocal flow of influences.

---

[114] In addition to works cited above, see e.g. (for the bibliography is immense) Peters, *Inquisition*, ch. 2. For an original angle see Brambilla, *Alle origini del Sant'Uffizio*, e.g. 103–10.

# 4    The value–instrumental interface in the Middle Ages

In the sister volume on *Rationalities in History* the symbiosis or mutual dependence of instrumental and value rationality is a major theme.[1] On the one hand, value rationality shapes and colours instrumental reasoning so that the latter's essentially universal character is hard to perceive. On the other hand, instrumental rationality helps explain how values are perpetuated over time. Instrumental techniques make ideas concrete and vivid and bring out the coherence of systems and the connections between their various parts, preventing defections from value systems and transmitting them from one generation to the next. The present chapter draws out and examines more closely, with reference to medieval data, particular aspects of this analysis.

The first part of the chapter, (a), exemplifies from medieval evidence the reproduction of values through instrumental technique. The next section, (b), focuses on medieval spirituality. The sister volume *Rationalities in History* suggests that there is an 'instrumental rationality of spirituality' just as much as of the phenomena grouped under the heading of 'modernity'.[2] That is certainly true of the Middle Ages, and one can go further and show that there was a *self-conscious* awareness of spirituality's instrumental aspects. The third section, (c), returns to the question of the universality of instrumental rationality, developing the argument that instrumental rationality can transcend cultures and religions without being perceptibly the same everywhere: it is common to human societies, but only comes out *seeming* similar insofar as the underlying values overlap.

Thus the propagation of belief in the Trinity – one God yet three persons – will be used as a case study of the reproduction of values, and medieval revivalist preaching as an example of instrumental rationality to match similar rationalisations of Protestant and Buddhist preaching.

---

[1] For the corresponding theoretical treatment and a more systematic comparative approach, see *Rationalities in History*, ch. 4.
[2] *Rationalities in History*, p. 123.

Then it will be argued with reference to Bernard of Clairvaux, Thomas Aquinas and Pope John XXII that the instrumental character of much medieval devotion and asceticism was clearly and consciously articulated in the Middle Ages, though it was contested in relation to poverty by a current of Franciscan thought. The last section addresses the question of the specificity and universality of rationalities, focusing on an 'interface value' characteristic of medieval religious orders. (In Chapter 1 'interface values' were defined as values that police the border between instrumental and value rationality.) It is argued that ideas about the discretion of superiors in religious orders and their powers to suspend the rules are almost the same as the idea of *epieikeia* developed by Aristotle in the context of the Greek city state; and that this concept, while capable of transcending cultures, is not a universal value: it can be contrasted with the rigidity (or consistency!) of modern Western legal systems on the one hand, and the infinite flexibility of Hindu law on the other.

## (A) REPRODUCTION OF BELIEF

Instrumental rationality as a modern analytical concept does need a little more definition if it is to be serviceable in analysing the reproduction of belief. Some of the ways in which it was promoted were by-products of other social actions rather than instrumentally rational attempts to promote a given value. The right framework for describing them is sociological functionalism, which works best with social forms which strengthen a system without consciously setting out to do so, in the course of following some other agenda.[3]

For example, one of the more powerful ways of inculcating the doctrine of the Trinity was reinforced by a papal decision which was aimed at settling a dispute about baptism. A decretal of Pope Alexander III[4] in the twelfth century laid it down that the actual words 'I baptise you in the name of the Father, and of the Son, and of the holy Spirit, Amen' were necessary for a baptism to be valid. The decretal says explicitly that to immerse the child three times in water in the name of the Father, Son, and holy Spirit without actually saying the words explicitly was not enough for the sacrament to take effect. The Trinitarian formula was, as we would say, a performative utterance. This rule and practice would ensure that belief in the Trinity was closely associated for parish priests with one of their most important social and religious functions. Probably they often explained the core of the ceremony to godparents too. The

---

[3] For a clear-headed account of functionalism, see Douglas, *How Institutions Think*, ch. 3, pp. 30–43.

[4] X 3.42.1; Friedberg, *Corpus Iuris Canonici*, vol. 2, p. 644.

canon law rule was publicised in a model sermon collection by Johannes Herolt, to be discussed below, which was very widely diffused in the late Middle Ages. He gives the Trinitarian formula, says that baptism is not valid without it, and refers to the decretal.[5] Though popularisation of the idea of the Trinity was presumably not the purpose of the decretal, that was surely one of the effects of it.

Again, in the early Middle Ages the doctrine of the Trinity was inculcated by legal documents affecting the lives of powerful laymen and ecclesiastical institutions (especially monasteries), though that was not their aim. Thus the study of diplomatic becomes relevant to the history of the Trinity. The formula known as the *Invocatio* was widespread in the early Middle Ages, though it tended to disappear in the twelfth century.[6] A Trinitarian formula was a one type of *Invocatio*.[7] It was employed, notably, in Charlemagne's charters. In the early Middle Ages documents had a more sacral character than they would after the massive increase in the use of written records from the twelfth century on.[8] People paid attention to these documents and the presence of a Trinitarian formula in a prominent place at the beginning would help make the doctrine concrete in the minds of ecclesiastics and perhaps also some of the lay donors. Such unintentional mechanisms for propagating beliefs are among the most effective. Here, however, our main concern is with deliberate mechanisms for reproducing, diffusing and intensifying convictions, such as education (not only via schools), argument, ritual and preaching.

### Education

Systems of values and convictions may be reproduced and propagated in various ways. One of the commonest and most obvious is upbringing. People and peoples do not necessarily retain the convictions inculcated in childhood and youth, but often they do. Now this can be simply a matter of habit and tradition. Not necessarily, though: if the values in question form a coherent system and if they are passed on by parents

---

[5] 'But the form of words is "I baptise you in the name of the Father and the Son and the holy Spirit", as is clear from the *Liber Extra*, "On Baptism", c. i. And without these words there can be no baptism' ('Sed forma verborum est hec: "Ego baptiso te in nomine patris et filii et spiritus sancti", ut patet Extra "De baptismo", c. i. Et sine his verbis non potest fieri baptismus') (Johannes Herolt, *Sermones discipuli de tempore* (Nuremberg, 1483 edn.), sermon LXXVI, third column of sermon. (In using this edition below I normalise *c* and *t*, *u* and *v*, and of course the punctuation.)

[6] Guyotjeannin, Pycke and Tock, *Diplomatique médiévale*, 72, 123.

[7] Santifaller, 'Über die Verbal-Invokation in Urkunden', 10–12 (this essay is a stand-alone monograph of twenty pages).

[8] This is a central argument of Clanchy, *From Memory to Written Record.*

and others with authentic certainty. When the older generation's views are hanging on somehow when their support has been shot away the new one abandons them easily; if different value systems are at war within the same society adolescents feel a strong sense of choice; but insofar as parents, teachers and mass media agree in presenting a coherent scheme of values and convictions and give some respectable reasons for them, a high proportion of their charges accept the basic package.

So far as the Middle Ages are concerned, the monastic practice of oblation of children[9] must surely have played a large part in the formation of some key beliefs, including a vivid awareness of the Trinity. Oblation meant that boys grew up in monasteries from the age of about 7 or 8; it seems to have been the normal way to become a monk before the middle decades of the twelfth century, when the idea of monastic life as a choice made by young adults came in, with the help of a strong impulse from the Cistercians. The monastery would have been their social world. The idea of the Trinity was integrated into the collective prayer life of the monastery, and thus presumably impressed itself on the minds of some of the youths and boys who had joined the monastery as young 'oblates'.[10] The awareness would have been especially sharp where religious houses or their churches were dedicated to the Trinity: a growing practice in north and central France from the ninth to the eleventh century.[11] There are other symptoms that devotion to the Trinity played a special role in the religious life of Benedictine monasteries in the tenth and eleventh centuries and that the feast of the Holy Trinity grew up in Benedictine monasteries in the eleventh century, when oblation of children was still the norm. Monasteries were like greenhouses where values and beliefs could grow strong.

### The laity and godparenthood

The Trinity is in fact a particularly interesting case. At least from the Carolingian era, it became bound up with the practice of

---

[9] The standard study is De Jong, *In Samuel's Image*.

[10] 'Already in the eighth, ninth and tenth centuries the devotion to the Trinity was finding expression in various external forms in quite a number of circles. This is shown by the liturgical Hours of monks, which were supposed to begin and end with an invocation of the Trinity, as well as by the Votive Mass that was being put together at this time' ('Daß schon im 8., 9., und 10. Jh. die Verehrung der Dreifaltigkeit in manchen Kreisen zu vielen äusseren Formen drängte, beweisen neben der Votivmesse, die um diese Zeit zusammengestellt wurde, das Stundengebet der Mönche, das mit iherer Anrufung beginnen und schließen sollte'); Browe, 'Zur Geschichte des Dreifaltigkeitsfestes', 67.

[11] *Ibid.*

godparenthood.[12] This institution involved both clergy and laity in what would normally be a special and memorable occasion. Moreover, godparenthood was remarkably popular with the laity: it created quasi-kinship bonds and these were evidently perceived as highly desirable. People would therefore be prepared to go to some trouble to be accepted as godparents. They would need to take a little trouble because knowledge of the Creed (and the Lord's Prayer) became a precondition, from the time of the Carolingian reforms, for acting as a godparent at baptism.

Anyone who knew the Creed (any of the creeds) would know something of the doctrine of the Trinity, so *grosso modo* one can be confident that some familiarity with the idea of the Trinity was a *sine qua non* for assuming a sought-after social role. Such rules are hardly ever enforced entirely but this one seems to have been taken rather seriously and probably had more impact than a lot of the Carolingian reforming legislation.

### Logical arguments

In any period, educated people and even some of the uneducated would be bound to wonder what it could mean to speak of 'three persons in one God'. The arguments with which intellectuals attempted to make sense of the belief are a form of instrumental rationality in that most of them were not individually imposed by the core conviction as such: theologians had room for manoeuvre in elaborating their reasons. In fact the doctrine seems to have been a massive stimulus to intellectual creativity: we have already noted John Marenbon's insight that much of the most interesting medieval philosophy arose out of efforts to make sense of the Trinity.[13]

### Appeals to senses and emotions

Even in the early Middle Ages official and unofficial rituals would have impressed the idea of the Trinity on the mind. The institution of the feast of the Holy Trinity by Pope John XXII in 1334[14] ensured that the belief

---

[12] The following remarks on godparenthood are based on Lynch, *Godparents and Kinship in Early Medieval Europe*, ch. 11, esp. p. 322.

[13] 'But problems about intellectual knowledge were most often tackled by theologians in two contexts which would startle the philosopher of today. One is the theory of trinitarian relations. . . . Augustine had suggested that analogies to the Trinity could be found in man's mind. This theme . . . provided the basis for elaborate later medieval investigations of the workings of the human intellect' (Marenbon, *Later Medieval Philosophy*, 94); 'the theologians did not merely take it for granted that God is triune – often their most complex explorations of the human soul were carried out simply in order to penetrate the mystery of the Trinity' (*ibid.*, 190–1).

[14] See below, p. 99.

would be reinforced by the 'devotional technologies' that accompanied such celebrations: incense, lights and generally an exceptionally memorable service, in which a high proportion of the laity and all of the higher clergy would have participated.

### Preaching, mass communication and the Trinity

Especially after the establishment of the Feast of the Holy Trinity in 1334 the doctrine would have been propagated in a large number of sermons based on models by specialists in the technique of reaching the imagination of large aggregates of people. Even before the invention of printing the doctrine would have been regularly brought before the minds of a high proportion of the population. One can legitimately speak of 'mass communication'.

The concept of preaching as mass communication has been disputed on the grounds that there is 'a large gap between text and performance'[15] and that 'the idea of "mass media" tends to have, lurking behind it, certain assumptions about the passivity of the audience – that such media can "programme" their beliefs'.[16] Preaching did not programme beliefs any more than modern mass communications do. Newspaper readers and television watchers are far from passive recipients of what they read and see. So if this is a reason not to call preaching a mass medium it is reason not to call newspapers a mass medium: people discuss them, react against them, and use them for fish and chips.

As for the 'gap between text and performance', that argument too applies equally to print – if for 'performance' you read Reception. The whole thrust of literary theory in the last decades of the twentieth century was to emphasise the multiplicity of different meanings that could be derived from texts – printed texts – at the reception end, and this insight will survive the relegation of those theories to the dustbin of intellectual fashion. French and American literary theory ('Deconstruction') tended to break off meaning from the intention of a text's author altogether – producing the same uncertainty about the end-user's understanding without needing to invoke 'performance'. A more historically minded German school loosened the link between the intention behind a text and the text's reception without cutting it altogether.[17] Hans-Georg Gadamer saw that textual meaning expands beyond the author's intentions: for instance, legislators actually know that the meaning of their statutes will be expanded as they are applied and made concrete in the

---

[15] Arnold, *Belief and Unbelief*, 48.    [16] *Ibid.*, 49.
[17] For a good introduction see Warning, *Rezeptionsästhetik*.

face of unforeseen test cases.[18] Wolfgang Iser criticised earlier literary theories that make it seem as if 'communication were conceivable only as a one-way street from text to reader', and argued that 'For this reason it seems imperative to find a way of describing reading as a process of dynamic reciprocal interaction of text and reader.'[19] All this is now commonplace. Reception theory was assimilated long since by sermon studies.[20]

Similarly, the question 'How do you know whether anyone took in what the preachers were saying?' has naturally been addressed by medieval sermon scholarship. Again, modern newspapers provide an apposite analogy. Historians of the future will virtually never know what an individual reader made of an individual article. If certain themes are constantly reiterated in newspapers with a large circulation, however, they will be certain that readers are distributed along a spectrum between those who understand everything and those who understand nothing: in short, that the iteration will have affected attitudes to a greater or lesser degree. It is much the same with model sermons diffused in many manuscripts.[21] The key point is that the differences between individual 'performances' cancel out if one is interested not in this or that occasion but in aggregate effects.

*A fortiori*, after printing had been invented model sermon collections were even more widely diffused than before. If preaching had been a mass medium before, with sermon collections being copied and recopied in very large numbers by hand, they were even more so now, thanks to the new technology. The sermons we will study here were accessible in print. Many copies were available and each could have been used again and again for sermons to different congregations, or (with variations) at widely spaced intervals.

It is necessary to be selective. Preaching on the Trinity is an overwhelming topic, and there can be no question of doing justice to it here. In 1334 Trinity Sunday, a week after Pentecost, had been established throughout Christendom as a top-category feast.[22] Sermons on the Trinity would therefore be associated with a major liturgical occasion. Trinity Sunday

---

[18] Gadamer, *Wahrheit und Methode*, 312.

[19] 'Texttheorien solcher Art legen immer wieder die Vermutung nahe, als ob die Kommunikation nur als eine Einbandstraße vom Text zum Leser vorstellbar wäre. Aus diesem Grunde erscheint es geboten, das Lesen als Prozeß einer dynamischen Wechselwirkung von Text und Leser beschreibbar zu machen'; Iser, *Der Akt des Lesens*, 176.

[20] d'Avray, *Death and the Prince*, 189–99.

[21] Here I paraphrase a paragraph of d'Avray, *Medieval Marriage Sermons*, since Arnold may have missed, or does not address, these arguments.

[22] Browe, 'Zur Geschichte des Dreifaltigkeitsfestes', 79; Hauck, *Kirchengeschichte Deutschlands*, 374.

preaching of the late Middle Ages certainly deserves a monograph in its own right, but it is reasonably safe to say that a fair proportion of the massive corpus of model sermons that would be found share two characteristics of late medieval preaching generally: the attempt to reach the imagination as well as the abstract intelligence (so: concrete modes of thought), and a tendency to draw out connections between different points on the map of religious belief.[23]

To give a taste of this large genre one preacher may be mentioned briefly: Johannes Herolt, OP, known as 'Discipulus', whose model sermons enjoyed a tremendously wide diffusion through the printing press in the later Middle Ages.[24] In his widely diffused collection of *de tempore* sermons there are three sermons for this Sunday, two of them linking it with baptism.[25] The connection is worth noting but must be left aside here. The following references (they are no more than that, an indication of the manner in which the subject is treated) are confined to the first of the three sermons.

Herolt tries to make the doctrine vivid to the imagination by using analogies (a traditional method): God is a fountain, producing a stream, and fountain and stream fill a pool.[26] The Trinity is also linked with a range of other ideas, so:

- death as the result of original sin: 'But you might say: in what way is man[27] created in God's image? I reply: first in respect of immortality, for just as God is immortal, so too is the soul. . . . Indeed, even with regard to the body man was created to be immortal, but because he sinned, on that account he became mortal'.[28]

---

[23] For the latter tendency in an earlier period, see d'Avray, *The Preaching of the Friars*, 246–7.

[24] 'It is hard to overstate the practical effect of, above all, the Sermones de Tempore, which survive in over 200 fifteenth-century manuscripts and which were printed about forty-five times between 1474 and 1500' ('die praktische Wirkung vor allem der Sermones de tempore, die in weit über 200 Hss des 15. Jh.s erhalten sind und zwischen 1474 und 1500 etwa 45 Drucke erlebten, wird man nicht leicht überschätzen'); Worstbrock, 'Herolt, Johannes (Discipulus)', 1126. As noted earlier, I have used the Nuremberg, 1483 edn, in the British Library IB.7312 copy of 'Sermones discipuli', Sermon no. lxxv.

[25] 'Sermo LXXV. In festo trinitatis'; 'Sermo lxxvi. In eadem dominica de trinitate et baptismo'; 'Sermo lxxvii. Iterum de trinitate et de signis que ante et post baptismum fiunt'. The edition is unpaginated and unfoliated but the sermon numbers in the upper margin make it relatively easy to navigate.

[26] E.g. passage beginning: 'Idem cognoscitur in fonte' and ending 'est eadem substantia' (Herolt, *Sermones*, LXXV, col. 3).

[27] 'man' = 'men and women' throughout.

[28] 'Sed diceres: Quomodo homo ad imaginem dei est creatus? Respondeo: primo quantum ad immortalitatem, quia sicut deus est immortalis, sic et anima. . . . Immo etiam

- man's relation to the whole created world: 'Secondly, man is created in the image of God in respect of lordship, for just as God is the lord of all, so man is the lord of all creatures, . . . for if man had remained in the state of innocence, all creatures would have been subject to him, that is the birds of the air and the fish of the sea and the animals on earth. But because man was disobedient to his creator, he lost to a great extent the obedience of creatures. Again God created everything in heaven and on earth because of man: this is clear. For angels serve men, and similarly the heavenly bodies serve man. For the sun produces day for your benefit, and the moon illuminates the night for you, fire tempers the cold for you, air gives you breath, water washes away bad smells for you and alleviates burning thirst for you, the land brings forth its fruits for you, grain and wine that is, the water brings forth for you fish, the sheep provides you with wool with which to cover your body, and so on. Therefore man is the lord of all creatures; therefore he is bound to praise God above all creatures.'[29]
- the powers of the soul: 'Thirdly, man is created in the image of the Trinity, and this in the three powers of the soul, that is, memory, intelligence, and will, that is, in such a way that memory is the chamber of the Father, where he dwells through continuous recollection; intelligence is the chamber of the Son, where he dwells through knowledge of the true faith; and will is the chamber of the holy Spirit, where he dwells through love, in such a way that man may conform his will to the divine will in true charity.'[30]

secundum corpus homo fuit creatus quod debuit esse immortalis, sed quia peccavit, propterea factus est mortalis' (*ibid.*).

[29] 'Secundo homo ad imaginem dei creatus est quantum ad dominationem, quia sicut deus est dominus omnium, sic homo omnium creaturarum, . . . quia si homo in statu innocentie permansisset, omnes creature ei subiecte fuissent, scilicet volucres celi et pisces maris et animalia in terris. Sed quia homo suo creatori inobediens extitit, ideo obedientiam creaturarum pro magna parte perdidit. Item deus omnia que sunt in celo et in terra propter hominem creavit: hoc patet. Nam angeli serviunt hominibus, similiter celi luminaria serviunt homini. Nam sol causat tibi diem, luna illuminat tibi noctem, ignis temperat tibi frigiditatem, aer dat tibi spiramen, aqua mundat tibi fetorem et mitigat tibi sitis ardorem, terra profert tibi fructus, scilicet frumentum et vinum, aqua profert tibi pisces, ovis profert tibi lanam cum qua tegis corpus tuum, et sic de aliis. Ergo homo est dominus omnium creaturarum, ergo tenetur deum laudare pre omnibus creaturis' (*ibid.*, cols. 3–4).

[30] 'Tertio homo creatus est ad imaginem trinitatis, et hoc in tribus potentiis anime, scilicet memoria, intelligentia et voluntate, scilicet ut memoria sit camera patris in qua habitet per continuam recordationem, intelligentia sit camera filii in qua habitet per vere fidei cognitionem, voluntas sit camera spiritus sancti in qua habitet per amorem, ut homo in vera caritate voluntatem suam conformet divine voluntati' (*ibid.*, col. 4).

- God the Father's mercy and love: 'But although God the Father is omnipotent, there are two things in him, and two in us, which seem to conquer him. The first is his heartfelt mercy. . . . The second is his feeling of love.'[31]
- prayer: 'The third is when we pray in tears.'[32]
- redemption: 'Again, you should know that although the Son is utterly wise, nevertheless he knowingly allows himself to be fooled in selling, buying and exchange. In selling, indeed, because in selling to us the kingdom of heaven he allows himself to be taken in beyond half the just price. For he had sold himself to the apostles for nets and little boats, to Zachaeus for half what the man possessed, to the widow for two small coins, to some people for a cup of cold water, as we read in Matthew 10, to some for good will. . . . Secondly, he allows himself to be taken in by us when we are selling, for he purchases our worthless things for a dear price. For he bought[33] our body for the great price of his blood . . . he bought our soul by laying down his soul . . . Thirdly he allows himself to be taken in by us in exchange, since he restores our goods to us one hundredfold.'[34]
- heaven, purgatory, hell, the world and mercy: 'But the goodness that is attributed to the holy Spirit is so great that no one can hide themselves from it . . . For in heaven it is saving mercy . . . in purgatory it is liberating mercy . . . in hell it is mitigating mercy, since God's punishment there stops short of what is deserved . . . in the world, however, it is sometimes preserving mercy, with the just, sometimes mercy that is patient, with evildoers, sometimes mercy that pulls people along – with the hard of heart, that is, who are pulled along by the carrot and the stick, sometimes the mercy of acceptance, with those who return . . . That mercy and goodness is a particular characteristic of the holy Spirit.'[35]

---

[31] 'Quamvis autem deus pater sit omnipotens, duo tamen sunt in ipso, et duo in nobis, que ipsum vincere videntur. Primum est sua pietas viscerosa. . . . Secundum est sua caritas affectuosa' (*ibid.*, col. 6).

[32] 'Tertium est oratio nostra lachrimosa' (*ibid.*).

[33] The change of tense is a stylistic guess: 'emit' can be either present or perfect.

[34] 'Item sciendum quamvis filius sit sapientissimus [sapientissmus *edn*], tamen scienter permittit se decipi in venditione, emptione et commutatione. In venditione quidem, quia vendens nobis regnum celorum permittit se a nobis decipi ultra dimidium iusti pretii. Ipsum enim vendiderat apostolis pro rethibus et parva navicula, Zacheo pro dimidia substantia, vidue pro duobus minutis, quibusdam pro calice aque frigide, ut habetur Math. x., quibusdam pro bona voluntate. . . . Secundo permittit se decipi a nobis in emptione, quia vilia nostra caro pretio emit. Nam corpus nostrum emit pretio magno sui sanguinis . . . animam nostram emit positione anime sue . . . Tertio permittit se a nobis decipi in commutatione, quia res nostras nobis in centuplo restituet' (*ibid.*, cols. 6–7).

[35] 'Sed bonitas que attribuitur spiritui sancto tanta est ut ab ea nullus se abscondere possit . . . Nam in celo est misericordia salvans . . . in purgatorio est misericordia

In the above we have combined precisely the two key elements of value rationality: a concrete mode of thought (much more vivid, obviously, in 'live' sermons well preached) and a network of interlinked ideas. The history of Trinitarian convictions in the Middle Ages illustrates how the vitality of beliefs is preserved by the deployment of instrumentally rational techniques to reproduce them in successive generations. These techniques ensure among other things that the beliefs in question are impressed on the mind in a vivid and concrete way. Instrumental rationality helps to turn weak opinions or received ideas into firmly held convictions and values. Looked at from the other end, however, one may say that the convictions generate instrumental techniques which ensure their survival. In fact what we have is a spiral process: conviction or value rationality produces techniques which recreate the convictions, which in turn foster the instrumental technology that protects them. Next, the examination of this spiral process will be continued with the emphasis on instrumental technologies and then, in (b), on awareness of the instrumental character of spiritualities.

### Revivalist preaching as instrumental rationality

Without the help of newspapers,[36] radio,[37] or television,[38] medieval revivalist preachers nevertheless managed to orchestrate the emotions of large numbers of people. Like later Protestant counterparts such as the early Methodist George Whitefield,[39] they used the technique of keeping on the move. This prevented familiarity breeding indifference, as could easily happen with routine Sunday preaching. Vincent Ferrer apparently visited fifty different places between 8 February 1418 and 5 April 1419.[40] An infrastructure of mendicant convents made this easier – eighteen of the places had at least one.[41] By contrast with the likes of Whitefield, the political establishment supported him: he had come at the invitation of the Duke of Brittany.[42]

---

liberans … in inferno est misericordia mitigans, quia deus ibi punit citra condignum … in mundo vero modo est misericordia conservans quantum ad iustos, modo misericordia expectans quantum ad malos, modo misericordia trahens quantum ad duros, qui per beneficia et flagella trahuntur, modo misericordia suscipiens quantum ad revertentes … Ista autem misericordia et bonitas spiritui sancto est propria et innata' (*ibid.*, col. 7).

[36] For newspapers and Protestant revivalist preaching in the USA, see Stout, 'Religion, Communications', at 112, 117.

[37] Cf. Harrell, 'Oral Roberts', 322–4. For Buddhist preaching and the radio, see Deegalle, *Popularising Buddhism*, 147; also 165–6.

[38] Harrell, 'Oral Roberts', 325–9; for Buddhist preaching and television, see Deegalle, *Popularising Buddhism*, 166–7.

[39] See *Rationalities in History*, ch. 4, pp. 116–17.

[40] Martin, *Les Ordres mendiants*, 317–18.     [41] *Ibid.*, 318.     [42] *Ibid.*, 317.

The local secular establishment provided a supportive infrastructure for fifteenth-century revivalist preaching. For a Vincent Ferrer or a Thomas Cornette expenses were likely to be paid.[43] The authorities would find places large enough to hold the crowd and they would erect a platform.[44] In short, the administrative side of revivalist preaching was likely to be organised by the secular authorities rather than by the revivalists themselves.

Moving back in time to the thirteenth-century revival known as the 'Great Allelluia', we find techniques that were instrumental to the point of being manipulative. Here we have the benefit of an admirable analysis by Augustine Thompson.[45] Thompson argues that the revivalists did not have an existing wave of religious emotion to ride: they had to make their own wave. They 'met regularly to determine the locations, days, and hours of their sermons' and appear on at least one occasion to have used their coordinated timetable for two preachers to fake mutual visions of each other preaching in different cities![46] Thompson describes the public conversion of two Bologna University masters at the end of (two different) sermons as 'too beautifully orchestrated to have been unplanned and spontaneous'.[47] Behind the drama was an impressive organisational infrastructure:

A preacher's impact depended on his audibility and visibility. Since most sermons of the Alleluia took place outside the cities, in fields or on banks of rivers, a stage of some type was essential. During the great assembly at Paquara [a revivalist meeting which aimed to restore peace] John of Vicenza employed a kind of look-out tower . . . of wood rising almost . . . 28 metres.[48]

For this Paquara event 'workmen had to construct two bridges over the Adige'; 'these preparations would have required a "road crew" of considerable size'.[49]

In the Middle Ages, as today, revivalist preaching catches the attention because of its dramatic and apparently spontaneous quality. It is important to point out that a lot more was required for popular success than personal charisma. Practical calculation to arrange the setting was a precondition for the appeal to the emotions.

That said, one should not exaggerate the importance of revivalist preaching. It spiced up but could not replace the routine sort. The

[43] *Ibid.*, 318; Martin, *Le Métier de prédicateur*, 54–5.
[44] Martin, *Le Métier*, 55; Martin, *Les Ordres*, 318–19.
[45] Thompson, *Revival Preachers*.     [46] *Ibid.*, 93–4.
[47] *Ibid.*, 97.     [48] *Ibid.*, 92.     [49] *Ibid.*, 93.

majority of sermons were delivered in a less dramatic mode on Sundays and major feast days. That too required an infrastructure, though of a quite different sort.[50] The same may be said *mutatis mutandis* of more modern Christianity. This routine preaching also presupposed and presupposes rational organisation. The friars established such a system in the thirteenth century and the various Protestant churches had and have their counterparts.[51] All that belongs to the history of rationalisation, but in a more trivial sense than the self-conscious means–ends calculations of the revivalists.

### Values and the chronology of medieval preaching

We have seen that medieval Christianity can be aligned with Protestantism in its rationalisation of revivalist preaching, and so in this respect contrasted with Judaism and pre-colonial Hinduism, despite similarities in other respects. Preaching is, however, a fundamental value in Buddhism, both in modern times and in very early teaching.[52] It has deep roots in medieval Christianity too, being embedded in New Testament texts and emphasised by Augustine and Gregory the Great, two of the writers who had most affected medieval values.[53] Revivalist preaching can therefore be explained as just such a set of techniques as that value was likely to generate.

The question then arises: how to explain the chronology of preaching in the Middle Ages? According to a standard view,[54] preaching that reached the masses did not become common until the second half of the Middle Ages. There is crusade preaching in the eleventh century,[55] Bernard of Clairvaux's preaching tour against heresy in the twelfth,[56] the wandering preachers (orthodox or dissident) inspired in one way or another by the apostolic life ideal,[57] and the preaching revival of Foulques of Neuilly

---

[50] Analysed e.g. in d'Avray, *The Preaching of the Friars*.

[51] For instance, for the Methodist system of preaching in the USA in the generation after Whitefield see Wigger, *Taking Heaven by Storm*, chs. 2–3.

[52] Mahâvagga, I.5.2–4, in *Vinaya Texts, Part I*, trans. Rhys Davids and Oldenberg, 85–8; cf. Deegalle, *Popularising Buddhism*, ch. 2: 'Buddha as the Best Preacher'; Freiberger, *Der Orden in der Lehre*, 195–6.

[53] Dessì and Lauwers, 'Introduction, *Praedicatores* et Prophètes' to *La Parole du Prédicateur*, 9.

[54] Which I endorsed with caveats in *The Preaching of the Friars*, 20.

[55] For early crusade preaching see e.g. Riley-Smith, *The First Crusade and the Idea of Crusading*, index s.v. 'preaching'.

[56] Cf. e.g. Mayne Kienzle, 'Medieval Sermons and their Performance', 117.

[57] Grundmann, *Religiöse Bewegungen*, 17–18, 38–45, 65.

at the end of the century.[58] Then comes the age of the friars, bringing revivalist as well routine preaching.

If preaching was a core value of medieval Christianity, why did it take so long to set up delivery systems? Some well-known differences between the last three medieval centuries and the preceding period probably provide the answers. Both revivalist and routine preaching were fostered by urbanisation, which made it easier to arrange events with large concentrations of listeners, collective organisation (towns issued invitations, the mendicant orders could coordinate a preaching campaign), and intellectual training (Foulques de Neuilly studied with the famous master Peter the Chanter at Paris; and mendicant preachers had all been through their order's schools and in some cases to university as well).

It is true that none of this was indispensable for preaching. It is possible indeed that in a much earlier period of medieval history (roughly, the seventh to the ninth century) there was a lot more preaching than we can actually prove to have been going on. Insofar as the basic pastoral unit was a 'minster', a kind of 'team-ministry' covering a larger area than a parish, better training for priests may have been available (through the minster community) and mini-preaching revivals launched from these bases might have been possible. Some such system is suggested by John Blair's study of the Anglo-Saxon Church,[59] and the model may be applicable also to the Continent.[60]

In the intervening period, however, the basic pastoral unit increasingly became the rural parish. If there had ever been a golden age of minster preaching in say the eighth or ninth centuries – which is likely to remain an unprovable possibility – it will have come to an end as the parish system developed. Parishes were smaller than the units they replaced and doubtless made the ritual life of the Church more accessible to more people, but the priests who served them might have very little education: most would have been trained on a sort of apprenticeship system.[61] This kind of infrastructure did not favour either routine or revivalist preaching. The general point is that the success of values in generating corresponding instrumental techniques depends on unconnected infrastructures, which may make it hard to implement the value. The value then becomes a 'delayed action' cause, which only operates when other variables fall into place.

---

[58] d'Avray, *Preaching of the Friars*, 22–4; Forni, 'La "Nouvelle Prédication"'.

[59] For the minster system in Anglo-Saxon England, in connection with evangelisation, see Blair, *The Church in Anglo-Saxon Society*, 164–5.

[60] The model would explain the evidence of book ownership and preaching presented by a recent thesis: see McCune, 'An Edition and Study of Select Sermons'.

[61] d'Avray, *Preaching of the Friars*, 19–20, with further references.

## (B) THE SELF-AWARE INSTRUMENTALITY OF MEDIEVAL SPIRITUALITY

### Aquinas on rituals

Self-conscious theoretical comments on the instrumental character of religious practices qualify for special attention. For some medieval writers theorised explicitly on the optional character of many devotional practices: these were not core values deriving from Jesus Christ but devices created by humans to serve those core values – instrumentally. For Thomas Aquinas, notably, external actions can be like signs which humans use as a means by which the mind may be raised to God in spiritual acts:

in divine worship it is necessary to use some bodily things, so that the human mind may be stimulated by them, by certain signs, as it were, to the spiritual acts through which it is joined to God. And therefore [the virtue of] religion does indeed have internal acts which are primary as it were and which pertain to religion in and of themselves: and on the other hand external acts which are secondary so to speak and which are subordinated to the interior ones.[62]

Later on we read that:

just as prayer is primarily (*primordialiter*) in the mind, but on a secondary level it finds expression in words ... so too adoration does indeed principally consist in an interior reverence for God, but secondarily in certain bodily signs of humility: thus we genuflect to show our weakness in comparison to God; we prostrate ourselves and in this way we as it were publicly acknowledge that in ourselves we are nothing.[63]

Elsewhere, Thomas Aquinas gives his thoughts on Christian rituals other than the sacraments. He is dealing with an objection that

in the Old Law [the Jewish Law before Christ] not only were sacraments established, but also certain other sacral things ... But in the New Law, even though some sacraments were instituted, still, no sacral things seem to have been instituted by the Lord: say things pertaining to the consecration (*sanctificationem*) of a temple or of vessels, or indeed for the celebration of some ceremony (*solemnitatem*). Therefore the new law did not regulate exterior things to a sufficient degree.[64]

He replies as follows:

in the sacraments of the new law grace is given, and this is only from Christ: and so it was necessary that they be instituted by him. But in sacral things no grace is

---

[62] *Summa theologiae*, 2-2 q. 81 a. 7, 'Respondeo' section, in Aquinas, *Opera omnia*, vol. 9, p. 184.
[63] *Ibid.*, 2-2 q. 84 a. 2 ad 2.
[64] *Ibid.*, 1-2 q. 108 a. 2 objection 2; *Opera omnia*, vol. 7, p. 284.

given: say in the consecration of a church or altar or of other things of this sort, or indeed in the actual celebration of ceremonies. And therefore the Lord left such things, which do not in themselves involve the necessity of interior grace, for the faithful to create as they prefer.[65]

Rituals other than the sacraments are within the realm of human discretion. This fits our concept of instrumental choice as the room for manoeuvre within a framework set by values. The implication is that God left Christians a good deal of room to create the ritual acts that worked.

Rituals fit comfortably within the framework of the Christian religion as Aquinas understands it, but apart from some special cases, above all the sacraments, it is left to humans to calculate what forms will best serve the core religious values.

### Gregory the Great's instrumental attitude to ritual

The 'instrumental' attitude to devotion or rather to the techniques calculated to foster it is quite deep-rooted in medieval Catholicism. It underlies a famous passage in which Pope Gregory the Great advises the missionaries in Anglo-Saxon England to adapt pagan temples and festivals:

the idol temples of that race [the English] should by no means be destroyed, but only the idols in them. Take holy water and sprinkle it in these shrines, build altars and place relics in them. For if the shrines are well built, it is essential that they should be changed from the worship of devils to the service of the true God. When this people see that their shrines are not destroyed they will be able to banish error from their hearts and be more ready to come to the places they are familiar with, but now recognising and worshipping the true God. And because they are in the habit of slaughtering much cattle as sacrifices to devils, some solemnity ought to be given them in exchange for this. So on the day of the dedication or the festivals of the holy martyrs, whose relics are deposited there, let them make themselves huts from the branches of the trees around the churches which have been converted out of shrines, and let them celebrate the solemnity with religious feasts. Do not let them sacrifice animals to the devil, but let them slaughter animals for their own food to the praise of God, and let them give thanks to the Giver of all things for his bountiful provision. Thus while some outward rejoicings are preserved, they will be able more easily to share in inward rejoicings.[66]

The basic attitude that underlies the passages from Gregory the Great and Aquinas, far apart though they may be in time, is that there are many external rituals and devotions which may promote the core values of their religion but which can be distinguished from them.

---

[65]  *Ibid.*, ad 2; *Opera omnia*, vol. 7, p. 285.
[66]  *Bede's Ecclesiastical History*, ed. Colgrave and Mynors, i. 30, pp. 106–9.

## Instrumental rationality and medieval Western monasticism

As with devotion, so with monasticism: something akin to the value/ instrumental rational pair of concepts underlies both writings and practice. A key distinction between precepts and counsels underlies two of the most articulate reflections on the life of 'religion' (i.e. of monks, regular canons and friars): the little treatise 'On Precept and Dispensation' by Bernard of Clairvaux, and the discussion of religious orders towards the end of the 'Secunda secundi' of Thomas Aquinas's *Summa theologica*. The realm where 'precepts' left off and 'counsels' took over was one of instrumental rationality.

In the early 1140s or earlier two monks from the Benedictine monastery of Chartres, Saint-Père de Vallée, wrote to Bernard with a series of questions about obedience to the monastic rule. Among his replies are some that bring out the difference between the Benedictine rule and absolute values, and the instrumental character of the letter of the rule.[67] Early on he explains that the provisions of the rule were not absolute values, apart from some exceptions that he lists:

Thus all the provisions of St Benedict's rule – apart of course from quite a few dealing with spiritual things, such as charity, humility, kindness, which clearly derive from God's authority rather than his, so that they cannot by any means be changed – apart from that all the rest are to be judged as advice or counsels so far as those who have not made a monastic profession are concerned, nor does failure to observe them do harm, while on the other hand they turn into precepts for those who do make their profession as monks . . . to the former they are quite appropriately held to be voluntary or man-made,[68] to the latter necessary and quasi-natural. I would of course call them 'necessary' in such a way that there should be no question of their prevailing against necessary and rational dispensations.[69]

Charity, humility, etc. are values. The other provisions of the rule are instrumental. They serve values, which is why they are subject to rational dispensations. In his way, Bernard of Clairvaux is saying in his own discourse that the rules of religious orders and other man-made ecclesiastical rules – he is no longer just referring to the Benedictine rule[70] – are the products of human reason and may be suspended in

[67] Cf. Fieback, '*Necessitas non est legi subiecta, maxime positivae*', 137, 145–6.
[68] My rather free translation of 'factitia'.
[69] Bernard of Clairvaux, *Tractatus de praecepto et dispensatione*, 1.2, in *Sancti Bernardi opera*, vol. 3, pp. 255–6.
[70] *Ibid.*, 2.4, p. 256: passage beginning 'Et quidem stabile dixerim' and ending 'dignae auctoritatis'.

particular cases when they do not serve the purpose for which they were designed:

Since they are handed down from saints, they are sanctified and continue unshaken, nor is it by any means allowed to any one of those subject to them to vary or alter them in any way. Since, however, they derive from men, the men who succeed those men, taking their place and their office by canonical election, may on occasion licitly, and without doing any damage, grant dispensations from them, where the situations, persons, places, or times require it. Here the reader should note carefully that I am carefully not saying that they can be changed lightly or arbitrarily even by these men, but that dispensations may be granted conscientiously (*fideliter*) and for a rational cause (*ex ratione*).[71]

The next sentence stresses again that these rules are not in themselves values: 'They can be subject to this same change, in such a manner, and from such men, because they are not good naturally or in and of themselves.'[72] He proceeds to develop a sort of monastic counterpart to Aristotle's doctrine of *epieikeia*: the provisions in rules for the monastic and religious life were meant to be instrumental in serving charity and should be obeyed so long as they work in that way, but if they should become counter-productive in particular circumstances then dispensation is in order:

For indeed, they were devised and instituted, not because it was forbidden to live in a different way, but because it was more expedient in this way, and obviously there was no other aim apart from the increase or safeguarding of charity. So long as they are in the service of charity, they are unchangeably stable, and cannot be altered in any way, without wrongdoing, even by those same religious superiors. But if, conversely, they should sometimes happen to seem to be contrary to charity, to those namely to whom the power is given to recognise this and to whom the task of taking care of this has been entrusted, is it not clearly the most just thing in the world, that those things which had been devised for the sake of charity, should also, for the sake of charity, where it seems to be expedient, be either omitted, or intermitted, or perhaps changed into something that works better.[73]

### Aquinas on the instrumental character of religious orders

Moving from the monastic to the scholastic world, we find Thomas Aquinas thinking along exactly the same lines as Bernard of Clairvaux. He brings out the instrumental character of Western 'monastic' asceticism in a section of his *Summa theologica* devoted to religious orders.[74] In

---

[71] *Ibid.*, 256–7.    [72] *Ibid.*    [73] *Ibid.*, 2.5, p. 257.
[74] Thomas Aquinas, *Summa Theologiae*, esp. 2-2, qq. 186–9; *Opera omnia*, vol. 10, pp. 486–553.

one article he asks whether it diminishes the perfection of an order to own anything, collectively of course. A sophisticated essay in ends–means calculation follows:

perfection does not consist essentially in poverty, but in the following of Christ . . . poverty is like an instrument or exercise for reaching perfection . . . For the lack of all resources, or poverty, is an instrument of perfection insofar as certain impediments to charity are removed when wealth is taken away. There are three of them in particular. The first is the worry that wealth brings with it. . . . The second is the love of wealth, which is increased through the posses-sion of wealth. . . . The third is the vain glory or elation to which wealth gives birth . . . The first of these cannot be totally separated from wealth, whether it is great or small; for the acquisition of maintenance of external things is bound to cause a little anxiety. But if the external things are only sought or possessed in a modest quantity, such as is sufficient for simple sustenance, this worry is not much of an impediment to man. Thus it is not incompatible with the perfection of a Christian life either. For God does not forbid all worry, but only unnecessary and harmful worry . . . But the possession of wealth in plenty causes a greater degree of worry, and a person's soul is greatly distracted by it and prevented from being totally committed to the service of God. – But the other two, namely the love of wealth and elation or boasting about wealth, are the consequences of abundant wealth only.[75]

Further down the calculation becomes more complex as Aquinas dif-ferentiates between the amount of collective wealth appropriate for the goals or ends of different sorts of religious orders:

granted such and such an end, a greater or lesser degree of poverty is appro-priate for a religious order; and each religious order will be the more perfect so far as poverty is concerned the more its poverty is proportionate to its end. For it is evident that for the external and bodily works of the active life a per-son needs a large supply of external goods; for contemplation, however, few are required. . . . Thus therefore it is clear that a religious order which is directed towards physical actions in the active life, say towards military activity or provid-ing hospitality, would be imperfect if it lacked collective wealth. Religious orders which are directed towards the contemplative life, however, are the more perfect the more their poverty diminishes their preoccupation with temporal things. For the more a religious order requires preoccupation with spiritual things, the more preoccupation with temporal things is an impediment in that order. For it is evident that an order which is instituted for contemplation and for passing on to others the fruits of contemplation through teaching and preaching [he is obvi-ously talking here about his own Dominican order] requires more preoccupation with spiritual things than a religious order instituted solely for contemplation. Therefore for the former sort of order the sort of poverty which causes the least preoccupation is appropriate.

[75] 2-2 q. 188 a. 7, Respondeo section; *Opera omnia*, vol. 10, pp. 530–1.

It is evident that the maintenance of things necessary for human use and procured at a suitable time is what causes the least preoccupation.[76]

Aquinas cannot resist making his own order sound the best, but that should not distract us from the instrumental character of his reasoning. The calculation of ends and means is further rationalised, into a system:

And therefore to the three degrees of the religious life[77] set out above three degrees of poverty are appropriate. For to those religious orders that are directed towards physical actions in the active life, possession of an abundance of collective wealth is fitting [he may have the Templars and Hospitallers primarily in mind here]. – To those orders which are directed towards contemplation, it is more appropriate to have moderate possessions, unless the members of that religious order must at the same time either themselves or through others provide hospitality and help the poor [here he probably has in mind various forms of the Benedictine life]. But to those which are directed towards the communication to others of the fruits of contemplation, it is fitting to have a life which is unencumbered by external preoccupations to the greatest possible degree. And this happens when the few things necessary for life are procured at an appropriate time and maintained.[78]

### Absolute value in Franciscan writings

There is a dispute going on behind the surface of these passages. The instrumentalist account of poverty given by the Dominican Aquinas contrasts sharply with the absolute value attached to it by many Franciscans and perhaps by Francis of Assisi himself. In the previous chapter a striking passage from the 'Writings of Leo', *Scripta Leonis*, was quoted.[79] Just before that passage we read that:

When brother Elias, with the ministers, was near the place where St. Francis was standing he called to him. St. Francis answered and, seeing the ministers, said: 'What do these brothers want?' Brother Elias replied: 'These men are ministers who have heard that you are making a new Rule and fear that you are making it too strict; they say and protest that they do not want to be bound to it. You are to make it for yourself and not for them.'[80]

As this 'Leo' source tells the story, Elias and the ministers represent the view that the Franciscan rule should not be treated like an absolute

---

[76] *Ibid.*, p. 531.
[77] The Latin is the same as 'religious order' and the variation in translation is to avoid awkwardness in the English.
[78] *Ibid.*
[79] See above, Ch. 3, p. 83, and *Scripta Leonis, Rufini et Angeli*, ed. and trans. Brooke, §114, p. 287.
[80] *Scripta Leonis, ibid.*

value – but their view was wrong, for Christ told Francis that the Rule should be observed to the letter and without gloss.[81] The men behind the source believed that their understanding of Franciscan poverty was an absolute value backed by the authority of a saint charismatically inspired by God. The contrast with Aquinas's instrumental calculations could hardly be sharper.

A conviction that their order's poverty was more than merely instrumental was passionately held by many Franciscans and lay at the root of much of the controversy within the order. Pope John XXII would attack the foundations of this conviction by his declaration (*Cum inter nonnullos*) in 1323 that Christ and the apostles did hold property (in common),[82] but before that he had already made clear his opinion that rules of religious orders had an instrumental character. He did so in the context of the earlier and distinct Franciscan controversy about how the rule should be observed. Here we see a conception of the religious life as a symbiosis of values and instrumental calculation in conflict with a more purely value-driven Franciscan world-view.

In 1317 John laid it down that Franciscans must obey their superiors when it came to deciding what kind of garment (habit) they should wear (this in the bull *Quorumdam exigit*).[83] It was also up to the superiors to settle disputes about granaries and wine cellars. The order's superiors will tell the friars who have been making difficulties what to wear instead of the skimpy habits which they claimed the rule demanded. Obedience should out-trump poverty, even for Franciscans, according to John XXII. John was echoing the Dominican Thomas Aquinas here, according to the exemplary analysis of the dispute by David Burr,[84] who goes on tell

---

[81] *Scripta Leonis, ibid.* Though it would be naive to assume that the incident took place as recounted, there is a genuine echo of Francis's attitudes here. In his 'Testament' he wrote the following: 'In virtue of obedience, I strictly forbid any of my friars, clerics or lay brothers, to interpret the Rule or these words, saying, "This is what they mean". God inspired me to write the Rule and these words plainly and simply, and so you too must understand them plainly and simply' (*St. Francis of Assisi: Writings and Early Biographies*, ed. Habig, 69). For some recent comment on the *Scripta Leonis* see Burr, *The Spiritual Franciscans*, 18–19 and corresponding endnotes; and index s.v. 'Scripta Leonis'.

[82] Extravag. Ioann. XXII 14.4; E. Friedberg, *Corpus Iuris Canonici*, vol. 2, pp. 1229–30; *Extrauagantes Iohannis XXII*, ed. Tarrant, no. 19, pp. 255–7. Cf. Nold, *Pope John XXII*.

[83] Text in *Extrauagantes Iohannis XXII*, ed. Tarrant, no. 6, pp. 163–81. This establishes the text that circulated as part of the 'Extravagantes Iohannes XXII', but one can reconstruct from her apparatus criticus the original papal version. See too the convenient edition in Friedberg, *Corpus Iuris Canonici*, vol. 2, pp. 1220–4, and Eubel, *Bullarium Franciscanum*, vol. 5, no. 289, pp. 128–30.

[84] Burr, *The Spiritual Franciscans*, 197; for context, *ibid.*, ch. 9.

what happened to some Franciscans already in prison for their views on poverty:

Those who withheld assent were asked a second question; Did they think that the pope had the authority to command what he had in fact commanded in *quorumdam exigit*? Most said that he did not... Required to explain themselves, they replied in different ways: it was because he had no power to change the gospel; because he could not absolve from virtue and demand vice; because he could not order anything opposed to the evangelical counsels; or because he could not order the violation of an evangelical vow.[85]

This is a crystal-clear example of value rationality in action. Without following the twists and turns of the rest of the story, it is worth mentioning that four of the imprisoned Franciscans were prepared to die for their convictions.[86] This tale of courage should not prevent us from understanding the theory of instrumental rationality proposed by John XXII.

The essence of John's theory is that the individual problems and situations are infinitely diverse and cannot all be subsumed under general principles. He is certainly not denying the validity of general principles or proposing anything akin to 'situation ethics', but he is convinced that generalities cannot capture all particularities, so not all decisions are decisions of principle: not, for example, decisions about what kind of habit a Franciscan should wear.

Translating the passage in question is not entirely simple because the version which circulated among canon lawyers is different from the original papal version, which itself has to be reconstructed from different versions;[87] even when there is agreement about the Latin there is disagreement about how to punctuate it. Nevertheless, the following translation[88] probably does justice to John's intentions:

For no certain knowledge can be obtained of all particular things, nor is it possible for there to be a body of teachings (*disciplina*) out of them, since they are infinite;[89] no art, no rule embraces all individual circumstances and all inessential aspects of things. In those things it is for inferiors to be subordinate to those superiors, to obey them and pay attention to them, not only where there is certainty but

---

[85]  *Ibid.*, 197.    [86]  *Ibid.*, 205–6.
[87]  There are original bulls, and versions in the two great papal registers of the time, the *Registra Avinonensia* and the *Registra Vaticana* (the latter is a fair copy, so where possible historians should use the former – though it is messier – as being closer to the papal source).
[88]  I have reconstructed it from the apparatus criticus in the edition of the canon lawyer's version edited by Tarrant.
[89]  I am grateful to James Binns for advice on the translation of this phrase.

also in doubtful and uncertain things. They [the superiors] are set over the arts by which they [the subordinates] obey and the rules by which they comply with the teachings,[90] so that their pre-eminent purpose may be furthered by the due services of those who obey. Thus a judge analyses and investigates everything; applies laws to cases, and draws distinctions between canonical decrees. Thus a disease that growing graver demands a doctor, thus virtue, holding steady to the mean, demands a wise and prudent man...[91]

According to John XXII, the Franciscan Rule is neither a value nor capable of covering every eventuality and decision, and therefore much must be left to the superior's discretion. In Weberian language, the rule is instrumental and another kind of instrumental reasoning comes into play in cases which the rule cannot reach, though both sorts of instrumentality should serve the ethos of the order and Christian values generally. So it was that in the Latin Church the view that monastic rules were instrumentally rational devices serving values, rather than values in and of themselves, prevailed over a Franciscan challenge. John is rejecting a 'pure' value interpretation of Franciscan poverty, but, as will be stressed in the next section, he is obviously not advocating pure instrumental calculation either: there are plenty of strong values in the background to this passage. It is a symbiotic combination of value and instrumental calculation. As such, it is a mixture of the universality we have associated with instrumental rationality per se, and of the specificity of a particular value rationality.

---

[90] Note that Friedberg and Eubel both punctuate the Latin in this part of the passage differently (from me and each other); if they are right, that would affect the details of the translation. Friedberg has: 'illisque intendere, non in certis solum, verum etiam in dubiis, et certis praesunt artibus, quibus obediant, praesunt regulis singulis, quibus obtemperent disciplinis'; Eubel: 'illisque intendere, non in certis solum, verum etiam in dubiis et incertis praesunt artibus, quibus obediant, praesunt regulis, quibus obtemperent, disciplinis'. The basic meaning is not fundamentally affected by these different possibilities.

[91] Passages in bold type draw attention to those places where I have adopted readings from Tarrant's apparatus criticus (*Extrauagantes*, ed. Tarrant, 174–5), thus reconstructing from it so far as possible the papal original, and thus diverging from her own final text, which gives the version that circulated among lawyers. 'Non enim particularium omnium certa potest dari scientia, neque **horum** cum infinita sint contingit fieri disciplinam; non ars, non regula circumstantias singulas accidentiaque cuncta complectitur. Habent in illis minores subesse maioribus, **illis obsequi,** illisque intendere, non in certis solum, uerum etiam **dubiis** et incertis. Presunt artibus quibus obediant, **presunt regulis** quibus obtemperent disciplinis, ut illarum finis egregius debitis obsequentium ministeriis subsequatur. Sic iudicans cuncta rimatur et discutit; leges casibus applicat; canonum decreta secernit. Sic **morbus** aggrauans medicum, sic uirtus, constans in medio, sapientem prudentemque deposcit...'. horum] eorum *after correction in Avignon Register;* secernit] *Assisi, Biblioteca comunale, X, an original of the bull:* fecerint *Avignon Register, Vatican Register (litterae communes series), Vatican Register (litterae secretae series) – yet it is the inferior reading.*

## (C) SPECIFIC AND UNIVERSAL RATIONALITY: A MEDIEVAL 'INTERFACE VALUE'

### Pope John XXII and Aristotle

This passage just quoted is uncannily close to a passage from Aristotle in which he asserts that there are areas in the field of ethics which precepts cannot reach.[92] At first I assumed that Aristotle must be the direct source, but the passages are not quite close enough to establish that.[93] If the thoughts were independent, the convergence is if anything more interesting. Either way it seems clear that John XXII shared a common value with respect to the borderline between general rules and instrumental calculation. Both thought that there was a zone unreachable by rules as such, in which people with authority had to exercise their discretion. In both cases the language is such as to allow us to assimilate this discretion to instrumental rationality, saturated with values but not reducible to them.

### Aristotle, religious orders and canon law

This passage of Aristotle should be linked with the latter's concept of *epieikeia*, and earlier in the present chapter the strong affinity between Aristotle's *epieikeia* and Bernard of Clairvaux's concept of monastic law was noted. (Law is here used in a broad sense, as defined by Max Weber to include any set of rules where there are people responsible for enforcement[94] – as there were in all medieval religious orders.) The

---

[92] Aristotle, *Nicomachean Ethics*, 2.2, Bekker 1103$^b$–1104$^a$; *The Complete Works of Aristotle*, ed. Barnes, vol. 2, pp. 1743–4.

[93] The passages are closest at the following point (which I do not translate as the exact Latin wording is the point): – John XXII: *Non enim particularium omnium. . . . rudentemque deposcit* (see above at n. 91); Latin Aristotle, Grosseteste translation: 'adhuc magis qui de singulis est sermo, non habet certitudinem. Neque enim sub artem neque sub enarracionem aliquam cadit. Oportet autem ipsos operantes ea que ad tempus, intendere; quemadmodum et in medicinali habet et gubernativa' (*Aristoteles Latinus*, XXVI I-3 fasciculus tertius, *Ethica Nicomachea, Translatio Roberti Grosseteste. . . A. Recensio Pura*, ed. Gauthier, 165; the *textus recognitus* does not differ significantly: sub artem] sub arte; sub enarracionem aliquam] sub enarracione aliqua (*Aristoteles Latinus*, XXVI I-3 fasciculus quartus, *Ethica Nicomachea, Translatio Roberti Grosseteste. . . B. Recensio Recognita*, Gauthier, 398). If John XXII was paraphrasing Aristotle, he had assimilated the sense and was not just quoting the words. There may be an intermediate source. Again, it is possible that he came to the same idea independently.

[94] 'For our purposes let the existence of a staff for the purposes of enforcement be the decisive thing for the concept of "Law" (which can be defined quite differently for other purposes). Naturally, this body of enforcers need not bear any resemblance to the kind with which we are familiar today' ('Uns soll für den Begriff "Recht" (der für andre

implications of their common approach, including the settings in life that help explain their convergence, can be set out schematically as follows:

1. City states (in Aristotle's eyes) and religious orders (in the eyes of St Bernard *et al.*) were designed to make those who belonged to them virtuous.
2. The laws of city states and the rules of religious orders were an instrument to produce this end: and in this sense they measured the efficacy of the laws/rules against more fundamental criteria of human goodness.
3. Both laws and the rules of orders were regarded as the work of human legislators (more historically probably in the case of medieval religious orders).
4. An awareness of the plurality of sets of rules and human authors must in both cases have brought home the 'positive' character of *polis* law/religious rules: it could not be identified with natural or divine law.
5. Neither believed that the laws/rules could cover all eventualities, so both left discretion to the relevant authorities.
6. This presupposed acceptance of the legitimacy of the authorities.
7. Both trusted the authorities to make exceptions from the laws.

When we translate these points into the analytical categories of this study, we find the two rationalities inextricably mixed: *grosso modo*, (1) is about value rationality, (3) and (4) are convictions about instrumental rationality, and (2), (5), (6) and (7) are convictions about the role of instrumental rationality in a value framework. The intermingling of the two rationalities as they are perceived in these texts is a further reminder that the interplay between types of rationality is the interesting thing sociologically and historically – as opposed to any attempt to merely label and segregate types of rationality.

Common 'interface values' link Aristotle's attitude to the law of the *polis* with St Bernard's idea of law in the lives of monks. The resemblance to Aristotle goes even further when one turns to Dominican writers of the thirteenth century, Humbert of Romans and Thomas Aquinas.[95] Aquinas's instrumental attitude to orders' rules was noted above. Their man-made character is foregrounded. Since Aquinas's thinking was saturated with Aristotelian attitudes, however, the convergence with Aristotle is less remarkable than is Bernard's.

---

Zwecke ganz anders abgegrenzt werden mag) die Existenz eines Erzwingungs-Stabes entscheidend sein. Dieser braucht natürlich in keiner Art dem zu gleichen, was wir heute gewohnt sind') (Weber, *Wirtschaft und Gesellschaft*, vol. 1, p. 18).
[95] For developments in the intervening period see Fieback, '*Necessitas*', 138–40.

Aquinas's own Dominican Order was governed by Constitutions which could be changed by elected 'general chapters' of the order,[96] so that they lacked the aura of rules going back to a saintly founder in the distant past. The legally 'positive' character of the Dominican constititions was obvious. It comes out clearly in Humbert of Romans's commentary on them.[97] Nevertheless the distance between Humbert and Bernard should not be stressed too much.[98] They both distinguished between the man-made quasi-legal framework of their orders and fundamental values, and they both believed in dispensation.

The concept of monastic dispensation is integrated into a wider synthesis by the thirteenth-century canonist Johannes de Deo.[99] In his panorama of different sorts of 'dispensations' – he interprets the concept very broadly – he includes a section on dispensations by abbots. For example:

Again, the abbot can give a dispensation to a monk who in contravention of the rule secretly receives something, XII q. 11 *Non dicatis*,[100] Extra De statu monachorum, *Cum ad monasterium*, ad finem,[101] a contrario sensu.[102]

Johannes de Deo's understanding of 'Dispensation' seems, as just hinted, to encompass a vast range of decision-making which is doing something other than executing the rules, but this itself may be symptomatic of

---

[96]  Cf. Denifle, 'Die Constitutionen des Predigerordens', 532 and 534.

[97]  As Heinrich Denifle put it: 'The Master General rightly commented . . . that the means do not contradict the end and so it was inappropriate for the order's statutes to be observed strictly whenever they frustrated the purpose for which the order was founded' ('General Humbert machte mit Recht . . . die Bemerkung, dass die Mittel nicht dem Zwecke widerstreiten und deshalb die Ordensstatuten nicht strenge dürften beobachtet werden, sobald sie den Zweck, um dessentwillen der Orden gestiftet wurde, verhindern') (Denifle, 'Die Constitutionen des Prediger-Ordens vom Jahre 1228', at 177).

[98]  Fiebach, '*Necessitas*', 144–5, tends to highlight the differences more than I would, but our readings of the two writers are actually very similar: it is a question of whether one calls the glass half full or half empty.

[99]  In his *Liber dispensationum*. See Díaz y Díaz, *Index Scriptorum Latinorum Medii Aevi Hispanorum* (Madrid, 1959), no. 1269, p. 271; also see below, Ch. 6, at pp. 153, 161–2.

[100]  Pars II C. 12. q. 1. c. 11 (Friedberg, *Corpus Iuris Canonici*, vol. 1, pp. 680–1).

[101]  X.3.35.6 (Friedberg, *Corpus Iuris Canonici*, vol. 2, p. 600): 'Nor should the abbot imagine that he has the power to grant a monk a dispensation to possess property; for giving up the ownership of property, like the maintenance of chastitiy, is so bound up with the monastic rule of life that not even the pope can grant an exception' (passage beginning 'Nec aestimet abbas' and ending 'licentiam indulgere'). Reasoning 'a contrario sensu' is normally of the following sort: 'if the sign says "No parking 7 a.m. to 7 p.m.", then parking at night is legal.' Here it seems too compressed to be clear. For 'a contrario' reasoning by Humbertus de Romanis in relation to the same decretal see Fieback, '*Necessitas*' at 150.

[102]  'Again, the abbot can grant a dispensation to a monk who has secretly accepted something which is against the rule' ('Item abbas potest dispensare cum monacho qui contra regulam aliquid occulte recepit. XII.q.11 *Non dicatis*; Extra 'De statu monachorum', *Cum ad monasterium*, ad finem, a contrario sensu') (MS BL Royal 5.A.i, fol. 145ᵛ).

a culture comfortable with the interplay of formal rules and individual discretion, and indeed of formal rules enabling individual discretion, and a lot of it.

Nearly everything said above about the laws of religious orders holds good also for medieval canon law generally, at least from the later twelfth century on.[103] The 'interface values' of later medieval canon law can also be summarised along the same lines as the law of religious orders: man-made law, a means to the end of promoting the virtuous life;[104] a law whose efficacy depended on its formality, the predictability and certainty of the rules, but which could be suspended by dispensation in exceptional circumstances.

Along a spectrum of legal 'interface values', the law of medieval religious orders and later medieval canon law thus lie somewhere near a mid-point between the modern civil law tradition (and also common law as practised in England) on the one hand, and Hindu law on the other. (As we shall see in Chapter 6, however, canon law formalised the Dispensation system, so it is well short of the Hindu law end of the spectrum.) In normal circumstances they had the formality of modern secular law: the rules were meant to be observed, and technicalities mattered. The rules provided certainty, and the technicalities were the software which made the system work. On the other hand, they resembled Hindu law, perhaps the most flexible of the great legal systems of world history, in that formal laws could be suspended by dispensation. In canon law, the papal plenitude developed into an almost unlimited power of suspending man-made religious law in special circumstances – an interface value with large practical implications. The next two chapters, dealing respectively with legal formality and its interface with substantive rationality, will examine more closely the forms of instrumental rationality which these interface values generated.[105]

---

[103] Detailed bibliography in the next two chapters, but for an admirable introduction see Brundage, *Medieval Canon Law*.

[104] Cf. the comment of Peter Landau on Hostiensis: 'Let us content ourselves with pointing out that according to Hostiensis's formulation it was imperative to hold fast to the care for souls as the final end and purpose of Canon Law' ('Begnügen wir uns mit dem Hinweis, dass nach der Formulierung bei Hostiensis die Sorge um das Seelenheil als letzter teleologischer Gesichtspunkt für das kanonische Recht festgehalten werden muss') (Landau, 'Schwerpunkte und Entwicklung', 30).

[105] While situating these medieval sacred laws and in particular Canon Law in the general sociology of literate legal systems, it could be added that mainstream Islamic law differs in that there is no authority entitled to dispense from a *binding* rule of Sharia'h law (though note the instrumental flexibility in the area of practices recommended but not imposed, and discouraged but not forbidden); and that in Jewish law a rabbi may identify the emergencies in which the Law may be suspended (say to save life on the Sabbath) as cases where God would will the suspension of his own laws, but does not suspend them on his own human authority or even that of his office.

## Conclusion

The topics of this chapter have one theme in common: that value and instrumental rationality constantly interacted in the Middle Ages. The causal flow went in both directions. A case study selected was the idea of the Trinity, which was propagated and reproduced from generation to generation by techniques such as preaching, which in turn also helped give it the concrete character that made it a conviction rather than just a concept. This symbiosis of value and instrumental rationality is entirely typical.

The causal flow from value to practical rationalisation was not automatic. Revivalist preaching was the product of a deep-rooted value which remained partially latent until urbanisation and new religious orders provided a catalyst. Revivalist technique drew strength from a long-held value but needed the favourable soil of central and late medieval conditions.

Three theoretical discussions about monastic and mendicant rules, by Bernard of Clairvaux, Thomas Aquinas and John XXII, were singled out for their explicit awareness of the instrumental character of these laws for the life of spiritual elites – an instrumentality that could only make sense in terms of the value system which generated it. The spiritual Franciscans were an exception: they felt their rule was more than man-made and had an absolute quality denied to such rules by Bernard, Thomas and their papal *bête noire*.

All of these three, the Cistercian, the Dominican and the Pope, see the rules of religious orders as specimens of 'formal legality': rules made by man, thus instrumental, but serving values, and strictly observed rather as if they were values in themselves, because they were guaranteed by solemn vows. Aquinas in particular stresses their variety. The rules vary according to a given order's function. None of them can be identified with the life of perfection; all are means to that end. John XXII draws attention to levels of specificity which the rules cannot reach – which formal legality cannot cope with. Bernard explained the rationale of dispensations. The decision of a superior to grant a dispensation from the rule may be an exercise of instrumental rationality (in our language), just as is the rule from which the dispensation is granted.

These interface values are close to Aristotle's idea of law, though not derived from it since their clear formulation by Bernard of Clairvaux antedates the main medieval reception of Aristotle. They were also the values underpinning late medieval canon law generally, with papal plenitude of power an important extra ingredient. The result was a working system which combined two sorts of instrumental rationality: the formality so strongly developed in the the civil law tradition, and the substantive orientation of Hindu law. The formal legality of Canon Law shares a common source with the civil law tradition: Justinian and Classical Roman law. The substantive flexibility obviously had not the slightest connection with Hinduism, mentioned here only for comparative purposes, and in fact also has a source in Classical Roman law: for the Emperor's role prefigured the Pope's. With this imperial inheritance was combined the claim to office charisma deriving from Christ's delegation of power to St Peter. The result was a formally legal system capable of running without the bureaucratic and fiscal foundations of its modern counterparts, a topic which must now be further explored.

# 5    Formal rationality and medieval religious law

Formal rationality is defined here as decision-making within a set of rules constructed to govern an aspect of life abstracted or demarcated from all other aspects, in such a way that the latter are not allowed to affect the decision-making process.[1] These sets of rules frequently serve some purpose beyond themselves, and lack an absolute character, as being man-made and in principle alterable. Insofar as this is true, and so long as the rules do not become values in their own right (as can indeed happen), formal rationality is a species of instrumental rationality.[2] Even as such, however, it tends to be shaped by values and convictions, as the whole preceding line of argument would lead the reader to expect.

Contrary to some modern interpreters of Weber,[3] there is no intrinsic connection between formal rationality and 'modernity'. Also, formal rationality can be saturated with values, and serve them instrumentally, even when it is not a value in itself. This can be illustrated from many different institutions of the medieval world. Here we will concentrate on monastic legislation and papal law.

## Formal rationality and the Carthusians

In the light of the previous chapter it may now be taken as a given that monastic rules are law, even though not a law imposed by the state, and this also holds good for liturgy, the subject of much monastic law.[4]

---

[1] Cf. *Rationalities in History*, ch. 5, for the general historical sociology corresponding to this chapter.

[2] Tambiah, *Magic, Science, Religion*, 144–5, appears to identify formal with instrumental rationality, but this could be a cause of confusion, for two reasons: (i) formal rules do sometimes turn into value rationalities, and (ii) even though formal rationality is very frequently instrumental, it is still only one of many forms of instrumental rationality – suspension of the rules when they are counterproductive being another: see Ch. 6.

[3] See Ch. 1, 'Preliminaries', p. 24.

[4] Cf. Boureau, *La Loi du royaume*: 'In the beginning of the norm was the liturgy . . . . in essence, the conduct of life that Benedict sees himself as regulating is the order of the liturgy: it is the service of God (*opus Dei*), and up until the twelfth century the internal

In the medieval West this monastic law could have a high degree of formal rationality, in the sense that the rules were conceived of as man-made choices (not identified with objective virtue *tout court*) which were nevertheless binding on those to whom they applied, providing them with principles of behaviour. Meta-regulations which regulated the process of changing the regulations are a symptom of this formal character. The constitutional law of the Carthusian order is a striking example, and we can see legislation working through to liturgical practice. The legal aspect of monastic life is recognised in a recent study of Carthusian legislation.[5] This refers to the 'essentially legislative' powers of the general chapter and of the 'production of a specific internal law' (*droit*).[6] Asceticism and liturgy provide much of the material for this legislation, which substituted formal rules for the individual discretion of private individuals or religious orders less concerned with precision and regularity in respect of the points in question. This legislative power was not simply assumed. Its basis was the formal surrender by bishops of 'all jurisdiction' on any charterhouse or charterhouses in their dioceses.[7] The decisions of chapters general made 'jurisprudence',[8] of which several compilations were made. The one that concerns us is the so-called *Tertia compilatio* of 1509.[9] This third compilation is cited, as formal law, in an interesting text, itself formal law at the local level of an individual house, in which there is a liturgy for taking runaway monks back into the community. The text in question is a custumal from Sheen in Surrey. A careful study by Donald Logan of runaway monks in England did not find any cases from Sheen, and rather few Carthusian cases altogether.[10] Although the order was among the most ascetic, with a strict rule of silence on top of austerities of diet and clothing, it was remarkably free from scandals, in great part no doubt because of its highly selective entry criteria,[11] and indeed perhaps also because of provisions in its constitution, according to which legislation tending to relax the rigours of life in the order was made extremely difficult to pass.[12] Still, should a Carthusian run away

---

legislation of monks concentrated almost exclusively on the definition and control of good liturgical practice' ('Au début de la norme, il y eut la liturgie. . . . pour l'essentiel, la conduite de vie qu'entend régler Benoît est d'ordre liturgique: c'est le service de Dieu (*opus Dei*) et jusqu'au XIIᵉ siècle, la législation interne des moines s'attache à peu près uniquement à la définition et au contrôle de la bonne pratique liturgique') (p. 74). See too Melville, 'Ordensstatuten und allgemeines Kirchenrecht'.

[5] Le Blévec, 'Une source d'histoire monastique'.
[6] *Ibid.*, 158.     [7] *Ibid.*, 159.     [8] *Ibid.*     [9] *Ibid.*, 159–60.
[10] Logan, *Runaway Religious in Medieval England*, 215–16.
[11] For the austerity and selective entry of the Carthusian order see Lawrence, *Medieval Monasticism*, 160–3.
[12] 'Any measure aiming to soften the rigour of the rule, on the other hand, had to get the unanimous approval of the definitors and afterwards the consent, by majority vote,

and come back to Sheen, not only a prison, 'actually a room set aside for troublesome monks',[13] but also a formal ritual awaited him:

When the community has been gathered the Prior orders the fugitive to be called. The latter totally prostrates himself on the ground. ¶. The Prior says to him: 'What do you seek?' ¶. The fugitive says: 'mercy, Fathers, and reconciliation'. ¶. Then the Prior makes a speech of exhortation to him with great seriousness, making him see the grave scandal both to the order and the whole clerical state; also the great peril to his soul and the great harm done to the house: in such a way as to bring him round to penance; and while he, remaining humbly prostrate, bewails his guilt and promises to make amends, then the Prior says: 'Thanks be to God'. And he orders Section 4 of the Third Compilation, tenth Chapter to be read, lest the man think that an injury is being done to him. It goes as follows: 'Runaways coming of their own accord to any house of the order shall be reconciled, and (as is customary) shall be imprisoned.'[14] Then the Prior says: 'Behold, son, your sentence.'[15]

The sentence is the straightforward application of the general principle to the individual case, where the general principle is not an absolute value but a positive, formal law made by a legislative body that could change it.

of the monks of the Grande Chartreuse. In addition, this softening had to be agreed by two other consecutive general chapters before it could be implemented officially' ('Toute mesure visant à adoucir la rigueur de la règle doit en revanche être approuvée à l'unanimité des définiteurs et recevoir ensuite le consentement, voté à la majorité, des moines de la Grande Chartreuse. De plus, cet adoucissement doit etre accepté par deux autres chapitres généraux consécutifs avant d'être officiellement mis en application') (Le Blévec, 'Une source', 161). For the elaborate and ingenious method of electing definitors see *ibid.*, 160.

13 Logan, *Runaway Religious*, 152. He notes that a prison 'became a standard part of Carthusian buildings, although from the surviving English sources it appears that it was little used, at least by apostates' (*ibid.*).

14 '¶. Fugitivi vero ad aliquam domum ordinis sponte venientes reconcilientur, et ut moris est incarcerentur, nec recipiantur nisi ad carceres, et dum ab eis educuntur, nullo modo possunt in eisdem domibus profiteri, aut obedientias habere, sine expressa licentia capituli generalis, vel prioris Cartusie; possunt tamen priores seu rectores, aut eis absentibus, eorum vicarii, si volunt eos retinere, aut remittere ad domos suarum professionum, earumdem domorum sumptibus et expensis' (*Tertia compilatio statutorum*, 10. 4, in *Statuta ordinis Cartusiensis* (Basel, 1510), unpaginated; BL call number 704.h.21).

15 'Congregato conventu prior advocari iubet fugitivum, qui statim toto corpore prosternitur in terram. ¶. Cui dicit prior: "Quid petis?" ¶. Fugitivus: "Misericordiam, patres, et reconciliationem." Tunc prior facit ei cum magna gravitate exortationem, ponens ante oculos grave scandalum et ordinis et totius status clericalis; magnum item periculum anime sue, et grave dispendium domus: sic quod [fol. 57ᵛ] flecti possit ad penitentiam; cumque humiliter manens prostratus culpam deplorat et emendam pollicetur, *tunc dicit prior*: "Deo gratias". Et iubet legi ex statutis # 4ᵐ Tertie Compilationis, capituli decimi, ne iniuriam sibi fieri putet, ubi sic habetur: "*Fugitivi ad aliquam domum ordinis sponte venientes reconcilientur et (ut moris est) incarcerentur*". Tunc prior: "Ecce fili sententiam tuam."' (BL, MS Lansdowne 1201, fol. 57ʳ⁻ᵛ; italicised passages are in red in the MS). NB. the previous note, for what seems to be the statute in question.

Examples of such changes may be taken from the early 1440s. In 1440 it was ordained that 'if the prior and vicar are absent, the oldest [monk], if his place is on the left-hand side of the choir, should move at the appropriate hour to the prior's side of the choir to begin the hymn *Te deum*'.[16] This was repeated in the following year, for even decrees that did not soften the rigours of life in the order had to be passed in two successive years to become the definitive.[17] Or to take another example of the minute regulation of liturgical life and community ritual:

When the refectory reader on chapter days takes the place of the priest of the week in the church by celebrating the conventual mass, we ordain that he should also take his place in the refectory, by blessing the tables, after lunch or dinner, by saying the grace in church; and let the task of reading in the refectory pass on that day to another whose turn is next, notwithstanding any contrary custom.[18]

Legislation about liturgical details also features in the Sheen ritual for the reintegration of runaways:

the prior leads him to the entrance of the church, beating him on the shoulders with a rod and saying *Have mercy on me, O God*,[19] preceded by the community, which continues the same psalm, the two halves of the choir singing in alternation. In the meantime, however, the wrongdoer lies prostrate before the entrance, saying nothing. But when the psalm is finished, with 'Kyrie eleison, Christe eleison, Kyrie eleison' [Lord have mercy, Christ have mercy, Lord have mercy], 'Our Father'. And we [say]: 'Save your servant; send him help from the holy place; may the enemy not gain the upper hand over him; Lord, hear my prayer; Lord God of powers, convert us; The Lord be with you; Let us pray. *Prayer*: God, to whom it belongs to have mercy always and to grant forgiveness, pardon your servant, and may your compassionate mercy loose him whom the chain of excommunication and of sins holds bound. *Prayer*. God, whose nature it is to show mercy and grant pardon, look kindly on your servant, and may your compassionate mercy absolve this man whom the chain of excommunication and of sins had bound.[20]

---

[16] 'Ordinamus quod priore et Vicario absentibus antiquior si fuerit de choro sinistro transferat se hora debita ad chorum prioris ad ymnum te Deum laudamus inchoandum' (*Capitula generalia Cartusiae, 1416–1442*, 176).

[17] Le Blévec, 'Une source', 161.

[18] 'Quando lector refectorii diebus capituli supplet in ecclesia vices sacerdotis ebdomadarij missam conventualem celebrando Ordinamus quod eciam suppleat in refectorio mensas benedicendo et post prandium vel cenam gratias in ecclesiam persolvendo et lectura refectorii transeat illa die ad alium in suo ordine contingentem quacumque consuetudine in contrarium non obstante.' *Capitula generalia*, ed. de Grauwe, 189. I am not sure why 'ecclesiam' is in the accusative.

[19] Psalm 50 or 51, according to different numbering systems.

[20] 'ducit eum prior ad ianuam ecclesie verberando Super scapulas eius cum virga dicendo: *Miserere mei deus*, conventu precedente et ipsum psalmum alternante choro continuante. Interim autem iacet reus prostratus ante ianuam nichil dicens. Finito autem psalmo cum 'Kyriel[eyson], Chris[te eleyson] Kyrieleyson' [fol. 58ᵛ], Pater Noster. Et nos: Salvum

## Formal rationality in canon law

Max Weber stresses the high degree of formal rationality in canon law: it is one of the major arguments in his oeuvre. His view of the matter is discussed elsewhere in relation to the post-medieval Congregation of the Council,[21] but his comments were intended to apply to the medieval period as well. Medieval canon law is a good illustration of a central argument of this book. On the one hand, it was understood to be man-made law, distinct from theology and dogma, yet laying down general principles for the governance of behaviour. Its rules were not coterminous with the system of values and convictions it was meant to serve. On the other hand, those values and convictions shape the whole character of the formal system.[22]

## Overlap between formal and material rationality

There was naturally much overlap in content between canon law and doctrine. A legal judgement could amount to a doctrinal judgement. An example of this is the declaration that a marriage contracted by consent was valid even though secular law did not recognise it as such. The case that gave rise to the statement of principle was of a Frankish nobleman who had married a woman from Saxony according to Saxon law and against the rules of Frankish law. Later he left her and married another woman. According to a synodal decision of 895, later incorporated into the authoritative *Liber extra* of 1234, 'that transgressor of the law of the Gospel should be subject to penance, and separated from his second wife, and compelled to return to his first one'.[23] Here the fundamental principle that consent makes a marriage leaves the law of the Franks without authority.

Fundamental moral principle is also decisive in a much later case, which came to Pope Alexander III.[24] A man took a woman into his

---

fac servum tuum; mitte ei auxilium de sancto; nichil proficiat inimicus in eo; Domine exaudi orationem meam; Domine deus virtutum converte nos; Dominus vobiscum. Oremus. *Oratio.* Deus, cui proprium est miserere semper et parcere, propiciare famulo tuo, et quem excommunicationis et peccatorum cathena constringit, miseratio tue pietatis absolvat . . .' (BL, MS Lansdowne 1201, fol. 58[r–v]).

[21] See *Rationalities in History*, section on 'The Congregation of the Council in a Comparative Perspective', ch. 5, pp. 153–4.

[22] My thanks to Dr Peter Clarke and Dr Barbara Bombi for comments on the remainder of the chapter.

[23] X. 4.1.1., Friedberg, *Corpus Iuris Canonici*, vol. 2, col. 661.

[24] X.4.1.15; Friedberg, *Corpus Iuris Canonici*, vol. 2, cols. 666–7. The reference given by Friedberg to 'Jaffé no. 9866' must be a misprint for 'Jaffé no. 8966'.

house and had children with her. He also promised in front of witnesses to marry her. In the meantime he slept with a neighbour's daughter when he spent a night at the latter's house. The neighbour found the two of them in bed together and made them get married by words of present consent. To whom then was the man married? Alexander leaves it to his delegate to elicit the facts but states the principles that must apply. To summarise: if the man had intercourse with his long-standing partner after he had promised to marry her and before the events at his neighbour's house, he was married to her. If not, he was married to the neighbour's daughter, provided that her consent had not been forced, which would invalidate his consent and nullify the marriage. In these cases fundamental principles guide the decisions.

All this is compatible with formal rationality as defined. In the formally rational systems of modern times there is naturally a huge overlap between what most consider morality and the formal legal rules. Most people under these jurisdictions think that murder and stealing are substantively wrong. That does not detract from the formal status of the laws against them. *Mutatis mutandis* the same applies to medieval canon law.

### Gratian and legal informality

Nonetheless – to deal with an objection coming from a different angle – not all medieval canon law can be classified under the heading of 'formal legal rationality'. One can find in Gratian, notably, elements reminiscent of sacred laws in which positive rules are hardly distinguished from ethical demands: laws which are probably mainly symbolic and almost unenforceable, in the same sense as some provisions of classical Chinese law. For example, Pars I D. 76 c. 5 says that it is fitting that there should be a fast after the festive season of Easter, the Ascension, and Pentecost, in case anyone has allowed themselves too much licence during the festive season, but it is not clear how such a fast could have been imposed on any laymen who did not feel like observing it. (Here Gratian's version of canon law is reminiscent of, for instance, Islamic law, which brings not only morality but worship and ritual practices within its remit: even such details as 'how far to raise one's hands at the beginning of the ritual prayer'.[25]) Sometimes the line between law and preaching virtually disappears. Gratian Pars I D 86 c. 2 says: 'Sins should be hated not men; let the proud be punished but the humble tolerated; and that which has

---

[25] Melchert, *The Formation of the Sunni Schools of Law*, 198. Cf. Johansen, 'Introduction: The Muslim Fiqh as a Sacred Law. Religion, Law and Ethics in a Normative System', in his *Contingency in a Sacred Law*, 60.

to be disciplined with some severity should be punished not in a spirit of anger but of healing.' Up to and including Gratian's time canon law by no means fully fits Weber's schema of formal legal rationality.

## Legal formality after Gratian

In the age after Gratian and especially from the time of Innocent III, the canon law system approximates more and more closely to Weber's ideal-type of formal legal rationality, without ever losing its connection with the medieval Church's value rationality, of which it was an instrument. In this period (roughly, from the mid-twelfth century on) a body of case law was built up by papal letters responding to concrete problems with wider applications. Whether they were conscious of 'legislating' by decretal is another matter.[26] They can hardly have been completely unaware that at times they lacked a precedent for their decision and that they were probably going to set one. The spectrum of awareness may have been rather like that of English common law judges, who do not expect to make case law every day but know that they can do so by laying down the law on some issue hitherto unresolved.[27]

Much of this formally legal case law had no specifically religious content as such. Thus, for example, the Decretals of Gregory IX had a section on arbitration (X.1.43). It lays down some rules that have no direct connection with ethics or theology, except that a formal rule is required to enable the settlement of disputes. The rule that there should be an odd rather than an even number of arbiters, so that there could be a majority decision, has no particular connection with medieval Catholicism as such.[28]

---

[26] Peter Clarke points out that 'one must be wary of seeing this case law as self-conscious legislation from the outset', as 'judicial business at the curia largely expanded in response to external demand' (Clarke, *The Interdict in the Thirteenth Century*, 6. Cf also Duggan, '*De consultationibus:* The Role of Episcopal Consultation', 209–10. Relevant to this whole question is the important study by Sägmüller, 'Die Entstehung und Bedeutung der Formel "*Salva Sedis Apostolicae Auctoritate*"'.

[27] One important difference: a common law judge can hardly make a decision settling an uncertain point of law and add that it is not to become a precedent, whereas popes could do exactly that, as the work of Anne Duggan (as in previous note, but also work in progress) rightly emphasises.

[28] 'A panel of arbitrators should have an uneven number, and, if they do not agree, the majority should prevail. [This heading was added later but shows the reception of the law.] From an African council . . . . If however, by a common decision of the bishops who are litigating, they should choose arbitrators, let either one be chosen or three, so that, if they choose three, they should accept the sentence of either all or of two' ('Arbitri sunt in dispari numero assumendi, et, eis discordantibus, statur sententiae maioris partis. Ex concilio Africano . . . . Si autem ex communi placito episcoporum, inter quos causa versatur, arbitros elegerint, aut unus eligatur aut tres, ut, si tres elegerint, aut omnium

The following law is a similar example of a rule which has no intrinsic connection to edification, except insofar as disorder might follow from the absence of any rule:

Wishing to put an end by the present constitution to an ancient dispute, we determine that anyone should appeal, if he wants to do so, from elections, postulations, provisions and any kind of extra-judicial acts, in which appeals are admitted, within ten days after he has become informed, if he believes he has suffered injury from them and desires to have the injury done to him put right through the benefit of an appeal.[29]

Why ten days? The precise figure may not be arbitrary, but whatever the reason it was probably not seen as a fundamental moral or religious imperative. This is positive law.

Another example of legal formality is the rule that if one of the judges delegate dealing with a case dies, the office of all of them expires, if the original commission had not specified the contrary.[30] Or again there are the rules governing 'prescription'. These deal with a problem that can arise under almost any legal system, not just religious ones. If someone has a claim to property that another has de facto owned, does it remain valid for all time, or does the claim eventually lapse? The time required for the claim to lapse is the period of prescription. Modern law in the civil and common law traditions allows prescription in defined forms, as did ancient Roman law. Medieval canon law too was faced with the problem.[31] It could arise without laypeople being involved at all. If a monastery has possessed a church, arranged for services in it, and drawn the income from it for a long time, and then a nearby baptismal church puts in a claim to it as a dependent chapel, a claim which would be valid if the time element were left out of account, who should possess the church?[32] The religious colouring of canon law did make some difference. The possessor 'must have acted honestly and without knowledge of the true state of the title'.[33] Some rights could never be acquired by prescription, such as a bishop's if exercised by a priest.[34] To a very considerable extent, however, the canon law was able to follow the Roman law.[35] It even allowed prescription to override unclaimed legal rights of the Roman Church, though the period was long, a hundred

---

sequantur sententiam, aut duorum') (X.1.43.1; Friedberg, *Corpus Iuris Canonici*, vol. 2, col. 230).

[29] Sext 2.15.8; Friedberg, *Corpus Iuris Canonici*, vol. 2, cols. 1017–18.

[30] Delegation and arbitration are grouped together under this rule: X.1.29.42; Friedberg, *Corpus Iuris Canonici*, vol. 2, col. 182: 'delegatorum vel arbitrorum'.

[31] In what follows, I follow the magisterial survey by Helmholz, *The Spirit of Classical Canon Law*, ch. 7.

[32] Cf. *ibid.*, 178–9.    [33] *Ibid.*, 188.    [34] *Ibid.*, 181.    [35] *Ibid.*, 183, 187, 190.

years (which was in fact the period laid down by Justinian).[36] The instrumental character of this legal formality is clear: the formal rules provided legal certainty, so that people knew where they were in relation to the law.

## Legal formality and value rationality

It is worth spelling out how this fits into the central argument that instrumental rationality usually takes its flavour from values and convictions. Here an old thesis of the canon law historian Rudolf Sohm is illuminating. Passionately Protestant himself, Sohm was sensitised to the difference between his values and those out of which the medieval Church had grown. The latter, the 'essence of Catholicism', had given birth to the medieval canon law system on which, paradoxically, he was a well-known expert.[37] For Sohm,

> The essence of Catholicism consists in the fact that it draws no distinction between the Church in the religious sense (the Church of Christ) and the Church in the legal sense. For Catholicism, the Church in the doctrinal sense (*Lehrsinn*) is at the same time the Church in the legal sense, and vice versa. The Church of Christ is for Catholicism an organisation with a legal constitution: the Christian community's life with God is regulated through Catholic ecclesiastical law.[38]

There is an insight here, coming out of Sohm's vivid sense of Luther's contrary vision. For Luther (and predecessors like Marsiglio of Padua), the spiritual character of the Church meant that worldly matters such as power, money and positive law were not its business: they could be left to the state; the Church itself would be pure, a matter for grace, faith and the hearts of individuals. A key assumption of the medieval Church, on the other hand, was that organisation and law, including the enforcement of law, were among the means by which Christ's sacrifice was translated into the salvation of individuals and of society. Just as the organisation and law of the state were means of achieving human ends

---

[36] *Ibid.*, 183–5.

[37] Nevertheless, he was capable of major empirical misjudgements where medieval canon law was concerned. He entered into a controversy about the nature of the marriage contract in medieval canon law with another great German Protestant canon law historian, Emil Friedberg. See Friedberg, *Verlobung und Trauung*, and Sohm, *Trauung und Verlobung*. Subsequent scholarship seems to have vindicated Friedberg.

[38] 'Das Wesen des Katholizismus besteht darin, daß er zwischen der Kirche im religiösen Sinn (der Kirche Christi) und der Kirche im Rechtssinn nicht unterscheidet. Die Kirche im Lehrsinn ist ihm zugleich Kirche im Rechtssinn, und umgekehrt. Die Kirche Christi ist ihm eine rechtlich verfaßte Organisation: das Leben der Christenheit mit Gott ist durch das katholische Kirchenrecht geregelt.' Sohm, 'Wesen und Ursprung des Katholizismus', 345.

in this life, so too with the Church: its organisation and law were means of achieving salvation. The Church was like a state in form; the nature of its remit was different, though sometimes only because its end was different. To understand this set of convictions and values we only need to think of modern attitudes of the state: purely conventional rules such as 'drive on the right' or 'stop at red' are on one end of a continuum, with laws against murder and stealing on the other end: both belong to the *raison d'être* of the state. So too, rules about arbitration and rules about indissolubility both belonged to the *raison d'être* of the Church as it was understood by mainstream ecclesiastics in the Middle Ages.

## Formal legal rationality in early papal decretals

It is worth attempting to trace the roots of formal legal rationality that we find in papal decretals of the age after Gratian. They can be traced back to the Roman empire, and they developed under the influence of Roman law.[39] For the sake of brevity we may confine ourselves here to legal formality in papal law.

Already in the late fourth and fifth centuries we seem to find the following: papal *responsa*, answers to questions which can be clearly differentiated from doctrinal (including moral doctrinal) pronouncements;[40] an intention that these answers should establish general law, rather than simply solve the individual questioner's problem,[41] and the reception of papal letters into the archives or 'Gesta' of individual episcopal churches, from which early canon law collections were compiled.[42] *Mutatis mutandis*, there are strong structural parallels with the age of Gratian.

The decretals in these early collections are largely if not entirely genuine: systematic production of forged papal decretals seems to have begun in the ninth century. They were not mixed up with penitential material, by contrast with the canon law collection of Burchard of Worms in the early eleventh century.

---

[39] Hess, *The Early Development of Canon Law*, 86–9; 'At the time of Pope Siricius (a. 385) there appears a form modelled on imperial constitutions; these are *decretals*, that is, "decretal letters"' ('Tempore Siricii papae (a. 385) forma apparuit, qua constitutiones imperiales imitabantur; sunt *decretales*, scilicet, "litterae decretales"') (Rabikauskas, *Diplomatica pontificia*, 23).

[40] The first surviving set of *responsa* are Pope Siricius' letter to the Bishop of Tarragona, in 385. For a convenient translation see Shotwell and Loomis, *The See of Peter*, Appendix [I], 699–708.

[41] Shotwell and Loomis, *The See*, Appendix [I], para. 20, pp. 707–8.

[42] Silva-Tarouca, 'Die Quellen der Briefsammlungen Papst Leos des Grossen', 37–9; Caspar, *Geschichte des Papsttums*, vol. 2, pp. 296–7; Wurm, *Studien und Texte zur Dekretalensammlung*, 111–12; Jasper and Fuhrmann, *Papal Letters in the Early Middle Ages*, 22–8; Kéry, *Canonical Collections of the Early Middle Ages*, esp. 1–13.

A ruling in a decretal letter of 405 by Pope Innocent I[43] can serve as an early example of legal formality which was an instrument of religious convictions while remaining distinct from them. It is a rescript laying down or at least declaring the law. This decretal was incorporated about a century later into the most important early medieval canon law collection, that of Dionysius Exiguus.[44]

And this was asked: what ought the practice to be with those who after baptism have been constantly given over to the pleasures of incontinence but who at the point of death ask for penance and the reconciliation of Communion at the same time? On this matter previous practice was more rigorist, while more recently the demands of mercy have made it less unbending. For previous custom held that penance should be granted to them but Communion denied. For, since there were frequent persecutions in those times, lest easily obtained permission to receive Communion should mean that men were confident of reconciliation to the church and that a deterrent against breaking under persecution be taken away, Communion was rightly refused – though penance was granted, lest they be denied everything whatsoever – and the logic of the situation at that time made forgiveness harder. But after our Lord had restored peace to his churches, with the terror now cast aside it seemed good for Communion to be given to those who had strayed, both because of the Lord's mercy, like a final meal for people setting out on a journey, and lest we might seem to emulate the harshness and rigorism of the heretic Novatian, who refused forgiveness. Therefore a final Communion is granted together with penance, so that people of this kind and at the point of death may with the Saviour's permission be freed from unending catastrophe.[45]

This has all the characteristics of formal legal rationality. Innocent is not stating an absolute principle. He makes it clear that the rules have changed on this issue. The changes have a rational justification, which he explains quite fully. The reasons he gives make it clear that both the old practice and the more recent one were instruments in the service of core values even though they are not values themselves.

## The limited efficacy of early papal law

Lack of a routine link with the localities was a great limitation on early papal law from an instrumental point of view. Papal *responsa* circulated

---

[43] Wurm, 'Decretales selectae', 46–78; cf. Wurm, *Studien und Texte zur Dekretalensammlung*, 131–3.

[44] See Wurm, *Studien*; Kéry, *Canonical Collections*, 9–13; Jasper and Fuhrmann, *Papal Letters*, 35–6.

[45] Innocent I, Decretal Letter to Exsuperius, Bishop of Toulouse, JK. 293, edited by Wurm, 'Decretales selectae', 65–7; Maassen, *Geschichte der Quellen und der Literatur des canonischen Rechts*, vol. 1, p. 244.

widely in canon law collections, but the influence of these rules upon ecclesiastical justice 'on the ground' is anybody's guess. Comparison with the later medieval centuries points to what was absent before the twelfth century: a network of lower courts with a professionally trained staff; university-type schools to give professional training in papal law (or in canon law generally); and above all routine availability of papal justice to settle ordinary disputes, disputes where legal principles were applied rather than developed through new case law.

## The vicissitudes of canon legal rationality

This is not the place to recapitulate the history of early medieval canon law.[46] Canon law collections are impressively rational in their way well into the Carolingian period, the expanded version of Dionysius Exiguus' collection presented by Pope Hadrian to Charlemagne being a high point. The following period is famous above all for forgery, the Pseudo-Isidorian decretals produced in Francia apparently to undermine the power of metropolitan bishops, out-trumping the latter by producing imaginary papal documents. The Carolingian and post-Carolingian periods also saw the spread of penitential handbooks, a genre which originated in Ireland and which is not characterised by the rational sobriety of the early compilations of conciliar and papal law.[47] Penitential material finds a place in syntheses of canon law, such as Burchard's, as noted above.

A new period of formal legal rationality began around the middle of the twelfth century. A symptom and agent of change was 'Gratian's Decretum'. A powerfully argued reconstruction of its genesis by Anders Winroth would make a second recension of the Decretum a key moment in the transformation of canon law.[48] Precise dates cannot be given for either recension, he argues, but they both probably fall between 1139 and 1158.[49] 'Gratian 2' (probably a different person from Gratian) massively expanded the original recension. In particular, he brought a systematic knowledge of the Roman law – that is, of the Justinian corpus, the Corpus iuris civilis – to bear on the canon law synthesis produced by the original

---

[46] For a quick survey, see Brundage, *Medieval Canon Law*, ch. 2. For fuller details, Kéry, *Canonical Collections*, and Jasper and Furhmann, *Papal Letters*. For the predecessors and sources of Gratian see Winroth, *The Making of Gratian's* Decretum, 15–17, and Landau, 'Gratian and the *Decretum Gratiani*', esp. 25–35.

[47] Cf. e.g. Lutterbach, *Sexualität im Mittelalter* for a flavour of their contents. For further references see Meens, *Het Tripartite Boeteboek*.

[48] Winroth, *The Making of Gratian's* Decretum.          [49] *Ibid.*, 144.

Gratian.[50] In the course of his investigation Winroth also redated the serious academic study of the Justinian corpus to the 1130s, a generation earlier than most scholars had hitherto assumed.[51] Winroth's brilliant theses are still under discussion.[52]

## Roman law and papal government

The rise of academic Roman law as redated by Winroth coincides closely with a massive expansion of papal government, driven by demand from below, a widespread tendency to fight litigation to the highest possible court, and a desire for authoritative case law. While there is no obvious direct causal connection between these two developments, there is an indirect one and a kind of elective affinity. The papacy found certain key Roman law concepts to be a powerful instrument for meeting the demand for high-level justice.[53] The elective affinity between the papacy and Roman law is unsurprising. The papacy had grown into a self-conscious and self-confident institution in the later Roman Empire and its aftermath and we have already noted its heavy debt to the example of imperial government.[54] The new interest in and knowledge of Roman law in the second third of the twelfth century was at the very least a happy coincidence so far as papal government was concerned. Roman law provided a model of rational legal formality that popes followed closely in the middle decades of the twelfth century and after.

As Gabriel Le Bras pointed out, the composition of papal rescripts partly mirrored Roman protocol: they had the same kind of general legal force as imperial rescripts, and their content (*fond*) owed much to Roman law.[55] The idea that the Pope could be judge of first instance in any ecclesiastical case mirrors the Roman emperors' power to cut out

---

[50] *Ibid.*, 195; also ch. 5, and *passim*. Note that 'most of the Roman texts added by the author of the second recension concern procedure' (*ibid.*, 174). For Roman law's influence on canon law see Legendre, *La Pénétration du droit romain*.

[51] Winroth, *The Making of Gratian's Decretum*, 157–74.

[52] See e.g. Larrainzar, 'La ricerca Attuale sul "Decretum Gratiani"', 74–83. Without going into the controversy, it may be useful clearly to distinguish three distinct arguments: (1) that manuscripts previously regarded as representing an abbreviation of the Decretum in fact embody the first recension; (2) that the second recension was not by Gratian but by a pupil; and (3) that Roman law studies took a great leap forward between the two recensions (note that some think that there were more than two). My thanks to Dr Barbara Bombi and Dr Peter Clarke for advice about this debate.

[53] Le Bras, 'Le Droit romain au service de la domination pontificale'. This should be read together with Le Bras's complementary piece on 'La Formation du droit romano-canonique'.

[54] See above, p. 131, for the rescript system. The letters of Gregory the Great show the system of judges delegate in operation – a Roman imperial system (see pp. 135, 137 below).

[55] Le Bras, 'Le Droit romain', 391.

at will any intermediate lower jurisdiction.[56] (It will be argued below that the version of this system operated by the papacy from the time of Innocent III on was more instrumentally rational than that of its classical predecessor.) Perhaps most important of all was the concept of delegated jurisdiction.[57]

In Roman law, 'Iurisdictio delegata' was 'The delegation of jurisdiction by the emperor to an official or a private person to examine a case (*delegatio causae*) and render judgement, either in the first instance or in appellate procedure. Such a jurisdictional delegate (*ex divina delegatione*) may subdelegate the matter to another judge.'[58] This exactly describes the papal system of delegated justice. The content of the jurisdiction was of course different: in the papal case it was largely confined to matters involving the clergy, the sacraments, doctrine, wills and marriage. But there are two further non-obvious differences between the structure of the system in the Roman empire and in the age of papal monarchy. First, the papacy could not afford an administration remotely comparable to that of the Roman emperors;[59] but secondly, its delegated justice nevertheless achieved a remarkable degree of rationality, in view of the limited material resources behind it. What we find – to oversimplify – is one half of Weber's ideal-type without the other: Roman law-inspired formal legal rationality without rational bureaucracy.

Weber created a composite ideal-type in which effective legal formality and bureaucracy were closely linked to each other. The case of the medieval papacy shows that the link was by no means a necessary one. Legal inventiveness could compensate for bureaucratic deficiencies. The bottom line was that the papacy could not afford a proper bureaucracy proportionate to the role it accepted. The imbalance in bureaucracy was redressed by ingenuity.

The papacy of the twelfth and thirteenth century did not come close to Weber's ideal-type of a bureaucracy. The classic study by Brigide Schwarz (discussed already in Chapter 1) has drawn attention to the many unbureaucratic features of the papal chancery.[60] Her study is a model of how the ideal-type method should be used. Precisely because she has a checklist of the features of a bureaucracy *à la* Weber, she notes what was missing: notably, an office where the chancery scribes could

---

[56] *Ibid.*: 'Il est juge ordinaire . . .'. For the working of this system in the Roman empire see Millar, *The Emperor in the Roman World*, esp. 516–49.
[57] Le Bras, 'Le Droit romain', 390: 'Les notions fondamentales . . . des rapports hiérarchiques', with further references.
[58] Berger, *Encyclopedic Dictionary of Roman Law*, 524.
[59] For 'Imperial Wealth', see Millar, *Emperor*, ch. 4.
[60] Schwarz, *Die Organisation kurialer Schreiberkollegien*, esp. 210–12.

work,[61] and a proper bureaucratic salary system. Chancery scribes were paid by fees for piece-work rather than a salary,[62] and they themselves paid their immediate superiors, who were chosen from their midst and returned to it after a short term of office,[63] rather like a Chair of the Board of Examiners in a modern university department. As noted in Chapter 1, until the early fourteenth century senior papal officials were paid in kind rather than by a money salary.[64] In the fifteenth century the system of sale of offices, neither bureaucratic nor efficient (except as a rather desperate expedient for raising money), must be added to the catalogue of practical irrationalities[65] – all thoroughly at odds with Weber's ideal-type of bureaucracy.

As a governmental system covering vast areas and many countries, furthermore, the papacy was underfunded. Its financial means were never remotely commensurate with the legal position that it assumed or rather which was thrust upon it by the litigants who beat a path to the Curia from the twelfth century on. Popes could not or not for long enforce a proper taxation system: direct taxes, initially at least supposed to be used for crusades, invited unpopularity and haemorrhaged money to monarchs who took a huge cut; the revenues of the papal state were not commensurate with an international government; census payments and the like for monasteries, and 'Peter's Pence' from England, brought in fairly modest sums; the Avignon system of taxes on benefices granted by the Pope brought in more, but much of the ground thus won was lost in and after the Great Schism.[66] In relation to its role the papacy was poor. How should one explain its extraordinary legal presence throughout Christendom?

## Governmental ingenuity: letters of justice

How then was it that, despite its lack of a proper bureaucracy in anything like the modern sense and despite its fundamental economic weakness, the papacy succeeded in establishing a system which turned Roman law concepts into a functioning system of government? The most remarkable thing about the papal legal system was the degree to which it was able

---

[61] *Ibid.*, 67–9.     [62] *Ibid.*, 211.     [63] *Ibid.*, 84.

[64] Baethgen, 'Quellen und Untersuchungen', 141–3; Dehio, 'Der Übergang von Natural- zu Geldbesoldung an der Kurie' (they relied on benefices as well): see above, pp. 4–5.

[65] Frenz, *Papsturkunden des Mittelalters und der Neuzeit*, 60.

[66] For papal income in the Middle Ages see Bauer, 'Die Epochen der Papstfinanz', and Lunt, *Papal Revenues in the Middle Ages*. It is true that the other kinds of income were increasingly exploited: see e.g. Tewes, 'Die päpstliche Datarie um 1500'.

to use amateur administrators[67] in place of a proper bureaucracy and yet retain central authority, even over remote parts of Europe and over relatively minor matters. It was an astonishing achievement. The secret seems to have been the combination of Roman law principles with a cleverly designed set of procedural rules that enabled the system to work without much bureaucratic back-up. The result was possibly unique in world history: a vast area, central authority, local knowledge and no true bureaucracy. The technicalities of the formal procedural rules established in the thirteenth century were the key. To understand this remarkable triumph of legal formality as instrumental rationality one needs to grasp technical details and think on to what they imply.[68]

The rules worked like this: a person or institution would decide to bring a case against another person or institution. Very often both parties would be clerics or ecclesiastical but laypeople could be involved: one could bring a suit for legal separation from a spouse, for instance. To bring a suit one picked a form of action from a formulary, rather as with English common law writs. (As with English common law writs, one would probably get expert legal advice: 'proctors' were available to guide litigants through the system.) Via a procedure to be explained in the next section, letters went out to local clerics with the right status and qualities – to ask them to judge the case. The Pope could ask more judges to act in a given case than were absolutely needed, so that (say) one out of two appointed judges could bow out if he had a good excuse.[69]

Judges delegate judged the case committed to them with papal authority. They would not be paid for their services by the papacy: they were *honoratiores*, in Weber's terminology, that is to say part-timers whose status left them little choice but to say 'yes', and who might be happy to do so because it was a sign of status emanating from the highest authority in Christendom. The system depended on the pool of qualified men with other sources of income to support them but with some time to spare: heads of religious houses, university masters, benefice holders with an academic background or much administrative experience and no

[67] In addition to personal connections and nepotism, as Dr Barbara Bombi pointed out in a personal communication.

[68] For the technical details of the system's working, see Sayers, *Papal Judges Delegate*; Herde, *Audientia litterarum contradictarum*; Müller, *Päpstliche Delegationsgerichtsbarkeit*; also his 'Entscheidung auf Nachfrage'. For a magisterial overall survey of the judge delegate system, see Herde, 'Zur päpstlichen Delegationsgerichtsbarkeit'.

[69] To give just one example, in Innocent IV's commission in 1249 to the Bishop of Hereford and the Archbishop of York to judge a royal marriage case, he says at the end 'si non ambo hiis exequendis potueritis interesse, alter vestrum ea nichilominus exequatur' (d'Avray, 'Authentication of Marital Status', 1000 (and cf. 993).

involvement with the dispute to be judged. It is true that to use that pool of talent would have been impossible without a general acceptance of the Pope's plenitude of power and right to command a cleric's time. Major cases could still end up being judged at Rome, by the Rota, or a cardinal, or by the Pope himself. Normally, however, these would be big cases. To judge the mass of routine cases in Rome would have required a judicial bureaucracy far larger than the papacy had at its disposal. Arguably, however, the judge delegate system did just as well, in that the judges had local knowledge. It is hard to find anything like this combination of local knowledge and central authority in world history.

The system was a long way from perfect even by the standards of the time. For instance, it was subject to delays,[70] partly because the theoretical exclusion of appeals did not prevent them in practice,[71] and the outcome was a settlement rather than a judgement. Yet precisely this may be regarded as a virtue of the system: at any rate, settlement out of court is something that modern civil justice tends to encourage – the preceding comments on the slow pace of litigation could equally apply to modern English, American and Continental legal systems, which have quite a high opinion of themselves. As will be clear below, the system probably often involved compromise and a sort of settlement at the initial stage too, when judges were being nominated. Moreover, the fact that people preferred to take the trouble and time rather than work through local ordinary judges speaks for itself. The system must have been thought relatively fair, and perhaps it was, if both parties tended to be involved in the selection of judges. It was a relatively cheap way of satisfying the demand for justice from the top.[72]

---

[70] Hageneder, *Die geistliche Gerichtsbarkeit*, 36: 'The trial proceedings were long drawn out. Mainly to blame was Roman-Canonical "due process", which was consistently employed in papal delegated jurisdiction' ('Die Prozesse zogen sich sehr in die Länge. Daran trug vor allem das römisch-kanonische Prozeßverfahren Schuld, das im Gericht der päpstlichen delegierten Richter stets zur Anwendung kam'); cf. p. 74.

[71] 'usually, despite the theoretical exclusion of the possibility of appeal (the formula 'appeal not permitted' or 'no appeal' is a standard component of rescripts appointing judges delegate), the proceedings were subsequently reopened again and again, and closure of the case was achieved, if at all, often by compromise' ('meistens folgten, trotz theoretischem Ausschluß der Appellation (die Formel *appellatione remota, cessante* ist stereotyper Bestandteil von Delegationsreskripten), endlose Neuaufnahmen der Verfahren, und ein Abschluß der Prozesse wurde, wenn überhaupt, häufig durch Vergleiche erreicht') (Herde, 'Zur päpstlichen Delegationsgerichtsbarkeit', 23).

[72] Cf. Hageneder, *Die geistliche Gerichtsbarkeit*, 73: 'It is already apparent from this rapid overview that judicial decisions from the Curia were much in demand throughout the whole of the late Middle Ages' ('Schon aus diesem kursorischen Überblick ist zu ersehen, wie man noch während des ganzen späten Mittelalters gerne von der Kurie gerichtliche Entscheidungen verlangte').

That the demand existed should not surprise us (any more than it should surprise us that English royal justice was often preferred to the justice of the county court in the Middle Ages). Local judges (bishops, bishops' officials and archdeacons in the ecclesiastical domain) might well have connections with one or other party to a dispute, in which case it might at the very least be hard to get them moving against their friends. Papal judges delegate could be picked to avoid just that. Not much is known about how they were picked but a plausible hypothesis suggests how it could have been done without detailed records. If the hypothesis is right, the system was a remarkable piece of governmental ingenuity. Another hypothesis with plausibility on its side suggests that even the process of drafting the letters appointing the judges required little input from papal bureaucracy. If so, that was a further instance of the streamlining of the system through the application of intelligence to make up for the lack of bureaucratic fire-power.

To contrast bureaucracy with formal legal rationality seems like a criticism of a Weberian thesis but in fact it is an application of his method. Composite ideal-types like the association of Bureaucracy and Legal Formality were intended like all his other ideal-types to direct attention to empirical data that would seldom correspond precisely with the schema. The ideal-type is an engine for empirical research directed by clear questions. As a case study of the method at work and to convince sceptics of the complementarity of social theory with empirical disciplines like papal Diplomatic it may be permitted to develop this particular analysis in some detail.

The judge delegate system was a triumph of ingenuity over bureaucratic inadequacy. It made *honoratiores* take most of the burden of providing centralised papal justice. There is also some reason to believe that the system was so set up as to take the task of choosing acceptable judges off the shoulders of the papacy. The sequence of steps that a litigant had to take made it rational for him to suggest judges that would be acceptable to the other party. If he did not do so, he would himself lose time and money.

Letters appointing judges delegate were read aloud at the *Audientia publica*, one of the most important products of Innocent III's reforms of the papal system. This was the moment at which the defendant's proctor could complain that the judges named in the letter were biased or inappropriate. Should such a complaint be made, the matter was decided in the *Audientia litterarum contradictarum*, a sort of extension of the *Audientia publica*, before a senior papal official called the *Auditor litterarum contradictarum*. If the judges nominated were indeed inappropriate he would be likely to uphold the objection. Should he do so, the plaintiff had to get the revised letter copied afresh, which would cost time and money.

How could the plaintiff avoid this? What was the rational course of action in view of the system Innocent III had put in place? It was strongly in the plaintiff's interest to choose judges acceptable to the defendant, and the natural way to do so would be to agree on them in advance: for otherwise the proctor of the defendant might protest just to cause delay, and the *Auditor litterarum contradictarum* might not know enough about the judges nominated to overrule the protest as frivolous. Judge delegate justice would have had some of the characteristics of arbitration.[73]

Details of the system's working suggest another way in which it could have been streamlined. The procedure for producing a papal letter which students of papal diplomatic know best from handbooks was elaborate. According to the textbook account, petitions were received in the 'data communis', which was probably an occasion rather than an office. A senior papal official (notary or later one of the *referendarii*, a step down) took the letter. Letters not important enough to come before the Pope were taken to the Vice-Chancellor. If the latter gave his approval, one of the notaries or of the *abbreviatores* working for him did a draft of the papal letter. The draft was then given to a papal scribe, who made a fair copy of it. The scribe put his name on the fair version and returned it with the petition to the official from whom he had received it. This was brought to the notary's chamber in which the draft had been done, and the letter was inspected. Then it went to the *corrector litterarum apostolicarum*, who made sure it fitted the forms of the papal chancery. Only then did it go to be read in the *Audientia*.[74]

To carry out this procedure for all letters (even apart from those that came before the Pope himself) would have been a heavy bureaucratic burden. There is reason to think, however, that for routine business most

---

[73] Cf. Herde, 'Zur päpstlichen Delegationsgerichtsbarkeit', 37: 'In the case of Letters of Justice it is likely – as the Constitutions of the Chancery and the expression "to obtain through the *Audientia*" strongly suggest – that negotiations about who to have as judges delegate, where the case should be heard, and about certain clauses of the letter took place at the initial stage of the process of getting a letter sent, in order to avoid the eventuality of an objection being levelled against the fair copy, which might in some circumstances lead to the preparation of a fresh letter, at considerable expense' ('Vermutlich wurden – das legen Kanzleikonstitutionen und der Ausdruck "*impetrare per audientiam*" nahe – im Falle von Justizbriefen die Verhandlungen über die delegierten Richter, den Gerichtsort und gewisse Klauseln schon im frühen Stadium der Briefexpedition geführt, um einen möglichen Widerspruch gegen die Reinschrift zu vermeiden, der unter Umständen zu einer kostspieligen Neuausfertigung der Urkunde führen konnte') (with further references); cf. Herde, 'Zur audientia litterarum contradictarum', 79.

[74] I follow Rabikauskas, *Diplomatica pontificia*, 76–8.

of the corners could be cut. It would appear from the recent careful analysis of the evidence by Thomas Frenz that at least from the time of John XXII most of the stages listed above could be omitted in the case of 'letters of simple justice' starting common-form cases which would come before judges delegate.[75] It was not necessary to present a formal petition. One could simply put the matter in the hands of a proctor.

Of course, it would be in the plaintiff's interest to be clear about what was wanted, and, ideally, to have the appropriate letter already in draft for the proctor to check. A large ecclesiastical institution might have its own version of the formulary for letters starting judge delegate cases – i.e. the *Audientia* formulary.[76] (The *Audientia* formulary in BL MS Lansdowne 397, fols. 147[r]–168[v] is probably a case in point: it is written in an English hand and travels together with documents relating to the church of Durham.[77])

The proctor would hand the letter to a scribe. It is even possible that he might himself be the scribe, though not after the pontificate of Martin V. The scribe's fair copy would be checked by the *corrector* and then the letter could go straight to the *Audientia*. This minimalist and relatively cheap route may have accounted for a large proportion of the papacy's legal business from the time of John XXII.

It is even possible that it did so earlier too. Long ago Geoffrey Barraclough, in one of his brilliant early articles on papal administration, hinted at a thirteenth-century procedure which would bear an uncanny similarity to the system Frenz believes was initiated by John XXII.[78] The regulation of John XXII which is the starting point of Frenz's

[75] Frenz, *Die Kanzlei der Päpste der Hochrenaissance*, 142–3, passage beginning 'Der Ursprung eines gesonderten Expeditionsweges' and ending '*per viam corectoris*'; then p. 145, passage beginning 'Betrachten wir nun' and ending 'aus einigen Bemerkungen in Kanzleikonstitutionen'; then pp. 145–6, passage beginning 'An die Stelle der Supplik ist' and ending 'offenbar auch eingehalten worden'.

[76] Cf. Herde, 'Papal Formularies for Letters of Justice'.

[77] Compare the handwriting of this formulary with that of fol. 230[r], the beginning of the 'Constitutiones Ricardi Episcopi Dunolmensis': it is almost certainly the same scribe, which shows that the formulary folios went with Durham material from the beginning; for a full list of the (very interesting) contents, suggestive of a Durham milieu, see *A Catalogue of the Lansdowne Manuscripts in the British Museum*, vol. 2, p. 114. Professor Peter Herde made available to me a fuller description by one of his pupils: my thanks to both.

[78] Barraclough, 'Formulare für Suppliken', 439: passage beginning 'Bei der vereinfachten Behandlungsweise' and ending 'nicht zu entbehren'; note also his remark in a footnote on the same page about 'the simplified procedure by which the Abbreviator did not prepare a draft, or prepared only a summary one, so that the fair copy was prepared on the basis of the petition without an intermediate stage' ('über die vereinfachte Behandlung, welche daraus bestand, daß vom Abbreviator kein (oder nur ein verkürztes) Konzept abgefaßt, die Reinschrift also direkt auf Grund der Petition hergestellt wurde').

argument may not necessarily have to be read as instituting a new state of affairs.

## Formality supplements bureaucracy

The fact that popes clearly could not keep track of the letters of justice that went out under their names also gives pause for thought. If they lacked the administrative apparatus to keep rational control of the papal documents the chancery produced,[79] did they really have the resources to go through the elaborate series of steps described above and in the handbooks for every routine letter of justice? It seems highly unlikely.

The same problem of keeping track of documents issued also arose with papal grants, the other great category of papal documents in the 'age of papal monarchy' (say from the mid-twelfth century to the Great Schism). These were papal letters granting benefits, such that the documents were worth keeping. They were easily distinguished from letters of justice and administrative letters generally even externally, for the seal was green silk thread, rather than string, the Pope's name at the start was all in capitals, the ascenders of the letters on the top line shot up high and looped the loop, a sign like an 8 with the bottom sliced off replaced the straight-line superscript abbreviation, and the line linking some letters was stretched out far.[80] Among the benefits conferred were benefices, where in some

---

[79] 'how were Church and Christendom to be ruled without an administration equal to the task and capable of checking and overseeing the documents produced by the Chancery to make sure that the assumptions on which they were based were correct and that they were implemented on the ground?' ('wie waren Kirche und Christenheit ohne einen entsprechenden Verwaltungsapparat, der den Urkundenausstoß der Kanzlei auf die Richtigkeit seiner Voraussetzungen und seine Durchsetzung *in partibus* hätte prüfen und überwachen können, zu regieren?') (Hageneder, 'Päpstliche Reskripttechnik', 194). This article develops views already articulated in important earlier papers, notably Hageneder, 'Probleme des päpstlichen Kirchenregiments' and 'Die Rechtskraft spätmittelalterlicher Papst- und Herrscherurkunden'. Also relevant is Meduna (a pupil of Hageneder's), *Studien zum Formular der päpstlichen Justizbriefe*.

[80] Rabikauskas, *Diplomatica pontificia*, 54–6. A couple of caveats are in place here: for one thing, an essentially administrative letter (what German scholars would call a 'Mandat' in German or scholars writing about English government a 'writ') might be of lasting value to one of the parties involved. Thus, for instance, an exemplar of an administrative letter to the Archbishop of Mainz telling him to make sure that those under him protected the Cistercian abbey of Heilsbronn was sealed on silk thread, but the exception proves the rule because the exemplar was kept at Heilsbronn, for whom this administrative command represented a benefit. In a similar case the scribe mixed the external script features of the two types of letters, no doubt, and understandably, unsure of how to categorise the letter. Then again, attention to the function (benefit versus administrative command) is more consistently reflected in the type of thread in the first half of the thirteenth century than the second. For discussion of these niceties see P. Herde, 'Die Urkundenarten im dreizehnten Jahrhundert', 59–61.

cases very substantial incomes might be involved. It could easily happen that two candidates would arrive with a papal 'provision' giving them some entitlement to a cathedral canonry or other benefice.

The solution was an increasingly carefully calibrated set of rules to determine which papal document outranked which: again formal legal rationality did not so much depend on bureaucracy as supply a partial alternative to it. The papacy needed to come up with something if it was not to turn away litigants and petitioners. It is a feature of medieval papal history that the institution seldom refused demands for its services (though it seldom initiated such processes). And indeed, the papacy did come up with solutions that brought order to the system without the help of the bigger bureaucracy that would otherwise have been needed.

A degree of informed control was ensured by the system of 'executing' papal letters of grace, especially provisions to benefices.[81] When a petitioner received a provision to a benefice, it was only a first step. The provision had to be 'executed', which meant that letters went out to appropriate local people telling them to ensure that the provision was translated into action, if the candidate had the best claim – it was a big 'if', for as we have seen, there might be other candidates: so the institution of a provisee had something of the character of a legal process.[82] Even if the claimant had a papal document which was high in the hierarchy of priority there might be reasons to disqualify him apparent to someone near at hand.[83] The letters naming the executors would seem to have gone through the *Audientia*.[84]

Furthermore, popes and canonists developed a series of ingenious legal expedients for papal documents (whether 'of justice' or 'of grace') so that it was clear which outranked which if it came to a clash. One such device was the 'notwithstanding' (*non obstantibus*) clause. This meant that a given papal document must be accepted notwithstanding any previous documents which said something different. The history of this clause has been traced from 'a time of experimental uncertainty under Alexander III and his successors to its normalisation under Innocent III'.[85] One should really talk of 'clauses' in the plural, because the device evolved

---

[81] '"Executor": a (or several) local ecclesiastical office holder, entrusted with the exectution of a papal grant, especially the provision of a benefice' ('Executor, ein (oder mehrere) Prälat(en) am Ort, die mit der durchführung eines päpstl. Gnadenerweises, bes. einer Pfründenprovision beauftragt werden') (Frenz, 'Executor', 160).

[82] Barraclough, 'The Executors of Papal Provisions', esp. p. 152.

[83] Hageneder, 'Päpstliche Reskripttechnik', 190–1 n. 31.

[84] Personal communication of Prof. Peter Herde; see also Frenz, *Die Kanzlei*, 72.

[85] 'Anhand des Urkundenmaterials läßt sich die Entwicklung der Formel von einer Zeit experimentierender Unsicherheit unter Alexander III. und seinen Nachfolgern bis zu ihrer Normierung unter Innocenz III. verfolgen'; Meduna, *Studien*, 171.

into a sophisticated hierarchy of documentary power. Specialists in papal diplomatic refer to these clauses as the *clausulae* or derogatory clauses.

To give an example: there was a *clausula* which overrode any future papal letter on the matter, provided that the future letter did not make special mention of the letter issued with this clause.[86] That covered the Pope against the danger of a future document being extracted without his officials connecting it with the subject of the letter currently being issued, while leaving him room for manoeuvre if he wanted to take a different tack, for he could always make special mention of the earlier letter and say he was overriding it.

On the other hand, a pope might on occasion want to ensure that a document met no obstacle, and might not be sure whether some previous relevant papal document had adopted the formula just discussed, invalidating in advance any future document that did not quote it or mention it. Once again the problem would be the impossibility of knowing what previous papal documents had been issued. So a clause was evolved to the effect that the current document overrode even any previous document which specified that only a special mention and quotation could override it. In short, the Pope's hands were never absolutely tied by a previous document and clauses were crafted to give coherence to the diplomatic of the documents through which the sovereignty was manifested.

The disadvantage of the system was the same as with any sovereign body. As with the British parliament (for instance), anything could be overridden in principle by a new act of authority. The ideology of sovereignty is in fact an aspect of the diplomatic of the papal bulls which use such clauses, especially the clause *ex certa scientia*, by which the Pope said that he was reaching a decision by his own personal knowledge.[87]

All this could of course be quite irritating for recipients of papal letters. They could never be certain that a later letter might not override the one on which they were relying. Yet within its own terms the system was ingenious. With time a framework of rules evolved capable of ensuring that there was never a stalemate between two papal documents dealing with the same subject. This distinctly ingenious system of rules to some extent neutralised the failure of the bureaucracy to keep track of outgoing documents: the ranking of papal documents like chess pieces cost nothing but thought.

The ranking of papal documents can be set out, at some risk of oversimplification, and with the proviso that many rules do not fit in the hierarchy even though they do not clash with it, in the following ascending order:

[86] *Ibid.*, 72.    [87] Cf. Hageneder, 'Die Rechtskraft', 412–14.

1. *Litterae communes* without *non obstantibus* clauses. These can be regarded as conditional documents which lost altogether the fairly low level of documentary power they had if the facts turned out not to match the account given by the person or institution which had requested the document. This conditional character might be expressed by a phrase such as 'if it is so' (*si ita est*) or 'if prayers are supported by the truth' (*si preces nitantur veritate*), or simply 'such that' (*sicut*).[88]

2. Letters with *non obstantibus* or *ex certa scientia* clauses. These ranked equal and in the event of a clash the later one would take precedence over the earlier one.

3. A letter with a *clausula* overriding not only past but future papal letters which did not make specific mention of it and quote it.

4. A letter subsequent to one in one of the last-mentioned two categories and making special mention of it.

5. A letter overriding all existing legal obstacles, including papal letters which could not be abrogated without special mention being made of them, even though the letter overridden is not specially mentioned or quoted.

The foregoing list gives only a taste of the system of rules, rules which belong both to the sphere of law and of diplomatic, which were developed to resolve conflicts between documents.[89] Thus, for instance, a papal privilege outranked a commission to judges delegate which would be derogatory to it – but not if the latter did made special mention of the privilege.[90]

Other rules were developed to determine which of two papal documents out-trumped the other when they were of equal status in themselves, the problem being to decide whether the moment when they were issued or the moment when they were activated and presented took priority. This remained uncertain territory for a long time but eventually criteria emerged. They are stated clearly by Baldus de Ubaldis:

---

[88] Hageneder, 'Päpstliche Reskripttechnik', 183. Hageneder notes that according to a decretal of Alexander III (X 1.3.2) the phrase *si preces nitantur veritate* was to be understood even when it was not specifically included. Contrast, however, Hageneder, 'Päpstliche Reskripttechnik', 188, where he speaks of 'a canon lawyers' legal opinion according to which a simple confirmation *without all the (conditional) clauses* [my italics] was equivalent to an '*ex certa scientia*' confirmation' ('einer kanonistischen Rechtsmeinung, nach der eine einfache Bestätigung ohne alle (Bedingungs-)Klauseln einer *ex certa scientia* Konfirmation gleichkomme'). This has imposing canon law authority behind it (see Hageneder, *ibid.*, 189 n. 25), but there seems to be an unresolved tension with X.1.3.2.

[89] For a good survey based above all on canon law commentaries see Dondorp, 'Review of Papal Rescripts'.

[90] *Ibid.*, 215.

Note that the controversy about these readings [of the decretal *Capitulum*, X 1.3.30] has been decided these days, for in letters of grace from which the right to the grace arises immediately one looks at when the document was dated, as in c. *Eum cui*, 'De Prebendis' (Sext 3.4.7) . . . but in rescripts for the activation (*exercitium*) of a court case or for litigation one looks at when the document was presented; for of course those letters receive their perfection from being activated.[91]

He quotes two papal decretals to back up the doctrine that it was the date on the document that gave priority where letters of grace were concerned.[92] They would have reached a wide public through a supplement to canon law, the Sext, which was 'published' in 1298; but considering that popes had been sending out large numbers of letters of grace for more than a century, this was rather late in the day: there must have been potential for confusion for a long time, whenever two claimants to a benefice turned up, and the one who demanded it from the bishop first had a document dated after the one brought by his tardy rival. The rationalisation of the system for prioritising papal letters was thus a gradual process. The evolution of *non obstantibus* clauses, etc. was a first step. As is normal with such legal and administrative processes, all sorts of unforeseen and complicated problems arose, and it took patient mental labour on the part of popes and canonists to resolve them.[93]

### Rules and values

Thus the thirteenth-century papacy used formal rules and procedures to exercise power at a distance, without the economic and bureaucratic resources that such power normally presupposes. Was this simply about power, instrumental rationality uncoupled from religious values? At this point it is useful to return to Rudolf Sohm.

---

[91] 'nota quod controversia istarum lecturarum est hodie decisa, nam in literis gratiosis ex quibus immediate oritur ius gratie inspicitur tempus date ut in c. *Eum qui* [read *cui*] De Prebendis lib. vi, . . . sed in rescriptis ad litis exercitium sive ad lites inspicitur tempus presentationis; nimirum quia iste litere ab exercitio recipiunt perfectionem' (from Baldus de Ubaldis, commentary on the *Liber extra*: *Clarissimi . . . Baldi perusini commentaria . . . super decretalibus* (Lyons, 1521); BL call number f.3 (2), fol. 43$^{rb}$ at X.1.3.30, *Capitulum*, next to '1' in left-hand margin). Cf. also Dondorp, 'Review', 234–5. His reference (p. 234) to 'Clemens VI' must be a mistake.

[92] 'ut in c. *eum cui* [sic for *cui*] "De prebendis", lib. vi (Sext 3.1.7), et in c. *Duobus*, "De rescriptis", eodem libro (Sext 1.3.14), a contrario sensu'. The meaning of 'a contrario sensu' may be that the decretal is about what happens when two documents were issued on the same day; from this it may be inferred that a document issued on an earlier date took priority.

[93] The analyses of Dondorp, 'Review', are the best way into understanding the complexities of the task and the progress made.

It will be remembered that Sohm felt that Christianity and formal law were antithetical. So far as he was concerned, the post-Gratian canon law system was a mistake. None of the ingenious rules explained above would have excited his admiration. Nevertheless he recognised that regulation of the Church by formal law was the manifestation of a world-view: 'the essence of Catholicism'. In short, it belonged to the realm of values, though it was in his eyes a bad value. That value is presupposed by the formal rules governing letters of justice and letters of grace, which would hardly have worked in practice without it.

The papacy might have dammed the flood of litigation that poured towards it in the twelfth century by simply failing to deal with it, and it need not have been so complaisant towards petitioners in search of church jobs. Another value-related preoccupation may explain why popes chose instead to accept all this business. Secular government was expanding and rationalising its procedures at much the same time. Kings like Henry II were not unwilling to settle ecclesiastical disputes like the one between Battle Abbey and the Bishop of Chichester.[94] Popes were probably aware that if the papal court was not willing to act as an ultimate jurisdiction prepared to settle litigation definitively, royal courts would step in, as they had of course been doing for centuries.[95] Similarly with benefices. Kings were accustomed to reward their own servants with ecclesiastical patronage. Popes could not stop that, but willingness to do their best for petitioners limited the loss to ecclesiastical independence.

### Practical dualism

This leads us to another value connected with letters of justice and grace and the rules that governed their working: the conviction that there was a distinction between a secular realm oriented towards this life and a religious realm oriented towards the next. So secular and ecclesiastical law could be distinct and parallel. There was a widespread assumption that there were two formally distinct spheres, even though their content overlapped. Thus, for example, marriage belonged to church law from one point of view (validity), and to the secular law from another point of view (say, legitimate inheritance).

---

[94] *The Chronicle of Battle Abbey*, ed. and trans. Searle, 146–209.
[95] Dr Peter Clarke suggests a different perspective in a personal communication: 'Conversely one might argue that Henry II was responding to the growth of papal and ecclesiastical administration (allowed freer rein during the anarchy of Stephen). Could one not counter-argue that papal government grew organically in response to external demand: i.e. rising volume of petitions and appeals?'

Theoretical writings of the time can give a misleading impression: some make it seem as though ecclesiastical authority was about to swallow up everything.[96] Even Pope Boniface VIII (d. 1303), who is often regarded as a hard-line advocate of papal monarchy in the secular domain, seems to have repudiated any such idea.[97] More to the point: if one looks at the actual business of the courts, rather than at theoretical abstractions, it is evident that in the overwhelming majority of cases there was never any question of the business of secular courts being claimed by ecclesiastical courts; there were some disputed areas (appointment to benefices, cases involving clerics) but they were untypical of the general run of legal practice. The value which this 'practical dualism' embodied does not seem as strange to us as it should: arguably it is alien to most other societies, including classical Greece, Islamic states, or classical China: in fact the church law–state law dualism and its modern descendants are exceptional in world history.

This 'practical dualism' is presupposed by the legal and administrative rules for letters of justice and letters of grace. It is so obvious that one can take it for granted. Great parts of legal life are outside their remit. Disputes about land or secular offices were outside the scope of papal letters of justice, and appointments to secular jobs outside the scope of papal letters of grace.

### Practical papalism

The whole system depended also on another pervasive value with a strong purchase on practice: acceptance of the Pope's power to command the time of moderately important men. In Weber's language, this is the charisma of office: the conviction that its divine origin gave it an overriding claim on obedience irrespective of the personal qualities of the individual holding it. Without *honoratiores* to implement them or

---

[96] Cf. e.g. Wilks, *The Problem of Sovereignty*.

[97] 'For this Peter [= Pierre Flotte] falsified our letter to the king, our letter which was not written in haste but only after repeated deliberations of the whole college [of cardinals] and with the counsel and consent of our brothers [i.e. the cardinals] .... He falsified it or made up falsehoods about it, for we do not know for certain that he tampered with our letter since that letter has been concealed from the barons and prelates, and he attributed to us a command that the king should recognize that he held his kingdom from us. We have been expert in the law for forty years and we know very well that there are two powers ordained by God. Who can or should believe then that we entertain or will entertain such a fatuous and foolish opinion? We declare that we do not wish to usurp the jurisdiction of the king in any way ... But the king cannot deny that, like all the faithful, he is subject to us by reason of sin.' (Boniface then refers to papal depositions of the French king's predecessors, because of their wrongdoing.) (Tierney, *The Crisis of Church and State*, no. 102, pp. 187–8.)

act as judges delegate, letters of grace and letters of justice would have been – dead letters. If he asked three men to act as judges delegate in a case, it was very hard for all three to excuse themselves. It is the same with requests to implement letters of grace. That there were usually people to do these jobs as *honoratiores* without salary presupposes implicit acceptance of the *plenitudo potestatis* at a matter of fact and practical level.

## Conclusion: formal legality without commensurate bureaucracy

It is ultimately the value framework which explains this peculiarity of later medieval papal law: formal legal rationality without a commensurate bureaucracy. As we have seen, Weber saw legal rationality and bureaucracy as complementary. But Weber's ideal-types were intended as a set of conceptual units which could be uncoupled and put together in new combinations. The office charisma of the papacy, the place of formal law in the 'essence of Catholicism' as perceptively understood by its critic Rudolph Sohm, and the practical dualism which allowed sacred and secular law to work side by side below the surface of superficial conflicts: all these values were part of the mix that made up the papal monarchical system. This value rationality (combined with a high degree of procedural inventiveness) explain how the one half of Weber's composite ideal-type could function without the other. It also helps us understand the relation between formal and substantive legal rationality in the medieval Church.

# 6     The formal–substantive interface and the dispensation system

## A shifting borderline

Formal legal rationality and substantive (or material) rationality are not usefully defined as opposites. Drawing the line between formal and substantive considerations is itself a matter of instrumental reasoning usually shaped in its turn by values and convictions – so the leitmotif of this book recurs. Furthermore, formal and substantive rationality often have a common basis in the assumption that the formal rules are not to be identified with morality *tout court*.[1]

### The formal and substantive rationalities of legal procedure

This is most evidently true with procedural rules. From the second half of the twelfth century on, an increasingly formal and elaborate law of procedure was built up in the Western Church, in tandem with the massive expansion of papal law and the development of professionally staffed local ecclesiastical courts. This is not the place to go into the details of the procedure, but it was 'complex and technical by the turn of the thirteenth century and became increasingly sophisticated and demanding during the century'.[2] In response, we find a growing interest in 'summary' procedures, which dispensed with some of the formal procedural steps.[3] Popes and canon lawyers saw the advantages of allowing formal corners to be cut if that was not prejudicial to real justice.[4]

---

[1] See *Rationalities in History*, ch. 6, for comparative historical sociology, but also for a continuation of the account of the history of dispensations into the period of the *Congregatio Concilii*, which opens a new phase of it.

[2] Brundage, *Medieval Canon Law*, 129; for an account of how it worked, *ibid.*, 129–34.

[3] Nörr, 'Von der Textrationalität zur Zweckrationalität'. As noted in the Introduction, Nörr is using 'Zweckrationalität' in a more specific sense than mine: in the usage adopted here (which is, I think, in the spirit of Weber's conceptual scheme) the formal rules of a full trial are a (formally rational) type of *Zweckrationalität*. This is a difference in concepts rather than about the contents of Nörr's argument.

[4] 'The decisive criterion is that of "cognisance of the truth", which we have already met in connection with Innocent IV, discussing *Decretals of Gregory IX*, X.5.1.26 and reporting

This was a trend from formal to substantive rationality. The key period was from the mid-thirteenth to the early fourteenth century. Milestones were the canon law commentary of Innocent IV,[5] the decree *Statuta* of Boniface VIII,[6] the decree *Dispendiosam* of the Council of Vienne in 1311/12,[7] and the clarificatory papal constitution *Saepe*.[8] The latter constitution 'specified what could be omitted in summary process and what could not', while leaving judges and litigants 'latitude to tailor a specific process to suit the circumstances of the problem before them'.[9] This is a good example of the complicated complementary relationship between formal and substantive rationality, which are very far from being antithetical alternatives. The same process of defining the scope of substantial legal rationality through formal rules can be observed in the development of the dispensation system.

### Dispensations, instrumental rationality and values

Instrumental reasoning also tends to come into play when the question arises: is an exception to this law justified? The kind of reasoning in canon law has a long history.[10] A comment by Pope Leo I in the fifth century, taken up into Gratian's *Decretum* in the twelfth, gives a coherent rationale for suspending the law:

Just as there are some things which cannot be overturned for any reason, so too there are many things which ought to be tempered either in view of the times, or because the situation makes it necessary, provided always that in matters which are doubtful or obscure we should know that we ought to follow a course which is not found to be either contrary to the precepts of the Gospel or against the decrees of the holy Fathers.[11]

---

other people's views. The question is whether the procedure serves the "cognisance of the truth" or not. "Truth" here means the dispute with which the trial was concerned, and refers to the facts on which the correct decision rests. No procedural law, summary process being no exception, is permitted to cut short those procedural actions that lead to a substantively correct judgement' ('Entscheidend ist das Kriterium der *cognitio ueritatis*, worauf wir schon bei Innozenz IV. gestoßen sind, als er zu X 5.1.26 über die Ansicht anderer berichtete. Es kommt darauf an, ob eine Prozeßhandlung der *cognitio ueritatis* dient oder nicht. Mit "Wahrheit" ist der Streitfall gemeint, um den der Prozeß geführt wird, sind die Tatsachen angesprochen, welche die richtige Entscheidung stützen. Kein Prozeßrecht, auch nicht das Recht des abgekürzten Verfahrens, darf jene Prozeßhandlungen beschneiden, die zum materiell richtigen Urteil führen') (*ibid.*, 21).

[5] *Ibid.*, 12–14, 18–19.    [6] *Ibid.*, 14–15.    [7] *Ibid.*, 15.    [8] *Ibid.*, 16–17.
[9] Brundage, *Medieval Canon Law*, 140, with further references to the detailed work of Kenneth Pennington.
[10] See e.g. Rößer, *Göttliches und menschliches*, ch. 4.
[11] 'Quia sicut quaedam sunt quae nulla possunt ratione convelli, ita multa sunt quae aut pro consideratione aetatum, aut pro necessitate rerum oporteat temperari: illa semper

Perhaps nowhere more than in medieval canon law has more intensive rational thought been given to the shaping of the relation between rule and exception. The limits of the authority to dispense from the law were set by fundamental values. The precise contours of these were a matter for debate, especially where the dispensing power of the Pope was concerned. He could not grant a dispensation to get out of a consummated marriage between a baptised couple; he could grant a dispensation to marry a third cousin; but where did a forbidden degree of consanguinity turn into incest, for which no dispensation could be granted? Thus the history of medieval dispensation shows us not only the interaction of substantive and formal rationality, but also the causal relation to both of values.

## 'Political' expediency in granting dispensations

Innocent IV in the mid-thirteenth century clearly believed that the substantive grounds for suspending rules could be expediency: the need for allies in the struggle against Frederick II. As noted at the beginning of this study, the laws banning marriages within the fourth degree of consanguinity or affinity in conclusive were no longer regarded as absolute values by this time, if they ever had been. They were justified, not merely cynically, as a means of promoting social charity by creating new bonds between clans.[12] In a given case, the need to bring a great family on side in the struggle of papacy against empire could no doubt seem from a papal point of view an overriding priority for the Church. Evidently such calculations were instrumentally rational, though they served what Innocent saw as a value, namely the triumph of the Church.

## Marriage dispensations and social cohesion

It was normal, however, to justify the need for a dispensation in terms of a high-minded end such as the promotion of social harmony. Thus, for example, a marriage dispensation incorporated in the fourteenth-century formulary of Walter Murner of Strasbourg justifies the exception as follows:

To the bishop, etc.... on the part of Burchard <...> a layman and Anne a woman, of your diocese, the petition presented to us states that they wish to be

---

conditione servata, ut in his quae vel dubia fuerint aut obscura, id noverimus sequendum, quod nec praeceptis evangelicis contrarium, nec decretis sanctorum Patrum inveniatur adversum' (Leo I, Epistola 167; PL 54, col. 1202; 'consideratione aetatum ... necessitate rerum] necessitate temporum ... consideratione etatum' in Gratian, *Decretum*, at D. 14 C. 2 as edited by Friedberg, *Corpus Iuris Canonici*, vol. 1, p. 33).

[12] d'Avray, 'Lay Kinship Solidarity and Papal Law'.

joined to each other in marriage, for certain and rational reasons and above all to avoid the scandals, dissensions and killings, which could probably occur among them and their blood relatives . . .[13]

The formulaic character of the document is evident: it is unlikely that the alternatives were marriage or homicide. On the other hand, it is not unlikely that the marriage or other such marriages actually did promote social cohesion by uniting families that might otherwise have been at odds with each other. At a high political level a notable example is the resolution of the great Mediterranean conflict between the Angevins of Naples and the Crown of Aragon, in great part through marriages for which dispensations were required.[14] Granted that the promotion of social cohesion was the main rationale of the consanguinity rules, dispensations on such grounds were entirely in the spirit of *epieikeia*. The decision whether to grant a dispensation in a given case might be an end–means calculation of whether the general rationale of the rule actually held good in this particular case. Other instrumental considerations which could not be put in the document but which were not necessarily nefarious – such as 'why not make these people happy since they have gone to so much trouble to ask for a dispensation' – might also weigh in the decision.

### The range of substantive rationality in medieval canon law

Dispensations were not the only interface between legal formality and substantive rationality in medieval sacred law. The idea of tolerating wrong to avoid a greater evil is another related strand of thought.[15] Exemption of religious houses or orders from episcopal authority is another.[16] They could have been discussed in this context. Still, dispensation adequately illustrates the relations between different sorts of rationality analysed here, especially since it could be understood broadly in the Middle Ages to include a wide range of instrumental decision-making. The thirteenth-century Spanish canon lawyer Johannes de Deo, in his interesting unpublished treatise on dispensation, seems to interpret the term broadly enough to include all areas where someone in authority has a free hand legally to make decisions.[17] Johannes says, for instance,

---

[13]  Meyer, *Die Pönitentiarie-Formularsammlung*, no. 845, p. 469.
[14]  Davies, 'Marriage and the Politics of Friendship'.
[15]  Roca, 'Der Toleranzbegriff im kanonischen Recht', 550; the article is also important for its survey of related concepts.
[16]  Rabikauskas, *Diplomatica pontificia*, 49–51, with further references.
[17]  For Johannes de Deo's 'De dispensationibus' I have used MSS BL Royal 5.A.i (= *L1*) and Royal 8.D.iii (= *L2*).

that a bishop can give a cleric permission to go on pilgrimage, citing a canon forbidding clerics (and laypeople) to go on pilgrimage without a bishop's permission.[18] This is 'dispensation' rather broadly defined.

## A photo-negative of legal formality

The history of dispensations has an exceptionally long history.[19] The idea seems to develop hand in hand with the notion that Church law was not coterminous with the law of God, but an extension of God's law which also had some of the features of what we would call positive, man-made law. The underlying logic was that a human authority could dispense from a law made by a human authority, if not from Divine law as such.

More specifically, dispensation from the law was a photo-negative of the law's formality.[20] For instance, dispensations for marriage within the forbidden degrees of consanguinity and affinity became normal and frequent.[21] When such dispensations for marriage within the forbidden degrees became common they could be formulated with great precision and construed strictly, so that there was a high degree of formality in the very act of dispensing on substantive grounds from the formal law. The proctors obtaining dispensations (in the fifteenth century at least seemingly often also the couples themselves[22]) understood the kinship system of canon law and knew that the impediments to be removed by

---

[18] 'Item potest dispensando indulgere clerico scilicet quod eat in peregrinatione', *De con. Di. v. Non* oportet [= PARS III D. 5 de con. c. 37]' (*L1*, fol. 139ʳ).

[19] The following studies have still not been superseded: Stiegler, *Dispensation*, and Brys, *De dispensatione in iure canonico*; cf. also Van Hove, *De privilegiis, de dispensationibus*, esp. 292–330.

[20] Nörr, 'Kuriale Praxis und kanonistische Wissenschaft', 36: 'The tighter the net of the law, the greater the need for the legal institution of the Dispensation and for related phenomena: otherwise the subject acts outside the law altogether (in a modern context the phenomenon of illegal labour inevitably comes to mind). A dispensation should not be regarded as an act of grace outside the legal order, but as a part of the latter' ('Je enger das Netz der Gesetze, desto notwendiger das Rechtsinstitut des Dispenses und verwandter Erscheinungen, sonst handelt der Untertan überhaupt am Gesetze vorbei und das Gesetz verliert seine Wirkung (wer denkt da heute nicht an das Phänomen der sogenannten Schwarzarbeit?). Die Dispensation stellt keinen Gnadenakt dar, der außerhalb der Rechtsordnung stünde, sondern sie ist Teil derselben').

[21] Kroppmann, *Ehedispensübung und Stauferkamp*; Schmugge, 'Kanonistik in der Pönitentiarie', 96, shows that in the years from 1455 to 1492 42,560 marriage dispensations were granted by the Penitentiary.

[22] Cf. Schmugge, 'Kanonistik in der Pönitentiarie', 98: 'Furthermore, the supplications for marriage dispensations in the Penitentiary registers also confirm the finding that the ecclesiastical marriage law was widely understood throughout Christendom, and that people knew how to adapt to it when it came to their choice of spouse and their marriage problems' ('Des weiteren bestätigen die Suppliken um eine Matrimonialdispens in den Pönitentiarieregistern auch die Festellung, dass die kirchliche Ehegesetzgebung in der gesamten Christenheit ... weitgehend rezipiert war und die Menschen sich bei Partnerwahl und Heiratsproblemen darauf einzustellen wussten').

dispensation had to be spelled out precisely or it would not work. It was not a matter of vague intentions but of exact specifications.

## The papal Penitentiary and legal formality

Formularies relating to the work of the papal Penitentiary[23] are another manifestation of the symbiosis of formal and substantive rationality in the late medieval history of dispensations. The Penitentiary is one of the most distinctive and also characteristic institutions of later medieval papal government;[24] through it, the granting of dispensations was routinised.[25] The very existence of formularies shows that the Penitentiary did not deal out 'Kadi-justice'[26] outside the realm of formal rules: in effect, the formularies contain a kind of law for granting exceptions. A number of these formularies have survived;[27] in fact they constitute a crucial source for

---

[23] Lea, *A Formulary of the Papal Penitentiary*; Lecacheux, 'Un formulaire de la pénitencerie'; Lang, *Die Urkunden*, doc. 226, pp. 171–2, for what he describes ('Einleitung', p. xci) as 'ein Auftrag aus einem Formelbuch'; Lang, 'Beiträge zur Geschichte der apostolischen Pönitentiarie'; Haskins, 'The Sources for the History of the Papal Penitentiary'; Goeller, *Die Päpstliche Pönitentiarie*; Meyer, *Die Pönitentiarie-Formularsammlung*. Despite all this work there is more to be done with Penitentiary formularies. Not all the formulary materials listed by Goeller have been edited, and Goeller himself could be forgiven for having missed important manuscripts. One formulary that appears not to have attracted the attention of scholarship hitherto is in BL Add. MS 24057. It has material that puts it later than the formulary of Thomas of Capua (d. 1239) edited by Lea, *A Formulary*: for instance, no. CCLV on fol. 33ʳ relates to the war between the Aragonese Frederick of Sicily (whom the Sicilians elected as king in 1296) and the displaced Angevin dynasty which the papacy supported. On the other hand, the BL formulary has only 511 chapters (table of contents fols. 3ʳ–8ᵛ; no. 511 is on fo. 54ᵛ, ending 'Et his est finis formularii penitentiarii domini pape teneantur' (despite the word 'finis' a couple of texts follow), whereas the formulary commissioned by Pope Benedict XII, at least as listed in Goeller, *Die Päpstliche Pönitentiarie*, vol. 1, pt. 1: *Darstellung*, pp. 32–3, has 570. My tentative guess is that the BL manuscript represents a stage well after the Lea formulary but prior to the Benedict XII formulary – though more work would be needed to verify this.

[24] The bibliography on the Penitentiary has burgeoned since the registers became available. See e.g. Erdélyi, 'Neue Forschungen zur Apostolischen Pönitentiarie'; Salonen and Krötzl (eds.), *The Roman Curia*; Schmugge, Hersberger and Wiggenhauser, *Die Supplikenregister der päpstlichen Pönitentiarie*; and Salonen, *The Penitentiary as a Well of Grace*; and Schmugge, *Ehen vor Gericht: Paare der Renaissance vor dem Papst*, for further references.

[25] More than 200 people worked at the Penitentiary (from the *penitentiarius maior* down): Schmugge, 'Kanonistik in der Pönitentiarie', 93). The granting of dispensations was not the only job of this organisation but it was a central function.

[26] 'Kadis' or 'Qadis' are Islamic judges. Weber and others used this phrase as a shorthand to mean justice administered on a case-by-case basis rather than in accordance with formal general rules. As Weber made explicitly clear, he did not think that Islamic justice was actually administered in the rule-free way, but merely used the word in its proverbial sense ('im sprichwörtlichen, nicht im historischen Sinn'; Weber, *Wirtschaft und Gesellschaft*, vol. 2, p. 657).

[27] Göller, *Die Päpstliche Pönitentiarie*, 20–57, 65–74. The second part of this work consists of editions of these texts: *Quellen*.

the history of the papal Penitentiary in the period before the pontificate of Eugenius IV, from which the first registers of supplications to the Penitentiary survive. The so called 'Summa of Nicolaus IV' contains papal rulings such as the following, setting the parameters for dispensations:

> The lord cardinal [penitentiary] can absolve in the due form and grant dispensations to those who have committed simony to enter a religious order, and other members of religious orders who consented to this or acted as intermediaries or who gained anything from this and who, erring through simplicity, received holy orders when this offence had not been purged and in them exercised his office.
> Martin IV.
> . . .
> Again, he can grant a dispensation without letters or witnesses in the confessional forum for the fourth degree of affinity, when the people who contracted marriage were in ignorance of this impediment at the time when the marriage was contracted, and if it was hidden. Gregory X.[28]

Incidentally, this shows how the secrecy and informality of the confessional could be combined with formal legal rationality.

As for dispensations where paperwork was required, no doubt the key thing was to frame the request in an established form of words. The grant of marriage dispensation quoted above from the formulary of Walter Murner probably borrows wording from a request framed for exactly that: to be incorporated into a grant.[29] Compare the Latin wording of the passage translated above (and a later part of the same document) with a petition from a different formulary[30] (which gives specimen petitions almost certainly based on real documents). The common form phrases are in bold type (first in English translation, then in the original Latin):

| *Formulary of Walter Murner*[31] | *Formulary in Cod. Arch. Vat. Arm. 53No. 17, fols. 26–35ᵛ, ed. Göller, no. 1*[32] |
|---|---|
| . . . the contents of the petition presented to us was that they . . . above all to avoid **the scandals**, dissensions and **homicides that could . . . arise** between them and their blood relatives, desire to be joined together in | In truth if their marriage were to be broken up, grave damage, **scandals** and **homicides could arise** in consequence. Your Holiness is therefore suppliantly asked . . . that . . . you may deign **mercifully to grant a** |

---

[28] Göller, Die Päpstliche Pönitentiarie, vol. 1, pt. 2: Quellen, 1.

[29] See above at pp. 152–3. Strictly speaking, the document is not a grant but an instruction to the bishop to give the dispensation and declare the children legitimate if he finds the facts to be as stated.

[30] Göller, *Die Päpstliche Pönitentiarie*, vol. 1, pt. 2: *Quellen*, 147–71.

[31] Meyer, *Die Pönitentiarie-Formularsammlung*, no. 845, p. 469; see above, p. 153 n. 13.

[32] Göller, *Die Päpstliche Pönitentiarie*, vol. 1, pt. 2: *Quellen*, 147.

marriage... We... grant to your foresightful self... **that... you may mercifully grant a dispensation** to the said Burchard and Anna... to contract marriage... and **licitly remain**... in it,... **deeming the children who have been and will be conceived to be legitimate.**

**dispensation** that they may **licitly remain** in the said marriage, **deeming the children who have and will be conceived to be legitimate...**

... nobis oblata petitio continebat, quod ipsi... presertim ad evitandum **scandala**, dissensiones et **homicidia**, qui [*sic*] inter eos et eorum consanguineos... **possent exoriri**, desiderant invicem matrimonialiter copulari,... Nos... circumspectioni vestre committimus, **quatenus**,... cum dictis Burcardo et Anna, quod... possint... matrimonium contrahere ... et in eo... **licite remanere, misericorditer dispensetis,... prolem susceptam et suscipiendam legitimam decernentes.**

Verum si divortium fieret inter eos, dampna gravia, **scandala** atque **homicidia possint** exinde **oriri**. Supplicatur igitur Sanctitas vester... **quatinus** eis... ut... in dicto... matrimonio **licite remanere** valeant, dignemini **misericorditer dispensare, prolemque susceptam et suscipiendam legitimam decernentes...**

Then again compare the following words from the second document with words from another in the same formulary:

*Formulary in Cod. Arch. Vat. Arm. 53, No. 17, fol. 26–35$^v$, ed. Göller, no. 1*[33]

*Formulary in Cod. Arch. Vat. Arm. 53, No. 17, fol. 26–35$^v$, ed. Göller, no. 3*[34]

**It is explained** to your Holiness on **behalf of...N. and B**. his wife, a **married couple** of *x* **diocese that formerly, not knowing that there was a certain impediment between them such as to prevent them being joined to one another in marriage, they contracted marriage** with each other **in public** using words in the present tense, in the face of the Church[35] **in accordance with the custom of the country** and **consummated** it by the union of the flesh and begat children from it; **afterwards it came to their notice...**

**It is explained on behalf of N. a layman, and B.**, a woman, **a married couple** of the diocese of Spoleto, **that formerly, not knowing that there was a certain impediment between them such as to prevent them being joined to one another in marriage, they contracted marriage** with one another **in public in accordance with the custom of the country; afterwards**, before they had **consummated** this marriage, **it came to their notice...**

---

[33] *Ibid.*, 147.    [34] *Ibid.*, 148.
[35] 'in facie ecclesie', though a stock phrase, is ambiguous: it could mean 'at the church door' or 'in the eyes of the Church': at this period I think the second meaning is predominant.

Exponitur S. V. pro parte...N. et B. eius uxoris **coniugum**..[36] **dioecesis, quod ipsi olim ignorantes aliquod impedimentum inter eos existere, quominus possent invicem matrimonialiter copulari, matrimonium** inter se per verba legitime de presenti in facie ecclesie **secundum morem patrie publice contraxerunt** illudque per carnis copulam consumarunt et prolem exinde procrearunt; **postmodum pervenit ad eorum notitiam**...

Exponitur S. V. pro parte N. laici et B. mulieris **coniugum** Spoletan. **diocesis, quod ipsi olim ignorantes aliquod impedimentum inter eos existere, quominus possint invicem matrimonialiter copulari, matrimonium invicem secundum morem patrie publice contraxerunt; postmodum** antequam huiusmodi matrimonium **consumarunt, ad eorum pervenit notitiam**...

It only made sense for petitions to follow fixed forms. There were *procuratores* to give the petitioners expert advice. These proctors were mostly lawyers and legally educated, so we should not be surprised to find that the Penitentiary registers, which incorporated wording from the petitions,[37] were full of terminology from canon and civil law.[38]

Expert advisers would know that a petition had the best chance of succeeding if it seemed to fit an existing a general category. Once we do have registers they bear out the impression of a system of well-established forms which requests to the Penitentiary needed to fit, with the 'On various forms' rubric providing the necessary 'miscellaneous' category.[39] The massive Penitentiary registers are a monument to the symbiotic relationship of formal and substantive rationality in papal government.

### Formal rationality in high-level dispensations

The legal formality in which dispensations could be encased could be strikingly evident at the highest social level, where we see it performing a

[36] The dots are in the edition: in papal documents they have a function a little like 'N.' in modern documents.

[37] Schmugge, 'Kanonistik in der Pönitentiarie', 95: passage beginning ' 'Generell ist festzustellen' and ending 'der Bittschrift enthalten'.

[38] *Ibid.*, 107, passage beginning 'Die an der Formulierung' and ending 'legistischer Texte'.

[39] Cf. Schmugge *et al.*, *Die Supplikenregister*, 23, passage beginning 'Die Registerschreiber ordneten' and ending '*in forma "Cupientes"*', and 96–7, passage beginning 'Auch in den anderen acht Kapiteln' and ending 'in Inhalt und Form' (pp. 96–7). Even so Schmugge *et al.* managed to bring a great part of the miscellaneous material under twelve headings of their own, starting with homicide and bodily harm ('Tötung und Körperverletzung') and ending with benefice income and delay of holy orders during academic study ('Pfründeneinkommen und Weiheaufschub während des Studiums') – adding, it is true, their own meta-miscellaneous ('Übriges') category (*ibid.*, 97).

function not mentioned so far: for the practice of framing dispensations from the forbidden degrees with formal precision, and construing them strictly, was designed to minimise the grey area between clearly valid and clearly invalid marriages. Some early fourteenth-century dispensations can illustrate the point. On 5 May 1318 John XXII granted a dispensation for Jeanne, daughter of Louis X of France, to marry Philip, son of the Count of Evreux. The couple had a common ancestor in one direction two degrees (i.e. generations)[40] away from Philip and three from Jeanne (who would thus be Philip's first cousin once removed), but the family trees met up with other ancestors too. The wording of the dispensation from these impediments is a piece of exact legal draftsmanship. The Pope's letter recapitulates the request for a dispensation for the couple's future marriage. In my translation 'stem' translates 'stirps', which is a point at which the family trees of two individuals meet up; there can of course be several.

notwithstanding the fact that the aforesaid Jeanne and the said Philip are known to be separated from one common stem in the third degree on her side and in the second degree only on his side, and from other stems also in two, several or different degrees of consanguinity or affinity: each in the third or the fourth, or one in the third and the other in the fourth . . . [41]

This was one notch less comprehensive than a dispensation granted on 21 June 1324 for the marriage of Charles IV of France to Jeanne the daughter of Louis of Évreux. They were first cousins, each only two generations away from the stem, so this was a considerable concession.[42] The Pope granted a watertight dispensation:

by a special grace, with certain knowledge [*ex certa scientia*] and with the plenitude of apostolic power, we grant a dispensation, notwithstanding in any way the aforesaid impediment with the aforesaid Jeanne, or any other impediments, introduced in any way by the constitutions of canon law or other human constitutions,

---

[40] For calculation by degrees see d'Avray, *Medieval Marriage*, 106, or the old account by Joyce, *Christian Marriage*, ch. 12, perhaps clearer than Goody, *The Development of the Family and Marriage in Europe*, 136–44.

[41] 'id non obstante quod Johanna predicta ab uno communi stipite tertio, et dictus Philippus secundo dumtaxat, et ab aliis stipitibus etiam duobus, pluribus diversisve uterque tertio vel quarto, aut unus tertio et alter quarto consanguinitatis vel affinitatis gradibus distare noscantur' (Coulon, *Lettres secrètes et curiales du pape Jean XXII*, fasc. 2, no. 576, col. 499).

[42] 'quia secundo consanguinitatis gradu ex utroque latere, respectu ejusdem stipitis vos invicem attinetis, matrimonium hujusmodi contrahere absque dispensatione Sedis Apostolice non valetis. Quare nobis tua serenitas humiliter supplicavit ut, tecum et cum eadem Johanna quod, impedimento hujusmodi aut quibusvis aliis, si qua forsan existant, nequaquam obstantibus, possitis copulari matrimonialiter dispensare de benignitate apostolica dignaremur' (*ibid.*, fasc. 4, no. 2106, col. 531).

for which the Apostolic See is accustomed to grant dispensations, especially with people of exalted rank, should such impediments perchance exist, whether they come about by reason of consanguinity in respect of the same stem or different stems – whether you are separated from the same stem by equal or unequal distances; or by reason of affinity or other affinities in the same or in a more distant degree; or of justice of public honesty;[43] or of spiritual relationship[44] or relationships: that you and the same Jeanne may be joined in marriage in God's name, and we announce that the children that will be received from you and the said Jeanne will be legitimate.[45]

Long, complex sentences are often a feature of the technical language of lawyers, and such dispensations were certainly, if paradoxically, formal legal documents: substantial rationality as legal formality! A lot was at stake here and there was history behind it. Charles had managed to get his first marriage to Blanche of Burgundy annulled in 1322 on grounds of impediments of kinship and spiritual relationship, a relatively rare thing by that time.[46] Though the spiritual relationship may have been the decisive issue, the kinship counted too and did so because the dispensation obtained for that first marriage did not cover all relationships between Charles and his wife. That in its turn was due to the circumstances in which the dispensation had been obtained, much earlier, in 1307. This dispensation was not tailor-made for Charles's marriage to Blanche, but framed for a bride as yet unspecified.[47] Although both Pope and King desired this annulment for reasons unconnected with the grounds for it, they were able to legitimise it quite adequately within their system, according to which the marriage was indeed invalid. The formal legal rules were strictly applied and it could not pass that test. Though the power to grant dispensations has no obvious parallel in common law or civil law, it does not belong to a world of arbitrary justice outside the constraints of rules and regularities. Dispensations do not make proper sense unless one is aware of the backcloth of complex and coherent legislation. The vulnerability of the dispensation of 1306 and the impregnability

---

[43] A technical term for another kind of impediment.
[44] Impediments arising out of godparenthood at baptism or sponsorship at confirmation: for details see Dauvillier, *Le Mariage dans le droit classique*, 153–5. The nature of the impediment had only been properly clarified relatively recently. See Jaffé, 'Die Ehepolitik Bonifazius VIII', 4 and 15 n. 8. It is a shame that this important thesis was never published (I have used typescript versions in the libraries of the Warburg Institute and the Monumenta Germaniae Historica).
[45] Coulon, *Lettres secrètes... Jean XXII*, fasc. 2, no. 2106, col. 532.
[46] For the depositions before the annulment see Robert de Chevanne, 'Charles IV le Bel et Blanche de Bourgogne', 313–50. My thanks to Stephen Davies for drawing my attention to this.
[47] *Regestum Clementis Papae V*, no. 2302, p. 182.

of the dispensation of 1324 must both be understood in terms of the rationality of formal law.

## The parameters set by values

Dispensations for marriage within the forbidden degrees became easier and easier to get, but a dispensation to get out of a valid marriage seems never to have been envisaged at an official level in the age of papal monarchy, though something of the kind can be found in the fantasy world of fiction, in the romance of *Ille et Galeron* by Gauthier d'Arras.[48] Away from fiction and in the real world, however, papal power was limited by the contours of a brick wall of value rationality.[49] As a thought experiment, one could imagine that the power to dispense from marriage vows would have been convenient for the papacy: a power such as was indeed exercised in the case of unconsummated marriages. Such a power would have been used in extreme circumstances, or in return for great favours. But there was no such road out of a consummated marriage. This is an example of the limits to the kinds of rationality discussed in the chapter: to both substantive and formal instrumental rationality.

The precise limits of papal authority were a matter of debate. Johannes de Deo, the under-researched thirteenth-century Spanish canon lawyer, addressed himself to the problem in his treatise on dispensations (a concept which he interpreted widely, as we have seen). According to some, he explains, the Pope can dispense from anything except articles of faith.[50] Others think that his power is more constrained: he cannot dispense 'against the Apostle, nor against divine law, nor against the Gospel, nor against the first four [general] councils – and they cite many laws in support of their position'.[51] ('The Apostle' was St Paul. It was thought, for instance, that St Paul's comment in Titus 1:5–7 that a presbyter should be the husband of one wife meant that a man who had married a widow

---

[48] d'Avray, *Medieval Marriage*, 96–8.    [49] *Ibid.*, 99–130.
[50] 'On dispensation by the lord pope. On this topic different doctors [i.e. of canon law] take different views. Some say that the pope can grant a dispensation in any case – even against what St Paul lays down – since he is in the place of St Peter and is the Vicar of Jesus Christ . . . Therefore they make no exception apart from articles of faith' ('De dispensatione domini pape. Super hoc diversi doctores [*added between lines*] diversa sentiunt. Quidam dicunt quod papa possit dispensare in omni casu etiam contra Apostolum, cum teneat locum beati Petri et sit vicarius Iesu Christi . . . Nolunt ergo excipere nisi articulos fidei tantum' (BL MS Royal 5.A.i [*L1*], fol. 134ʳ).
[51] 'Item alii dicunt contra, scilicet quia non potest dispensare contra Apostolum nec contra ius divinum nec contra ewangelium nec contra iiii concilia, et inducunt [*L2:* dicunt *L1*] pro se multa iura' (BL MS Royal 5.A.i [*L1*], fol. 134ʳ).

or who had married more than once could not become a priest, even if he was now single: this being treated as an absolute rule, not just a rule of positive ecclesiastical law.[52]) Others again define his dispensing power in terms of the powers that only the Pope possesses: where such things are concerned he must, however, give explicit consent, whereas in lesser matters (in respect of which lesser prelates too can grant dispensations) he can grant tacit consent.[53] Johannes de Deo seems to have tended towards the minimising wing: he does not think that the Pope can override St Paul and allow a man who had been married to a widow, or married more than once, to become a deacon or anything above that in the ecclesiastical hierarchy.[54]

The Pope's room for manoeuvre in granting dispensations was never thought to be unlimited. The general trend among Decretal commentators seems to have been towards a maximising interpretation of the dispensing power.[55] Ultimately papal practice defined the line,[56] but popes surely knew it was there. As we have seen, there was no question of the power to dispense from the bonds of a consummated marriage between baptised persons.

---

[52] d'Avray, *Medieval Marriage*, 132 and ch. 3 *passim*. Cf. Ch. 2 above, at p. 54.

[53] 'Again, others say that in matters that pertain to him alone he can uniformly (?) grant dispensations without infringement of the law: so the following: He alone restores to office those who have been solemnly deposed from it [*a list of things only the Pope can do follows*] . . . In these matters therefore and in similar cases he can grant dispensations, but only by doing so explicitly; in other lesser matters, in which lesser prelates too can grant dispensations, silence too is taken as consent' ('Item alii dicunt quod in eis que spectant ad ipsum solum possit indistincte [*L2:* indiffinite *L1?*] dispensare sine offensa iuris, que sunt hec: Solum restituit solenniter depositos . . . In his ergo et similibus possit dispensare, sed expresse tantum [*L2: om. L1*]: [fol. 135ʳ] in aliis minoribus etiam taciturnitas habetur pro consensu, in quibus etiam minores prelati possunt dispensare' (BL MS Royal 5.A.i [*L1*], fols. 134ᵛ–135ʳ).

[54] 'We must now look at the matters where he cannot grant dispensations *de iure* even if he can de facto. He cannot or should not act against St Paul and grant a dispensation to allow a man of two marriages [i.e. a remarried widower or husband of widow] to be promoted to deacon, priest, bishop or above' ('Restat ergo videre in quibus de iure non possit [*L2:* possunt *L1*] dispensare etsi de facto possit. Contra Apostolum non possit dispensare vel debet: quod bigamus promoveatur in diaconum [diaconem *L1, L2*] vel sacerdotem vel episcopum vel supra') (BL MS Royal 5.A.i [*L1*], fol. 136ʳ; etsi] et si *could be read but the sense is probably 'even if' rather than 'whether' as an indirect question*). Cf. d'Avray, *Medieval Marriage*, Document 3. 1, pp. 249–50.

[55] Brys, *De dispensatione*, 225–6.

[56] 'the pope's habitual actions beyond and contrary to the doctrine received in the schools would first sow doubt about whether the doctrine was correct, and then change the doctrine itself' ('modus agendi Pontificum ultra et contra doctrinam in scholis receptam, primo dubium ingeret circa doctrinae rectitudinem, deinde et ipsam doctrinam mutabit') (*ibid.*, 140; cf. 225).

## Conclusion

The dispensation system is an example of the field of force, generated by values and convictions, which defined the sphere of instrumental rationality, whether formal or substantive. Once again the usefulness of distinguishing types of rationality is demonstrated by the opportunity such analysis opens of understanding their interplay. The interplay of formal and substantive rationality is a symbiotic system within the larger symbiotic system of intrumental and value rationality.

# General conclusion

Parts of foregoing chapters will have pressed too close to the rocky ground of detailed medieval scholarship for the comfort of some readers; this Conclusion, on the other hand, may seem to go up to an unpleasantly high altitude of abstraction. There is a reason: *Medieval Religious Rationalities* shares a common structure with its more theoretical and comparative sister volume *Rationalities in History*. The aim of this final section is to resume the main themes of the present book in such a way as to bring out the line of argument that the two volumes share.

Both books distinguish different ways of reasoning in order to establish the relations between them: which is symbiotic rather than antithetical. The most fundamental distinction is between conviction rationality, also called value rationality, and instrumental rationality. Both kinds of thinking can be called 'rational'. With both, generalities as well as specificities are involved – principles and abstractions are part of our concept of rationality; and in both cases the reasons for thinking and acting held before the mind are also the actual causes of the thoughts or actions. Actions are *irrational* insofar as the causes of thoughts or actions are different from the reasons for them. It is crucial not to confuse irrational thoughts and actions with convictions, which, however reprehensible we may find them, fit the category of value rationality. The present book tries to discover how values and instrumental calculation affect each other, and to illustrate these relations in detail with medieval examples.

Instrumental rationality is what many people mean by 'rationality' *tout court*. In particular, economists and rational choice theorists tend to reduce rationality to this one species. Instrumental rationality includes calculations about ends and means or causes and consequences, including logical consequences. This kind of rationality seems to be a human universal. To see it as a sort of foundation on which different cultural rationalities are built is, however, an unhelpful analogy. It is more useful to think of the universal 'instrumental' rationality as a superstructure built on the foundations of different conviction/value rationalities. As noted below, the techniques used to bring sermons to the masses in the later

Middle Ages, both the *basso continuo* of model sermon production and the virtuoso performances of famous revivalists, can be classed as instrumental rationality, as can the techniques associated with Scholasticism – explicit logic and the *quaestio* form.

The distinction between these two fundamental types of rationality is therefore far from being a dichotomy. They are causally connected and constantly interact. In this flow of mutual influences, conviction rationality tends to exercise a certain primacy. Conviction rationality is explained here in terms of the following features.[1]

The first feature is that systems of values and convictions are holistic, with the different elements interrelated and interlocking. We saw that in orthodox medieval religion apparently discrete convictions about penance, marriage, Christ's suffering humanity, the Trinity, the exchange of spiritual gifts, papal power and belief in miracles were all tightly interlinked. The argument about the holistic character of the medieval Church's belief system and of the antecedent probability which each part derived from the others could easily have been extended to many other convictions and leading ideas within the system.

Here the medieval Church is a particular case of a general sociological fact about rationalities. In value systems, the various convictions support one another as if in an electricity grid, so that the antecedent probability of any one element being true is secured by the truth of the other elements, and (to change the metaphor) this bar of antecedent probability is too high for most arguments against any one element of the system to surmount. To put it the other way around: when any one conviction is attacked, the prior probability is so much in its favour that even an apparently convincing objection can be set aside mentally on the grounds that it will probably turn out to be wrong in the long run. The system can be attacked as a whole, but this too is very difficult because rational argument usually depends on isolating one distinct issue for discussion.

The second feature of value rationalities in the ideal-type used here is that convictions are anchored in experience or simulacra of experience – strong mental likenesses of the objects of the convictions. They are concrete and seem 'real', rather then just verbal, propositional, notional, abstract. The interrelated and interlaced medieval convictions listed above were all in one way or another made concrete and vivid to medieval Christians.

These two features of value systems tend to go together. Experience or a simulacrum of it affects estimates of antecedent probability. If an

---

[1] This analysis goes beyond Weber's *ipsissima verba* – but he is a source of stimulus here, not the object of an intellectual history.

objection to a system of convictions runs counter to strong mental images based on experience, as well as to what other firm convictions would lead one to infer, that objection may carry little weight. The two characteristics together mean that conviction rationalities are hard to shake.

They have immune systems against hostile arguments. From the thirteenth century, the rigorous demands for proof of miracles imposed in the new-style canonisation processes and the theoretical analysis of the nature and rationale of miracles by Aquinas and others would have reinforced one another. Within this intellectual context a generalised scepticism about miracles *à la Hume* would not be an appealing attitude for the uneducated.

For all their durability, systems of values and convictions do nevertheless ebb and flow in history. For instance, a system of values can be launched far beyond its original setting by a charismatic leader like the eighth-century Aldebert about whom Boniface worried, or a Valdes, or a Francis of Assisi, or a Luther. Personal experiences may be the crucible in which such leaders form new convictions, as with Aeneas Silvius Piccolomini's conversion from Conciliarism. Crises or challenges may develop out of seeds within the value system itself, as Waldensianism, Joachimite prophetic heresy, the radical dissident ideas about Poverty of the Franciscan Spirituals and other later medieval heresies that arose out of reflection within the system that was then challenged. Lutheranism was the first such challenge to succeed dramatically. On the other hand, belief systems may also disappear when their institutional infrastructure disintegrates, or is destroyed. The medieval Cathars could not continue as a vibrant religion when all the *perfecti* had been burned.

Changes of conviction that look dramatic on the surface may sometimes mask substantive continuities, as when someone seeks for the same value in a succession of churches or political parties. Belief in sacrifice as a religious ritual and in the value of a hero leader's death probably provided continuities between Pagan and Christian Anglo-Saxon England. The orality of pre-Christian England could have smoothed the transition to Christianity, too: there were no formulae fixed in writing to set against the new system. No monocausal explanation covers all these dynamics.

The fate of value systems over time is, however, much affected by how effectively they are served by instrumental techniques. Values and convictions may be tenacious, but they will not gain new adherents unless propagated by instrumental techniques, which may take many different forms: preaching, polemics, rituals, and so forth. Value systems need to reproduce themselves from one generation to the next. Consequently there is an instrumental rationality to education in values, whether religious or secular.

The relationship between values and instrumental rationality is symbiotic. The analytical distinction drawn by Weber between value rationality and instrumental rationality should not lead to segregation of the topics (nothing could have been further from his intentions). Values and convictions have a force which is lacking in merely abstract and propositional modes of thoughts, but instrumental techniques of devotion, ritual, asceticism and so forth may be required to maintain their concrete character and to reproduce them from one generation to the next. We saw how the idea of the Trinity was transmitted by the instruction associated with godparenthood, by scholastic philosophy, by ritual, notably a major new feast established in 1334, and by preaching which employed concrete analogies and linked the doctrine to other elements in the belief system. Medieval Catholicism reproduced and advanced its value systems by technically well-planned revivalist preaching.

It is important to stress the instrumentally rational character of these techniques (used not just by the medieval Church but also by other churches and world religions) to counteract the assumption that instrumental rationality is especially associated with secular modernity. Gregory the Great gave an explicitly instrumental rationale for his instructions about ritual in newly converted England. Thomas Aquinas explicitly articulates the idea that religious devotions and the rules of religious orders have an instrumental character.

Insofar as two value systems of any kind share underlying values, they are likely to employ strikingly similar instrumental techniques. Sometimes the similarity may be more apparent than real, but it can be genuine. The similarity may extend to 'interface convictions' – convictions about the contours of the interface between the two rationalities, in areas such as ethics and law. Thus Aristotle in the fourth century BCE saw city state law as a human instrument in the service of the virtues. The virtues were the real values, the laws instruments to promote them. A judge could use discretion to ignore the letter of the law in individual cases. We find 'interface values' similar to Aristotle's and antedating the reception of his *Ethics* in the Middle Ages, underpinning the laws of religious orders and canon law generally: the rules of these legal systems were instruments distinct from the ideals they served. They were taken very seriously – but dispensation was possible. the dispensation system was underpinned by an interface value similar to Aristotle's *epieikeia*.

One type of instrumental technique that transcends the secular–religious divide is formal legal rationality. This has indeed been associated especially with secular 'modernity', but, as Weber noted, it is strikingly characteristic of the legal and administrative systems of the Catholic

Church. Its origins go back to late antiquity and the conciliar and papal decretal law of the Christian empire – a canon law which owed much to imperial legal structures. The level of formal rationality fluctuated between that early precocious age and the age of Innocent III, when the system began to reach maturity.

The formal legal rationality of late medieval canon law differs from that of 'modernity' in a crucial respect: it was much less dependent on a properly salaried bureaucracy. That is important because papal administration deviated in a series of crucial respects from the ideal-type of bureaucracy as formulated by Weber, and in the direction of irrationality – defined in this particular context as the failure to match means to ends effectively. Even without its striking inefficiencies the papacy lacked the resources to pay an administrative service to govern Latin Christendom. It nevertheless in a real sense managed to hold this massive system of sacred law together. An ingenious set of formal rules enabled the system to run at minimal cost in view of its scale. In modern societies formal legal rationality depends on a salaried bureaucracy: in the medieval Church, formal legality partly replaced salaried bureaucracy. An underlying value, belief in papal office charisma, was the other key. The instrumentally ingenious formal rules and the religious value were interdependent.

Legal formality is contrasted with substantive legal rationality, as its opposite ideal-type. Some have identified substantive rationality with values, thinking to follow Weber. This is to misinterpret him, and it leaves one with an unviable analytical terminology which fails to accommodate, say, cases where temporary political considerations are allowed to override formal legal rules. Here substantive legal rationality can be highly instrumental. In some systems, notably with later medieval dispensations, the choice between following the formal rules or suspending them in a given case is an instrumental judgement left to the tribunal. This instrumental judgement was to be made, however, in the light of the system of values and convictions. The formal legality of ecclesiastical law and the system of dispensing on substantive grounds took root in the same soil, and both reached a high plateau in the thirteenth century. As with the relation of values to instrumental rationality, so too with the formal and substantive rationality of medieval canon law: the relationship was symbiotic. There were formal rules and formulae to regulate dispensations from the rules.

Thus one distinguishes different types of rationality to understand the reciprocal influences. Values and convictions are propagated through instrumental techniques, or else they contract and wither away. The myriad forms of instrumental rationality are explained in part by the variety of conviction systems: the more the values differ, the more different the instrumental techniques they generate look. Value rationalities create formal rationalities to serve as their instruments, and sometimes suspend them, in the light of instrumental calculation shaped by those same values. Instead of dichotomies and antitheses, therefore, the analysis of rationalities leaves one with a repertory of causal explanations to try out for size on concrete historical cases. These Weberian ideal-types help to make sense of detailed and technical medieval data: for empirical historians, they are not constraining but enabling.

# Bibliography

Albert of Aachen, *Historia Ierosolimitana: A History of the Journey to Jerusalem*, ed. and trans. S. Edgington (Oxford, 2007).

Althoff, G., 'Zur Bedeutung symbolischer Kommunikation für das Verständnis des Mittelalters', *Frühmittelalterliche Studien*, 31 (1997), 370–89.

Anderson, P., *Passages from Antiquity to Feudalism* (London, 1978).

Andrews, F., *The Early Humiliati* (Cambridge, 1999).

Angenendt, A., *Geschichte der Religiosität im Mittelalter*, 2nd edn (Darmstadt, 2000).

*Grundformen der Frömmigkeit im Mittelalter*, 2nd edn (Enzyklopädie Deutscher Geschichte, 98; Munich, 2004).

Aquinas, *see* Thomas Aquinas.

Aristotle, *Aristoteles Latinus, XXVI I-3 fasciculus tertius, Ethica Nicomachea, Translatio Roberti Grosseteste . . . A. Recensio Pura*, ed. R. A. Gauthier (Leiden etc., 1972).

*Aristoteles Latinus, XXVI I-3 fasciculus quartus, Ethica Nicomachea, Translatio Roberti Grosseteste . . . B. Recensio Recognita*, ed. R. A. Gauthier (Leiden, 1973).

*The Complete Works of Aristotle*, ed. J. Barnes, 2 vols. (Princeton, 1984).

*Nicomachean Ethics*, trans. H. Rackham (Cambridge, Mass., 1982).

Arnold, J. H., *Belief and Unbelief in Medieval Europe* (London, 2005).

*Inquisition and Power: Catharism and the Confessing Subject in Medieval Languedoc* (Philadelphia, 2001).

Aronstam, R. A., 'Penitential Pilgrimages to Rome in the Early Middle Ages', *Archivum historiae pontificiae*, 13 (1975), 65–83.

Asbridge, T., *The First Crusade: A New History* (London, 2005).

Atiyah, P. S., and Summers, R. S., *Form and Substance in Anglo-American Law: A Comparative Study of Legal Reasoning, Legal Theory, and Legal Institutions* (Oxford, 1987).

Atkinson, C. W., *Mystic and Pilgrim: The Book and the World of Margery Kempe* (Ithaca, NY, 1983).

Auerbach, E., *Mimesis: Dargestellte Wirklichkeit in der abendländischen Literatur*, 7th edn (Bern, 1982).

Baethgen, F., 'Quellen und Untersuchungen zur Geschichte der päpstlichen Hof- u. Finanzverwaltung unter Bonifaz VIII', in *Quellen und Forschungen aus italienischen Archiven und Bibliotheken, herausgegeben vom Preussischen Historischen Institut in Rom*, 20 (Rome, 1928–9), 114–237.

Baker, J. H., *An Introduction to English Legal History*, 4th edn (Bath, 2002).

Baldus de Ubaldis, *Clarissimi... Baldi perusini commentaria... super decretalibus* [of Pope Gregory IX, books 1–3] *novissime impressa, cum pluribus additamentis... doctorum* (Lyons, 1521; BL call number L.23 f.3 (2)).

Barraclough, G., 'The Executors of Papal Provisions in the Canonical Theory of the Thirteenth and Fourteenth Centuries', *Acta Congressus Iuridici Internationalis, Romae, VII saeculo a Decretalibus Gregorii IX et XIV a codice Iustiniano promulgatis, 12–17 Novembris 1934*, vol. 3 (Rome, 1936), 109–35.

'Formulare für Suppliken aus der ersten Hälfte des 13. Jahrhunderts', *Archiv für katholisches Kirchenrecht*, 150 [= Vierter Folge, dreiundzwanzigster Band] (1935), 435–56.

Bartlett, R., *The Hanged Man: A Story of Miracle, Memory and Colonialism in the Middle Ages* (Princeton, 2004).

*The Natural and the Supernatural in the Middle Ages* (Cambridge, 2008).

'From Paganism to Christianity in Medieval Europe', in Berend (ed.), *Christianization*, 47–72.

'Reflections on Paganism and Christianity in Medieval Europe', *Proceedings of the British Academy*, 101 (1999), 55–76.

*Trial by Fire and Water: The Medieval Judicial Ordeal* (Oxford, 1986).

Bataillon, L.-J., *La Prédication au XIIIᵉ siècle en France et Italie: Études et documents* (Aldershot, 1993).

'Un Sermon de S. Thomas d'Aquin sur la parabole du festin', repr. in his *La Prédication au XIIIᵉ siècle*, essay XVI, 451–6.

Bauer, C., 'Die Epochen der Papstfinanz', *Historische Zeitschrift*, 138 (1928), 458–503.

Bauer, P., *Die Benediktinerabtei Plankstetten in Geschichte und Gegenwart* (Plankstetten, 1979).

Bede, Venerable, *Bede's Ecclesiastical History of the English People*, ed. B. Colgrave and R. A. B. Mynors (Oxford, 1969).

Beebe, K., 'Felix Fabri and his Audiences: The Pilgrimage Writings of a Dominican Preacher in Late-Medieval Germany', D.Phil. thesis (Oxford University, 2007).

Bell, R. M., *Holy Anorexia* (Chicago, 1985).

Berend, N. (ed.), *Christianisation and the Rise of Christian Monarch: Scandinavia, Central Europe and Rus' c. 900–1200* (Cambridge, 2007).

Berger, A., *Encyclopedic Dictionary of Roman Law* (Transactions of the American Philosophical Society, 43, part 2; Philadelphia, 1953).

Bériou, N., *L'Avènement des maîtres de la parole: La prédication à Paris au XIIIᵉ siècle*, 2 vols. (Collection des Études Augustiniennes, Série Moyen Âge et Temps Modernes, 32; Paris, 1998).

'Saint François, premier prophète de son ordre dans les sermons du XIIIᵉ siècle' in Bérious and d'Avray, *Modern Questions*, 285–308.

and d'Avray, D. L., with Cole, P., Riley-Smith, J., and Tausche, M., *Modern Questions about Medieval Sermons: Essays on Marriage, Death, History and Sanctity* (Biblioteca di Medioevo Latino, 11; Spoleto and Florence, 1994).

Bernard of Clairvaux, *Tractatus de praecepto et dispensatione, 1.2, in Sancti Bernardi opera*, vol. 3, ed. J. Leclercq et al. (Rome, 1963), 255–6.

Bertram, M., *Stagnation oder Fortbildung? Aspekte des allgemeinen Kirchenrechts im 14. und 15. Jahrhundert* (Bibliothek des deutschen Historischen Instituts in Rom, 108; Tübingen, 2005).

Bianchi, L., *Il vescovo e i filosofi: La condanna parigina del 1277 e l'evoluzione dell'aristotelismo scolastico* (Quodlibet, 6; Bergamo, 1990).

Bijsterveld, A.-J. A., 'Looking for Common Ground: From Monastic *Fraternitas* to Lay Confraternity in the Southern Low Countries in the Tenth to Twelfth Centuries', in E. Jamroziak and J. Burton (eds.), *Religious and Laity in Western Europe, 1000–1400: Interaction, Negotiation, and Power* (Europa Sacra, 2; Turnhout, 2006), 287–314.

Biller, P, 'Goodbye to Waldensianism?', *Past and Present*, 192 (2006), 3–33.

'The Historiography of Medieval Heresy in the United States of America and Great Britain, 1945–1992', in Biller, *The Waldenses*, essay II.

*The Measure of Multitude: Population in Medieval Thought* (Oxford, 2000).

*The Waldenses, 1170–1530* (Aldershot, 2001).

'The Waldenses in the Fourteenth and Fifteenth Centuries: The Current State of Knowledge', in Biller, *The Waldenses*, essay I.

Binmore, K., *Just Playing: Game Theory and the Social Contract II* (Cambridge, Mass., 1998).

*Natural Justice* (Oxford, 2005).

*Playing for Real: A Text on Game Theory* (Oxford, 2007), 164.

Bischoff, B., 'Studien zur Geschichte des Klosters St. Emmeram im Spätmittelalter (1324–1525)', *Mittelalterliche Studien: Ausgewählte Aufsätze zur Schriftkund und Literaturgeschichte*, 2 (Stuttgart, 1967), 115–55.

Blair, J., *The Church in Anglo-Saxon Society* (Oxford, 2005).

Blouin, F. X., et al., *Vatican Archives: An Inventory and Guide to the Historical Documents of the Holy See* (New York, 1998).

Boniface, St, *Die Briefe des heiligen Bonifatius und Lullus*, ed. M. Tangl (Monumenta Germaniae Historica Epistolae Selectae I; Berlin, 1916 edn.).

Borgolte, M. (ed.), *Stiftungen in Christentum, Judentum und Islam vor der Moderne: Auf der Suche nach ihren Gemeinsamkeiten und Unterschieden in religiösen Grundlagen, praktischen Zwecken und historischen Transformationen* (Berlin, 2005).

Borofsky, R., Kane, H. K., Obeyesekere, G., and Sahlins, M., 'CA Forum on Theory in Anthropology: Cook, Lono, Obeyesekere, and Sahlins [and Comments and Reply]', *Current Anthropology*, 38 (1997), 255–82.

Borst, A., *Die Katharer* (Schriften der Monumenta Germaniae Historica, 12; Stuttgart, 1953).

Boucock, C., *In the Grip of Freedom: Law and Modernity in Max Weber* (Toronto, 2000).

Boudon, R., 'A propos du relativisme des valeurs: Retour sur quelques intuitions majeures de Tocqueville, Durkheim et Weber', *Revue française de sociologie*, 47 (2006), 877–97.

Boureau, A., *L'Empire du livre: Pour une histoire du savoir scolastique (1200–1380)* (Paris, 2007).

*La Loi du royaume: Les moines, le droit et la construction de la nation anglaise (XIᵉ–XIIIᵉ siècles* (Paris, 2001).

Brambilla, E., *Alle origini del Sant'Uffizio: Penitenza, confessione e giustizia spirituale dal medioevo al XVI secolo* (Bologna, 2000).

Braunmüller, B., 'Conföderationsbriefe des Klosters St. Emmeram in Regensburg', in *Studien und Mitteilungen aus dem Benedictiner-Orden, mit besonderer Berücksichtigung der Ordensgeschichte und Statistik,* 3 Jahrgang, I. Band (1882), 113–19.

Breuer, S. *Bürokratie und Charisma: Zur politischen Soziologie Max Webers* (Darmstadt, 1994).

*Die Briefe des heiligen Bonifatius und Lullus,* ed. M. Tangl (Monumenta Germaniae Historica Epistolae Selectae, 1; Berlin, 1916 edn).

Browe, P., 'Zur Geschichte des Dreifaltigkeitsfestes', *Archiv für Liturgiewissenschaft,* 1 (1950), 64–81.

Brubaker, R., *The Limits of Rationality: An Essay on the Social and Moral Thought of Max Weber* (London, 1984).

Bruce, S., *Choice and Religion: A Critique of Rational Choice Theory* (Oxford, 1999).

Brundage, J., *Medieval Canon Law* (London, 1995).

Brys, J., *De dispensatione in iure canonico, praesertim apud Decretistas et Decretalistas usque ad medium saeculum decimum quartum,* Universitas Catholica Lovaniensis Dissertationes ad gradum doctoris in facultate theologica consequendum conscriptae, II/xiv (Bruges, 1925).

Buchner, F. X., *Das Bistum Eichstatt: Historisch-statistische Beschreibung, auf Grund der Literatur, der Registratur des Bischöflichen Ordinariats Eichstätt sowie der pfarramtlichen Berichte,* vol. 2 (1938).

Burr, D., *The Spiritual Franciscans: From Protest to Persecution in the Century after Saint Francis* (University Park, Pa., 2001).

Bynum, C. W., *Holy Feast and Holy Fast: The Religious Significance of Food to Medieval Women* (Berkeley, 1987).

*Wonderful Blood: Theology and Practice in Late Medieval Northern Germany and Beyond* (Philadelphia, 2007).

Cameron, E., *Waldenses: Rejections of Holy Church in Medieval Europe* (Oxford, 2001).

*Capitula generalia Cartusiae, 1416–1442: Archives Générales du Royaume, Bruxelles, No. 14206/6 (formerly Bibliothèque Royale de Belgique, Bruxelles, MS II, 1959),* ed. Jan de Grauwe(Analecta Cartusiana, 100: 24; Salzburg, 1994).

Carroll, A. J., SJ, *Protestant Modernity: Weber, Secularization and Protestantism* (Scranton, Pa., 2007).

Caspar, E., *Geschichte des Papsttums von den Anfängen bis zur Höhe der Weltherrschaft,* 2 vols. (Tübingen, 1930–3).

*Catalogue générale des manuscrits latins,* vol. 6 (Nᵒˢ 3536 à 3775ᴮ) (Paris, 1975).

*A Catalogue of the Lansdowne Manuscripts in the British Museum* (London, 1819).

Chazelle, C., *The Crucified God in the Carolingian Era: Theology and Art of Christ's Passion* (Cambridge, 2001).

Cheney, C. R., and Jones, M., *A Handbook of Dates for Students of British History*, rev. edn (Cambridge, 2000).

Christianson, G., *Cesarini: The Conciliar Cardinal. The Basel years, 1431–1438* (Kirchengeschichtliche Quellen und Studien, 10; St. Ottilien, 1979).

*The Chronicle of Battle Abbey*, ed. and trans. E. Searle (Oxford, 1980).

Clanchy, M. T., *Abelard: A Medieval Life* (Oxford, 1997).

*From Memory to Written Record: England 1066–1307*, 2nd edn (Oxford, 1993).

Clark, J. G., 'Monastic Confraternity in Medieval England: The Evidence from the St Albans Abbey *Liber Benefactorum*', in E. Jamroziak and J. Burton (eds.), *Religious and Laity in Western Europe, 1000–1400: Interaction, Negotiation, and Power* (Europa Sacra, 2; Turnhout, 2006), 315–31.

Clark, S., *Thinking with Demons: The Idea of Witchcraft in Early Modem Europe* (Oxford, 1997).

Clarke, P. D., *The Interdict in the Thirteenth Century: A Question of Collective Guilt* (Oxford, 2007).

Clement V, see under *Regestum*.

Coleman, J. S., *The Foundations of Social Theory* (Cambridge, Mass., 1990).

Coulon, A., *Lettres secrètes et curiales du pape Jean XXII (1316–1334) relatives à la France* (Bibliothèques des Écoles Françaises d'Athènes et de Rome, 3ème série, deuxième fascicule, Feuilles 26 à 50, colonnes 401 à 800 (Paris, 1900).

*Lettres secrètes & curiales du pape Jean XXII (1316–1334) relatives à la France* (Bibliothèques des Écoles Franc̦aises d'Athènes et de Rome 3ème série, quatrième fascicule, *Feuilles 1 à 23, colonnes 1 à 364*; Paris, 1906).

Courth, F., 'Trinität', in *Lexikon des Mittelalters*, viii (Munich, 1997), cols. 1011–14.

Cucina, C., 'Il pellegrinaggio nelle saghe dell'Islanda medievale', *Rendiconti della Accademia Nazionale dei Lincei: Classe di scienze morali, storiche e filologiche*, ser. 9, 9/1 (1998), 83–155.

Dales, R. C., *Medieval Discussions of the Eternity of the World* (Brill's Studies in Intellectual History, 18; Leiden and New York, 1990).

Dalton, O. M., *The History of the Franks by Gregory of Tours*, vol. 2 (Oxford, 1927).

Dauvillier, J., *Le Mariage dans le droit classique de l'église depuis le Décret de Gratien (1140) jusqu'à la mort de Clément V (1314)* (Paris, 1933).

Davidson, D., *Essays on Actions and Events* (Oxford, 2001 edn).

'Incoherence and Irrationality', in *Problems of Rationality*, 189–98.

'The Objectivity of Values' (1995), in *Problems of Rationality* (Oxford, 2004), 39–57.

'Paradoxes of Irrationality', in *Problems of Rationality*, 169–87 (reprint of a paper first published in 1982).

*Problems of Rationality* (Oxford, 2004).

Davies, S., 'Marriage and the Politics of Friendship: The Family of Charles of Anjou, King of Naples (1285–1309)', Ph.D. thesis (London University, 1998).

Davis, J., 'Webb, Beatrice', in H. C. G. Matthew and Brian Harrison (eds.), *Oxford Dictionary of National Biography* (Oxford, 2004), vol. 57, pp. 802–27.

Davis, L. D., 'Hincmar of Reims as a Theologian of the Trinity', *Traditio*, 27 (1971), 455–68.

d'Avray, D., 'Alexander Murray', in Alexander Murray, *Doubting Thomas in Medieval Exegesis and Art*, prefaces by Letizia Ermini Pani and Lester K. Little and introd. by David d'Avray and a bio-bibliography of the author (Unione Internazionale degli Istituti di Archeologia Storia e Storia dell'Arte in Roma; Rome, 2006), 11–16.

'Authentication of Marital Status: A Thirteenth-Century English Royal Annulment Process and Late Medieval Cases from the Papal Penitentiary', *English Historical* Review, 120 (2005), 987–1013.

*Death and the Prince: Memorial Preaching before 1350* (Oxford, 1994).

'A Franciscan and History', reprinted in Bériou and d'Avray, *Modern Questions*, 259–84.

'Lay Kinship Solidarity and Papal Law', in P. Stafford, J. L. Nelson, and J. Martindale (eds.), *Law, Laity and Solidarities: Essays in Honour of Susan Reynolds* (Manchester, 2001), 188–99.

*Medieval Marriage Sermons: Mass Communication in a Culture without Print* (Oxford, 2001).

*Medieval Marriage: Symbolism and Society* (Oxford, 2005).

'Papal Authority and Religious Sentiment in the Late Middle Ages', in D. Wood (ed.), *The Church and Sovereignty, c.590–1918: Essays in Honour of Michael Wilks* (Studies in Church History Subsidia, 9; Oxford, 1991), 393–408.

*The Preaching of the Friars: Sermons Diffused from Paris before 1300* (Oxford, 1985).

'Printing, Mass Communication, and Religious Reformation: The Middle Ages and After', in J. Crick and A. Walsham (eds.), *The Uses of Script and Print, 1300–1700* (Cambridge, 2004), 50–70.

'The Transformation of the Medieval Sermon', D.Phil. thesis (Oxford University, 1976).

Deegalle, M., *Popularising Buddhism: Preaching as Performance in Sri Lanka* (Albany, NY, 2006).

De Grauwe, J. (ed.), *Capitula generalia Cartusiae, 1416–1442: Archives Générales du Royaume, Bruxelles, No. 14206/6 (formerly Bibliothèque royale de Belgique, Bruxelles, MS II, 1959)* (Analecta Cartusiana, 100: 24; Salzburg, 1994).

Dehio, L.,'Der Übergang von Natural- zu Geldbesoldung an der Kurie', *Vierteljahrschrift f. Social und Wirtschaftsgeschichte*, 8 (1910), 56–78.

De Jong, M., *In Samuel's Image: Child Oblation in the Early Medieval West* (Leiden, 1996).

Denifle, H., 'Die Constitutionen des Predigerordens in der Redaction Raimunds von Peñafort', in H. Denifle and F. Ehrle, *Archiv für Literatur-und Kirchensgeschichte des Mittelalters*, 5 (1889), 530–64.

'Die Constitutionen des Prediger-Ordens vom Jahre 1228', in H. Denifle and F. Ehrle, *Archiv für Literatur-und Kirchensgeschichte des Mittelalters*, 1 (1885), 165–227.

Denzinger, H., and Bannwart, C., *Enchiridion symbolorum, definitionum et declarationum de rebus fidei et morum*, 13th edn (Freiburg im Breisgau, 1921).
and Schönmetzer, A., *Enchiridion symbolorum: Definitionum et declarationum de rebus fidei et morum* (Barcelona, 1965).
Dessì, R. M., and Lauwers, M., *La Parole du prédicateur $V^e$–$XV^e$ siecle* (Nice, 1997).
Díaz y Díaz, M. C., *Index Scriptorum Latinorum Medii Aevi Hispanorum* (Madrid, 1959).
Dickson, G., 'The Advent of the *Pastores* (1251)', in Dickson, *Religious Enthusiasm*, essay VI.
*The Childrens Crusade: Medieval History, Modern Mythistory* (Basingstoke, 2008).
'The Genesis of the Children's Crusade (1212)', in Dickson, *Religious Enthusiasm*, essay IV.
*Religious Enthusiasm in the Medieval West* (Aldershot, 2000).
Dixon-Smith, S. A., 'Feeding the Poor to Commemorate the Dead: The Pro Anima Almsgiving of Henry III of England, 1227–72', Ph.D. thesis (University College London, 2003).
Dondorp, H., 'Review of Papal Rescripts in the Canonists' Teaching', *Zeitschrift der Savigny-Stiftung für Rechtsgeschichte*, 107, *Kanonistische Abteilung*, 76 (190), 172–253.
Douglas, M., *A Feeling for Hierarchy* (Marianist Award Lecture; University of Dayton, 2002).
*How Institutions Think* (Syracuse, NY, 1986).
*Natural Symbols* (London, 1996 edn).
Du Cange, C., et al., *Glossarium mediae et infimae Latinitatis* (Graz, 1954 reprint).
Duggan, A. J., '*De consultationibus:* The Role of Episcopal Consultation in the Shaping of Canon Law in the Twelfth Century', in B. C. Brasington and K. G. Cushing (eds.), *Bishops, Texts and the Use of Canon Law around 1100: Essays in Honour of Martin Brett* (Aldershot, 2008), 191–214.
Dunbabin, J., *A Hound of God: Pierre de la Palud and the Fourteenth-Century Church* (Oxford, 1991).
Ekelund, R. B., Jr., Hébert, R. F., Tollison, R. D., Anderson, G. M., and Davidson, A. B., *Sacred Trust: The Medieval Church as an Economic Firm* (New York and Oxford, 1996).
Elster, J., *Sour Grapes: Studies in the Subversion of Rationality* (Cambridge, 1983).
Erdélyi, G., 'Neue Forschungen zur Apostolischen Pönitentiarie', in *Quellen und Forschungen aus italienischen Archiven und Bibliotheken*, 86 (2006), 582–9.
Eubel, C., *Bullarium Franciscanum*, vol. 5 (Rome, 1898).
Evans-Pritchard, E. E., *Nuer Religion* (Oxford, 1956).
*Witchcraft, Oracles and Magic among the Azande*, abridged with an introduction by E. Gillies (Oxford, 1976).
*Extrauagantes Iohannis XXII*, ed. J. Tarrant (Monumenta Iuris Canonici Series B: Corpus Collectionum, 6; Vatican City, 1983).
Favereau, O., 'The Missing Piece in Rational Choice Theory', *Revue française de sociologie*, 46 (2005), supplement, 103–22.

Fea, C., *see* Pius II.

Felten, F. J., 'Auseinandersetzungen um die Finanzierung eines Kreuzzuges im Pontifikat Johannes XXII. (1316–1334)', in M. Pacaut, O. Fatio, and M. Grandjean (eds.), *L'Hostie et le denier: Les finances ecclésiastiques du haut Moyen Âge à l'époque moderne* (Publications de la Faculté de Théologie de l'Université de Genève, 14; Geneva, 1991), 79–99.

Feltoe, C. L., *see* Leo the Great.

Fieback, A., '*Necessitas non est legi subiecta, maxime positivae*: Über den Zusammenhang von Rechtswandel und Schriftgebrauch bei Humbert de Romanis O.P.', in G. Melville (ed.), *De Ordine Vitae: Zu Normvorstellungen, Organisationsformen und Schriftgebrauch im mittelalterlichen Ordenswesen* (Vita Regularis: Ordnungen und Deutungen religiosen Lebens im Mittelalter, vol. 1; Münster, 1996), 125–51.

Flori, J., *La Première Croisade: L'occident chrétien contre l'Islam (Aux origines des idéologies occidentales)* (Brussels, 1992).

Fogelin, R. J., *A Defence of Hume on Miracles* (Princeton, 2003).

Forni, A., 'La "Nouvelle Prédication" des disciples de Foulques de Neuilly: Intentions, techniques et réactions', in *Faire Croire: Modalités de la diffusion et de la réception des messages religieux du xii^e au xv^e siècle* (Collection de l'École Française de Rome, 51; Rome, 1981), 19–37.

Foxhall, L., and Lewis, A. D. E. (eds.), *Greek Law in its Political Setting: Justifications not Justice* (Oxford, 1996).

Freiberger, O., *Der Orden in der Lehre: Zur religiösen Deutung des Sangha im frühen Buddhismus* (Studies in Oriental Religions, 47; Wiesbaden, 2000).

Freise, E., Geuenich, D., and Wollasch, J., *Das Martyrolog-Necrolog von St. Emmeram zu Regensburg* (Monumenta Germaniae Historica, Libri Memoriales et Necrologia, NS iii; Hanover, 1986).

Frenz, T., 'Executor', in *Lexikon des Mittelalters*, iv (Munich, 1989), 160.

*Die Kanzlei der Päpste der Hochrenaissance (1471–1527)* (Bibliothek des Deutschen Historischen Instituts in Rom, 63; Tübingen, 1986).

*Papsturkunden des Mittelalters und der Neuzeit* (Stuttgart, 1986).

Friedberg, E., *Corpus Iuris Canonici*, 2 vols. (Leipzig, 1879–81; facs. repr. Leipzig, 1922 and Graz, 1959).

*Verlobung und Trauung, zugleich als Kritik von Sohm: Das Recht der Eheschliessung* (Leipzig, 1876).

Friedman, J. (ed.), *The Rational Choice Controversy: Economic Models of Politics Reconsidered* (New Haven, 1996).

Frutaz, A. P., 'La famiglia pontificia in un documento dell'inizio del sec. XIV', in *Palaeographica Diplomatica et Archivistica: Studi in onore di Giulio Battelli, a cura della Scuola Speciale per Archivisti e Bibliotecari dell'Università di Roma*, vol. 2 (Storia e Letteratura: Raccolta di Studi e Testi, 140; Rome, 1979), 277–323 (excluding plates).

Gadamer, H.-G., *Wahrheit und Methode: Grundzüge einer philosophischen Hermeneutik* (Tübingen, 1975 edn).

Garnett, G., *Marsilius of Padua and the Truth of History* (Oxford, 2006).

Geertz, C., 'Thick Description: Toward an Interpretive Theory of Culture', in id., *The Interpretation of Cultures: Selected Essays* (London, 1973; repr. 1993).

Giddens, A., 'Jürgen Habermas', in Q. Skinner (ed.), *The Return of Grand Theory to the Human Sciences* (Cambridge, 1985), ch. 7.

Given, J. B., *Inquisition and Medieval Society: Power, Discipline, and Resistance in Languedoc* (Ithaca, NY, 1997).

Glauche, G., *Katalog der lateinischen Handschriften der Bayerischen Staatsbibliothek München: Die Pergamenthandschriften aus Benediktbeuern Clm 4501–4663* (Catalogus Codicum Manu Scriptorum Bibliothecae Monacensis, 3, NS Pars 1; Wiesbaden, 1994).

Göller, E., *Die Päpstliche Pönitentiarie von ihrem Ursprung bis zu ihrer Umgestaltung unter Pius V, i/1: Darstellung; i/2: Quellen* (Bibliothek des Kgl. Preuss. Historischen Instituts in Rom, 3–4; Rome, 1907).

Gombrich, R., *Theravada Buddhism: A Social History from Ancient Benares to Modern Colombo* (London, 1988).

Goodich, M. E., *Miracles and Wonders: The Development of the Concept of the Miracle, 1150–1350* (Aldershot, 2007).

'Reason or Revelation? The Criteria for the Proof and Credibility of Miracles in Canonisation Processes', in G. Klaniczay (ed.), *Procès de canonisation au Moyen Âge: Apects juridiques et religieux* (Collection de l'École Française de Rome, 340; Rome, 2004), 181–97.

Goody, J., *The Development of the Family and Marriage in Europe* (Cambridge, 1983).

Grabmann, M., *Die Geschichte der scholastischen Methode*, 2 vols. (Freiburg im Breisgau, 1909–11).

Graeber, D., *Toward an Anthropological Theory of Value* (New York, 2001).

Grant, E., *God and Reason in the Middle Ages* (Cambridge, 2001).

Green, P., and Shapiro, I., *Pathologies of Rational Choice Theory: A Critique of Applications in Political Science* (New Haven, 1994).

'Pathologies Revisited: Reflections on our Critics', in J. Friedman (ed.), *The Rational Choice Controversy: Economic Models of Politics Reconsidered* (New Haven, 1996), 235–76.

Grundmann, H., *Religiöse Bewegungen im Mittelalter: Untersuchungen über die geschichtlichen Zusammenhänge zwischen der Ketzerei, den Bettelorden und der religiösen Frauenbewegung im 12. u 13. Jahrhundert und über die geschichtlichen Grundlagen der deutschen Mystik* (Hildesheim, 1961).

*Religious Movements in the Middle Ages: The Historical Links between Heresy, the Mendicant Orders, and the Women's Religious Movement in the Twelfth and Thirteenth Century, with the Historical Foundations of German Mysticism*, trans. S. Rowan (Notre Dame, 1995).

Gunawardana, R. A. L. H., *Robe and Plough: Monasticism and Economic Interest in Early Medieval Sri Lanka* (Tucson, Ariz., 1979).

Guyotjeannin, O., Pycke, J., and Tock, B.-M., *Diplomatique médiévale* ([Turnhout], 1993).

Hageneder, O., *Die geistliche Gerichtsbarkeit in Ober- und Niederösterreich: Von den Anfängen bis zum Beginn des 15. Jahrhunderts* (Forschungen zur Geschichte des Oberösterreichts, 10; Linz, 1967).

'Päpstliche Reskripttechnik: Kanonistische Lehre und kuriale Praxis', in Bertram (ed.), *Stagnation oder Fortbildung?*, 181–96.

'Probleme des päpstlichen Kirchenregiments im hohen Mittelalter (Ex certa scientia, non obstante, Registerführung)', *Lectiones Eruditorum Extraneorum in Facultate Philosophica Universitatis Carolinae Pragensis Factae*, fasciculus 4 (Prague, 1995), 49–77.

'Die Rechtskraft spätmittelalterlicher Papst- und Herrscherurkunden *"ex certa scientia"*, *"non obstantibus"* und *"propter importunitatem petentium"'*, in P. Herde and H. Jakobs (eds.), *Paptsurkunde und europäisches Urkundenwesen: Studien zu ihrer formalen und rechtlichen Kohärenz vom 11. bis 15. Jahrhundert* (Archiv für Diplomatik, Schriftgeschichte Siegel- und Wappenkunde, 7; Cologne, 1999), 401–29.

Haimerl, F. X., *Mittelalterliche Frömmigkeit im Spiegel der Gebetbuchliteratur Süddeutschlands* (Münchener Theologische Studien, I.4; Munich, 1952).

Hamilton, S., *The Practice of Penance* (Woodbridge, 2001).

Harrell, D. E., 'Oral Roberts: Religious Media Pioneer', in Sweet (ed.), Communication, 320–34.

Hart, H. L. A., *The Concept of Law*, 2nd edn (Oxford, 1994).

Haskett, T. H., 'The Medieval Court of Chancery', *Law and History Review*, 14 (1996), 245–313.

Haskins, C. H., 'The Sources for the History of the Papal Penitentiary', *American Journal of Theology*, 9 (1905), 421–50.

Hauck, A., *Kirchengeschichte Deutschlands*, vol. 5, pt. 1 (Leipzig, 1911).

Helmholz, R. H., *The Spirit of Classical Canon Law* (Athens, Ga., 1996), ch. 7.

Herde, P., *Audientia litterarum contradictarum: Untersuchungen über die päpstlichen Justizbriefe und die päpstliche Delegationsgerichtsbarkeit vom 13. bis zum Beginn des 16. Jahrhunderts* (Bibliothek des Deutschen Historischen Instituts in Rom, 31, 32; Tübingen, 1971).

'Papal Formularies for Letters of Justice (13th–16th Centuries): Their Development and Significance for Medieval Canon Law', in Bertram, *Stagnation oder Fortbildung?*, 223–47.

'Die Urkundenarten im dreizehnten Jahrhundert', in his *Beiträge zum päpstlichen Kanzlei-und Urkundenwesen im 13. Jhd.* (Münchener historische Studien, Abteilung geschichtliche Hilfswissenschaften, Bd. 1, 2nd edn; Kallmünz Opf, 1967), 57–71.

'Zur audientia litterarum contradictarum und zur "Reskripttechnik"', *Archivalische Zeitschrift*, 69 (1973), 54–90.

'Zur päpstlichen Delegationsgerichtsbarkeit im Mittelalter und in der frühen Neuzeit', *Zeitschrift der Savigny Stiftung für Rechtsgeschichte*, 119, *Kanonistische Abteilung*, 88 (2002), 20–43.

Herolt, Johannes, *Sermones discipuli de tempore* (Nuremberg, 1483; BL IB.7312).

Hess, H., *The Early Development of Canon Law and the Council of Serdica* (Oxford, 2002).

Hilton, R., *Bond Men Made Free: Medieval Peasant Movements and the English Rising of 1381* (London, 1977).

*Class Conflict and the Crisis of Feudalism: Essays in Medieval Social History* (London, 1985).

Hissette, R., *Enquête sur les 219 articles condamnés à Paris le 7 mars 1277* (Philosophes Médiévaux, 22; Louvain-la-Neuve, 1977).

Hollis, M., and Lukes, S., *Rationality and Relativism* (Cambridge, Mass., 1982).

Hume, D., *An Enquiry Concerning Human Understanding*, ed. T. L. Beauchamp (Oxford, 2000).

Hyams, P. R., *Rancor and Reconciliation in Medieval England* (Ithaca, NY, 2003).

Iaria, S., 'Enea Silvio Piccolomini und Pius II: Ein Vergleich im Hinblick auf den Konziliarismus mit einem Seitenblick auf die Kirchenreform', in C. Märtl and J. Dendorfer (eds.), *Nach dem Basler Konzil: Die Neuordnung der Kirche zwischen Konziliarismus und monarchischem Papat (ca. 1450–1475)* (Pluralisierung und Autorität, herausgegeben vom Sonderforschungsbereich 573, Ludwig-Maximilians-Universität München, 13; Berlin, 2008), 97–120.

'Silvio Piccolomini und das Basler Konzil', in K. Arnold, F. Fuchs and S. Füssel (eds), *Enea Silvio Piccolomini nördlich der Alpen: Akten des interdisziplinären Symposions vom 18. bis 19. November 2005 an der LMU München* = *Pirckheimer-Jahrbuch für Renaissance- und Humanismusforschung*, 22 (2007), 77–96.

Imber, C., *Ebu's-su'ud: The Islamic Legal Tradition* (Edinburgh, 1997).

Iser, W., *Der Akt des Lesens: Theorie ästhetischer Wirkung* (Munich, 1976).

Israel, J., *Radical Enlightenment: Philosophy and the Making of Modernity 1650–1750* (Oxford, 2001).

Jaffé, E., 'Die Ehepolitik Bonifazius VIII', diss. (Albert-Ludwigs-Universität, Freiburg im Breisgau, 1922).

Jamroziak, E., 'How Rievaulx Abbey Remembered its Benefactors', in Jamroziak and Burton (eds.), *Religious and Laity in Western Europe*, 63–76.

and Burton, J. (eds.), *Religious and Laity in Western Europe, 1000–1400: Interaction, Negotiation, and Power* (Europa Sacra, 2; Turnhout, 2006).

Jasper, D. and Fuhrmann, H., *Papal Letters in the Early Middle Ages* (Washington, DC, 2001).

Jerolmack, C., and Porpora, D., 'Religion, Rationality and Experience: A Response to the New Rational Choice Theory of Religion', *Sociological Theory*, 22 (2004), 140–60.

Joas, H., *The Genesis of Values* (Cambridge, 2000).

Johannes Herolt, *see* Herolt.

Johansen, B., *Contingency in a Sacred Law: Legal and Ethical Norms in Muslim Fiqh* (Studies in Islamic Law and Society, 7; Leiden, 1999).

John XXII, Pope, *see under* Coulon; *Extravagantes*.

Jones, J. W., *The Law and Legal Theory of the Greeks: An Introduction* (Oxford, 1956).

Joyce, G. H., *Christian Marriage: An Historical and Doctrinal Study* (London, 1933).

Kaelber, L., *Schools of Asceticism: Ideology and Organization of Medieval Religious Communities* (University Park, Pa., 1998).

Kant, I., *Grundlegung zur Metaphysik der Sitten*, ed. T. Valentiner (Stuttgart, 1984 edn).

Keen, M., *Chivalry* (New Haven, 1984).

Kennedy, D., 'Legal Formality', *Journal of Legal Studies*, 2 (1973), 351–98.

Kern, P., *Trinität, Maria, Inkarnation: Studien zur Thematik der deutschen Dichtung des späteren Mittelalters* (Philologische Studien und Quellen, 55; Berlin, 1971).

Kéry, L., *Canonical Collections of the Early Middle Ages (ca. 400–1140): A Bibliographical Guide to the Manuscripts and Literature* (Washington, DC, 1999).

Kieckhefer, R., 'The Specific Rationality of Medieval Magic', *American Historical Review*, 99 (1994), 813–36.

Kienzle, B. (ed.), *The Sermon* (Typologie des Sources du Moyen Âge Occidental, 81–3; Paris, 2000).

Klaniczay, G., *Procès de canonisation au Moyen Âge: Apects juridiques et religieux* (Collection de l'École Française de Rome, 340; Rome, 2004).

Kleinberg, A., 'Canonization without a Canon', in Klaniczay (ed.), *Procès de canonisation au Moyen Âge*, 7–18.

'Proving Saints: Selection and Authentication of Saints in the Later Middle Ages', *Viator*, 20 (1989), 183–205.

Kleinschmidt, E., *see* Rudolf von Schlettstadt.

Körner, A., 'Antiklerikale Ideen und religiöse Formen: Arbeiterkultur in Frankreich und Deutschland, 1830–1890', in Berthold Unfried (ed.), *Riten, Mythen und Symbole: Die Arbeiterbewegung zwischen 'Zivilreligion' und Volkskultur* (Leipzig, 1999), 60–89.

*Das Lied von einer anderen Welt: Kulturelle Praxis im französischen und deutschen Arbeitermilieu, 1840–1890* (Frankfurt, 1997).

Kronman, A. T., *Max Weber* (London, 1983).

Kroppmann, H., *Ehedispensübung und Stauferkamp unter Innozenz IV: Ein Beitrag zur Geschichte des päpstlichen Ehedispensrechtes* (Abhandlung zur mittleren und neueren Geschichte, 79; Berlin, 1937).

La Borderie, A. de, et al., *Monuments originaux de l'histoire de Saint Yves* (Saint-Brieuc, 1887).

Lacey, N., *A Life of H. L. Hart: The Nightmare and the Noble Dream* (Oxford, 2004).

Lambert, M., *The Cathars* (Oxford, 1998).

*Medieval Heresy: Popular Movements from the Gregorian Reform to the Reformation*, 3rd edn (Oxford, 2002).

Landau, P., 'Gratian and the *Decretum Gratiani*', in W. Hartmann and K. Pennington (eds.), *The History of Medieval Canon Law in the Classical Period, 1140–1234: From Gratian to the Decretals of Pope Gregory IX* (Washington, DC, 2008).

'Schwerpunkte und Entwicklung des klassischen kanonischen Rechts bis zum Ende des 13. Jahrhunderts', in Bertram (ed.), *Stagnation oder Fortbildung?*, 15–31.

Lang, A., *Die Urkunden über die Beziehungen der päpstlichen Kurie zur Provinz und Diozese Salzburg (mit Gurk, Chiemsee, Seckau und Lavant) in der Avignonischen Zeit: 1313–1378. Acta Salzburgo-Aquilejensia, Quellen und Forschungen zur österreichischen Kirchengeschichte, herausgegeben von der österreichischen Leo-Gesellschaft in Wien, Serie I, Band I, erste Abteilung: 1316–1352* (Graz, 1903).

'Beiträge zur Geschichte der apostolischen Pönitentiarie im 13. und 14. Jahrhundert', *Mitteilungen des Instituts für österreichische Geschichtsforschung*, Ergänzungsband 7 (Innsbruck, 1907), 20–43.

Langlois, J. D., Jr., ' "Living Law" in Sung and Yüan Jurisprudence', *Harvard Journal of Asiatic Studies*, 41 (1981), 165–217.

Langmuir, G. I., *History, Religion and Antisemitism* (Berkeley, 1990).

Lansing, C., *Power and Purity: Cathar Heresy in Medieval Italy* (Oxford, 1998).

Lapsanski, D., *Perfectio evangelica: Eine begriffsgeschichtliche Untersuchung im frühfranziskanischen Schrifttum* (Veröffentlichungen des Grabmann-Institutes, NS 22; Munich, 1974).

Larrainzar, C., 'La ricerca attuale sul "Decretum Gratiani"', in E. De Leon and N. Alvarez de las Asturias (eds.), *La cultura giuridico-canonica medioevale: Premesse per un dialogo ecumenico* (Pontificia Università della Santa Croce Monografie Giuridiche, 22; Milan, 2003), 45–88.

Laudage, J., 'Rittertum und Rationalismus: Friedrich Barbarossa als Feldherr', in J. Laudage and Y. Leiverkus (eds.), *Rittertum und höfische Kultur der Stauferzeit* (Cologne, 2006), 291–314.

Lawrence, C. H., *Medieval Monasticism: Forms of Religious Life in Western Europe in the Middle Ages* (London, 1989).

Lea, H. C., *A Formulary of the Papal Penitentiary in the Thirteenth Century* (Philadelphia, 1892).

Le Blévec, D., 'Une source d'histoire monastique: Les délibérations du chapitre général des chartreux', in C. Carozzi and H. Taviani-Carozzi (eds.), *Le Médiéviste devant ses sources: Questions et méthodes* (Paris, 2004), 157–69.

Le Bras, G., 'Boniface VIII, symphoniste et modérateur', in C.-E. Perrin (ed.), *Mélanges d'histoire du Moyen Âge dédiés à la mémoire de Louis Halphen* (Paris, 1951), 383–94.

'Le Droit romain au service de la domination pontificale', *Revue historique de droit français et étranger*, 4th ser., 27 (1949), 377–98.

'La Formation du droit romano-canonique', in *Actes du Congrès de Droit Canonique: cinquantenaire de la Faculté de Droit Canonique Paris, 22–26 avril, 1947* (Paris, 1950), 335–8.

Lecacheux, P., 'Un formulaire de la pénitencerie apostolique au temps du Cardinal Albornoz (1357–1358)', *École française de Rome, Mélanges d'archéologie et d'histoire*, 18; 1898), 37–49.

Legendre, P., *La Pénétration du droit romain dans le droit canonique classique de Gratien à Innocent IV, 1140–1254* (Paris, 1964).

Le Goff, J., *Naissance du Purgatoire* (Paris, 1981).

Leo the Great, *The Letters and Sermons of Leo the Great, Bishop of Rome*, trans. C. L. Feltoe (Select Library of Nicene and Post-Nicene Fathers of the Christian Church, 2nd ser., ed. P. Schaff and H. Wace, 12; repr. Grand Rapids, Mich., 1989).

Lhotsky, A., *Thomas Ebendorfer: Ein österreichischer Geschichtschreiber, Theologe und Diplomat des 15. Jahrhunderts* (Schriften der Monumenta Germaniae Historica, 15; Stuttgart, 1957).

Libera, A. de, *Penser au Moyen Âge* (Paris, 1991).

Lieu, S. N. C., *Manichaeism in the later Roman Empire and Medieval China* (Wissenchaftliche Untersuchungen zum neuen Testament, 63, 2nd rev. edn (Tübingen, 1992).

'Lire Max Weber': issue of the *Revue française de sociologie*, 46/4 (2005).

*Livre des deux principes*, ed. C. Thouzellier (Paris, 1973).

Lobrichon, G., *La Bible au Moyen Âge* (Les Médiévistes français, 3; Paris, 2003).

Logan, F. D., *Runaway Religious in Medieval England c.1240–1540* (Cambridge, 1996).

Longère, J., *La Prédication médiévale* (Études augustiniennes; Paris, 1983).

Lukes, S., 'Some Problems about Rationality', in Wilson (ed.), *Rationality*, 195–213.

Lunt, W. E., *Papal Revenues in the Middle Ages*, 2 vols. (New York, 1934).

Luscombe, D., *Medieval Thought* (Oxford, 1997).

*The School of Peter Abelard: The Influence of Abelard's Thought in the Early Scholastic Period* (Cambridge, 1969).

Lusiardi, R., 'Stiftung und Seelenheil in den monotheistischen Religionen des mittelalterlichen Europa: Eine komparative Problemskizze', in Borgolte (ed.), *Stiftungen in Christentum, Judentum und Islam*, 47–69.

Lutterbach, H., *Sexualität im Mittelalter: Eine Kulturstudie anhand von Bußbüchern des 6. bis. 12. Jahrhunderts* (Cologne, 1999).

Lynch, J. H., *Godparents and Kinship in Early Medieval Europe* (Princeton, 1986).

Maassen, F., *Geschichte der Quellen und der Literatur des canonischen Rechts im Abendlande bis zum Ausgange des Mittelalters*, vol. 1 (Gratz, 1870).

MacIntyre, A., *After Virtue: A Study in Moral Theory* (London, 1981).

Makdisi, J., 'Legal Logic and Equity in Islamic Law', *American Journal of Comparative Law*, 33 (1985), 63–92.

Manselli, R., 'Chi era Francesco d'Assisi? Discorso conclusivo', in S. Gieben (ed.), *Francesco d'Assisi nella storia, secoli XIII–XV*, vol. 1 (Rome, 1983), 349–59.

Mansfield, M. C., *The Humiliation of Sinners: Public Penance in Thirteenth-Century France* (Ithaca, NY, 1995).

Marenbon, J., *Later Medieval Philosophy (1150–1350)* (London, 1991).

*Medieval Philosophy: An Historical and Philosophical Introduction* (London, 2007).

*The Philosophy of Peter Abelard* (Cambridge, 1997).

Martin, H., *Le Métier de prédicateur en France septentrionale à la fin du Moyen Âge (1350–1520)* (Paris, 1988).

*Les Ordres mendiants en Bretagne (vers 1230–vers 1530)* (Paris, 1975).

Märtl, C., and Dendorfer, J. (eds.), *Nach dem Basler Konzil: Die Neuordnung der Kirche zwischen Konziliarismus und monarchischem Papat (ca. 1450–1475)* (Berlin, 2008).

Mayne Kienzle, B., 'Medieval Sermons and their Performance: Theory and Record', in Muessig (ed.), *Preacher, Sermon and Audience*, 89–124.

McCulloh, J. M., 'Jewish Ritual Murder: William of Norwich, Thomas of Monmouth, and the Early Dissemination of the Myth', *Speculum*, 72 (1977), 698–740.

McCune, J., 'An Edition and Study of Select Sermons from the Carolingian Sermonary of Salzburg', Ph.D. thesis (London University, 2007).

McKnight, B. E., and Liu, J. T. C., *The Enlightened Judgements, Ch'ing-ming Chi: The Sung Dynasty Collection* (Albany, NY, 1999).

Meduna, B., *Studien zum Formular der päpstlichen Justizbriefe von Alexander III. bis Innocenz III. (1159–1216): Die non obstantibus-Formel* (Vienna, 1989).

Meens, R., *Het Tripartite Boeteboek: Overlevering en betekenis van vroegmiddeleeuwse biechtvoorschriften (met editie en vertaling van vier tripartita)* (Hilversum, 1994).

Melchert, C., *The Formation of the Sunni Schools of Law, 9th–10th Centuries C.E.* (Leiden, 1997).

Melville, G., 'Ordensstatuten und allgemeines Kirchenrecht: Eine Skizze zum 12./31. Jahrhundert', in P. Landau and J. Müller (eds.), *Proceedings of the Ninth International Congress of Medieval Canon Law, Munich, 13–18 July, 1992* (Monumenta Iuris Canonici, Series C: Subsidia 10; Vatican City, 1997), 691–712.

and Staub, M. (eds.), *Enzyklopädie des Mittelalters*, 2 vols. (Darmstadt, 2008).

Merryman, J. H., *The Civil Law Tradition: An Introduction to the Legal Systems of Western Europe and Latin America*, 2nd edn (Stanford, 1985).

Meyer, M., *Die Pönitentiarie-Formularsammlung des Walter Murner von Strassburg: Beitrag zur Geschichte und Diplomatik der päpstlichen Pönitentiarie im 14. Jahrhundert* (Spicilegium Friburgense, 25; Freiburg Schweiz, 1979).

Millar, F., *The Emperor in the Roman World (31 BC–AD 337)* (London, 1977).

Molin, J.-B., and Mutembe, P., *Le Rituel du mariage en France du XII$^e$ au XVI$^e$ siècle* (Théologie historique, 26; Paris, 1974).

Mommsen, W. J., *The Age of Bureaucracy: Perspectives on the Political Sociology of Max Weber* (Oxford, 1974).

*Max Weber and German Politics, 1890–1920*, trans. Michael S. Steinberg (Chicago, 1984).

Muessig, C. (ed.), *Preacher, Sermon and Audience in the Middle Ages* (Leiden, 2002).

Müller, H., 'Entscheidung auf Nachfrage: Die delegierten Richter als Verbindungsglieder zwischen Kurie und Region sowie als Gradmesser päpstlicher Autorität', in J. Johrend and H. Müller (eds.), *Römisches Zentrum und kirchliche Peripherie: Das universale Papsttum als Bezugspunkt der Kirchen von den Reformpäpsten bis zu Innozenz III* (Neue Abhandlungen der Akademie der Wissenschaften zu Göttingen, Philologisch-Historische Klasse, NS 2, Studien zu Papstgeschichte und Papsturkunden; Berlin, 2008), 109–31.

*Päpstliche Delegationsgerichtsbarkeit in der Normandie: 12. und frühes 13. Jahrhundert*, 2 vols. (Studien und Dokumente zur Gallia Pontificia = Études et documents pour servir à une Gallia Pontificia, 4; Bonn, 1997).

Murray, A., *Excommunication and Conscience in the Middle Ages* (John Coffin Memorial Lecture; London, 1991).

'Piety and Impiety in Thirteenth-Century Italy', in G. J. Cuming and D. Baker (eds.), *Popular Belief and Practice* (Studies in Church History, 8; Cambridge, 1972), 83–106.

*Reason and Society in the Middle Ages* (Oxford, 1978).

*Suicide in the Middle Ages*, vol. 1 (Oxford, 1998).

Neske, I., *Katalog der lateinischen Handschriften der Bayerischen Staatsbibliothek: Die Handschriften aus St. Emmeram in Regensburg*, vol. 2: *Clm 14131–14260* (Catalogus codicum manu scriptorum Bibliothecae Monacensis, tom. IV, series nova, Pars 2, 2; Wiesbaden, 2005).

*Katalog der lateinischen Handschriften der Bayerischen Staatsbibliothek München: Clm 28615a–28786* (Catalogus codicum manu scriptorum Bibliothecae Monacensis, tom. IV, Pars 10; Wiesbaden, 1984).

Nold, P., *Pope John XXII and his Franciscan Cardinal: Bertrand de la Tour and the Apostolic Poverty Controversy* (Oxford, 2003).

Nörr, K. W., 'Kuriale Praxis und kanonistische Wissenschaft: Einige Fragen und Hinweise', in Bertram (ed.), *Stagnation oder Fortbildung?*, 33–8.

'Von der Textrationalität zur Zweckrationalität: Das Beispiel des summarischen Processes', *Zeitschrift der Savigny-Stiftung für Rechtsgeschichte*, 112, *Kanonistische Abteilung*, 81 (1995), 1–25.

Obeyesekere, G., *The Apotheosis of Captain Cook: European Mythmaking in the Pacific* (Princeton, 1997).

Oesterlé, G., 'Consummation', in *Dictionnaire de droit canonique*, vol. 4 (Paris, 1947).

Oexle, O.-G., 'Memoria, Memorialüberlieferung', in *Lexikon des Mittelalters*, vol. 6 (Munich, 1993), 510–13.

'Memoria und Memorialüberlieferung im früheren Mittelalter', *Frühmittelalterliche Studien*, 10 (1976), 70–95.

Papineau, D., 'The Evolution of Means–Ends Reasoning', in his *The Roots of Reason: Philosophical Essays on Rationality, Evolution, and Probability* (Oxford, 2003), 83–129.

*Patrologia Latina*, ed. J.-P. Migne, 221 vols. (Paris, 1844–64).

Patschovsky, A., 'Die Trinitätsdiagramme Joachims von Fiore (†1202): Ihre Herkunft und semantische Struktur im Rahmen der Trinitätsikonokraphie, von deren Anfängen bis ca. 1200', in A. Patschovsky (ed.), *Die Bildwelt der Diagramme Joachims von Fiore: Zur Medialität religiös-politischer Programme im Mittelalter* (Ostfildern, 2003), 55–114.

Paulus, N., *Geschichte des Ablasses im Mittelalter vom Ursprunge bis zur Mitte des 14. Jahrhunderts*, vol. 1 (Paderborn, 1922).

Payer, P. J., 'The Humanism of the Penitentials and the Continuity of the Penitential Tradition', *Medieval Studies*, 46 (1984), 340–54.

Pegg, M. G., *A Most Holy War: The Albigensian Crusade and the Battle for Christendom* (Oxford, 2008).

Pelikan, J., *The Christian Tradition: A History of the Development of Doctrine*, iv, *Reformation of Church and Dogma (1300–1700)* (Chicago, 1984).

Peter Damian, *Die Briefe des Petrus Damiani*, i, ed. K. Reindel (Monumenta Germaniae Historica: Die Briefe der deutschen Kaiserzeit, 4; Munich, 1983).

Peter, F., and Schmid, H. B. (eds.), *Rationality and Commitment* (Oxford, 2007).

Peter Lombard, *Magistri Petri Lombardi... Sententiae in IV libris distinctae*, ed. [I. Brady, anonymously], 2 vols. (Spicilegium Bonaventurianum, 4–5; Grottaferrata, 1971–81).

Peters, E., *Inquisition* (New York and London, 1988).

Piché, D., with Lafleur, C., *La Condamnation parisienne de 1277* (Paris, 1999).

Pius II, 'Bulla Retractationis', ed. C. Fea, *Pius II. Pont. Max. a calumniis vindicatus ternis retractionibus eius quibus dicta et scripta pro concilio Basileensi contra Eugenium PP. IV. ejuravit* (Rome, 1823).

Plöchl, W. M., *Geschichte des Kirchenrechts*, iv (Munich, 1966).

Ponting, C., '*R. v. Ponting*', *Journal of Law and Society*, 14 (1987), 366–72.

Potestà, G. L., *Il tempo dell'Apocalisse: Vita di Gioacchino da Fiore* (Rome, 2004).

Pouliot, F., *La Doctrine du miracle chez Thomas d'Aquin: Deus in omnibus intime operatur* (Paris, 2005).

Quinto, R., *Scholastica: Storia di un concetto* (Subsidia mediaevalia Patavina, 2; Padua, 2001).

Rabikauskas, P., *Diplomatica pontificia (praelectionum lineamenta)*, 6th edn (Rome, 1998).

Ranke, Leopold von, *Die Roemischen Paepste in den letzten vier Jahrhunderten*, 2 vols. (Leopold von Ranke's historische Meisterwerke, 15–16; Vienna, n.d.).

*Regestum Clementis Papae V, Annus Secundus (Regestorum Vol. LIV)*, ed. Monachi Ordinis S. Benedicti (Rome, 1885).

*Revue française de sociologie*, 47/4 (2006) (issue devoted to the sociology of values, with special reference to Europe).

Reynolds, S., 'Social Mentalities and the Case of Medieval Scepticism', *Transactions of the Royal Historical Society*, 6th ser., 1 (1991), 21–41.

Riley-Smith, J., *The First Crusade and the Idea of Crusading* (London, 1993).

Robb, F., 'The Fourth Lateran Council's Definition of Trinitarian Orthodoxy', *Journal of Ecclesiastical History*, 48 (1977), 22–43.

Robert de Chevanne, M. J., 'Charles IV le Bel et Blanche de Bourgogne', *Bulletin philologique et historique (jusqu'à 1715) du comité des travaux historiques et scientifiques*, 1936, 1937 (Paris, 1938), 313–50.

Roca, M. J., 'Der Toleranzbegriff im kanonischen Recht', *Zeitschrift der Savigny-Stiftung für Rechtsgeschichte*, 121, *kanonistische Abteilung*, 90 (2004), 548–61.

Roper, L., *Oedipus and the Devil: Witchcraft, Sexuality and Religion in Early Modern Europe* (London, 1994).

Rosen, F., 'The Political Context of Aristotle's Categories of Justice', *Phronesis*, 20 (1975), 228–40.

Rößer, E., *Göttliches und menschliches, unveränderliches und veränderliches Kirchenrecht, von der Entstehung der Kirche bis zur Mitte des 9. Jahrhunderts: Untersuchungen zur Geschichte des Kirchenrechts mit besonderer Berücksichtigung der Anschauungen Rudolf Sohms* (Görres-Gesellschaft . . . Veröffentlichungen der Sektion für Rechts- und Staatswissenschaft, 64; Paderborn, 1934).

Rubin, M., *Corpus Christi: The Eucharist in Late Medieval Culture* (Cambridge, 1991).

*Gentile Tales: The Narrative Assault on Medieval Jews* (New Haven, 1999).

Rubinstein, A., *Modeling Bounded Rationality* (Cambridge, Mass., 1998).

Rudolf von Schlettstadt, *Historiae Memorabiles: Zur Dominikanerliteratur und Kulturgeschichte des 13. Jahrhunderts*, ed. E. Kleinschmidt (Cologne, 1974).

Runciman, W. G., *A Critique of Max Weber's Philosophy of Social Science* (Cambridge, 1972).

Sabatier, P., *Vie de S. François*, 13th edn (Paris, 1894).

Sägmüller, H. B., 'Die Entstehung und Bedeutung der Formel "*Salva Sedis Apostolicae Auctoritate*" in den päpstlichen Privilegien um die Mitte des 12. Jahrhunderts. Eine Studie zur Geschichte der Entwicklung des päpstlichen Gesetzgebungsrechtes', *Acta Congressus Iuridici Internationalis . . . Romae, 12–17 Novembris 1934*, vol. 3 (Rome, 1936), 155–71.

Sahlins, M., *How 'Natives' Think: About Captain Cook, for Example* (Chicago, 1995).

*St Francis of Assisi: Writings and Early Biographies. English Omnibus of the Sources for the Life of St. Francis*, ed. M. A. Habig (London, 1973).

Salonen, K., *The Penitentiary as a Well of Grace in the Late Middle Ages: The Example of the Province of Uppsala, 1448–1527* (Annales Academicae Scientiarum Fennicae, 313; Helsinki, 2001).

and Krötzl, C. (eds.), *The Roman Curia, the Apostolic Penitentiary and the Partes in the Later Middle Ages* (Acta Instituti Romani Finlandiae, 28; Rome, 2003).

Santifaller, L., 'Über die Verbal-Invokation in Urkunden', *Sitzungsberichte der Österreichische Akademie der Wissenschaften, philosophisch-historische Klasse*, 237/ii (Vienna, 1961).

Satris, S. A., 'The Theory of Value and the Rise of Ethical Emotivism', *Journal of the History of Ideas*, 43 (1982), 109–28.

Sayers, J., *Papal Judges Delegate in the Province of Canterbury, 1198–1254: A Study in Ecclesiastical Jurisdiction and Administration* (Oxford, 1971).

Schluchter, W., 'Einleitung. Religion, politische Herrschaft, Wirtschaft und bürgerliche Lebensführung: Die okzidentale Sonderentwicklung', in W. Schluchter (ed.), *Max Webers Sicht des okzidentalen Christentums: Interpretation und Kritik* (Frankfurt am Main, 1988 edn), 11–128.

*The Rise of Western Rationalism: Max Weber's Developmental History*, trans. and intro. Guenther Roth (Berkeley, 1981).

(ed.), *Max Webers Sicht des okzidentalen Christentums: Interpretation und Kritik* (Frankfurt am Main, 1988 edn).

Schmugge, L., *Ehen vor Gericht: Paare der Renaissance vor dem Papst* (Berlin, 2008).

'Kanonistik in der Pönitentiarie', in Bertram (ed.), *Stagnation oder Fortbildung?*, 93–115.

Hersberger, P., and Wiggenhauser, B., *Die Supplikenregister der päpstlichen Pönitentiarie aus der Zeit Pius' II* (Tübingen, 1996).

Schneyer, J. B., *Repertorium der lateinischen Sermones des Mittelalters für die Zeit von 1150–1350*, 11 vols. (Münster, 1969–90).

Schwarz, B. *Die Organisation kurialer Schreiberkollegien von ihrer Entstehung bis zur Mitte des 15. Jahrhunderts* (Tübingen, 1972).

*Scripta Leonis, Rufini et Angeli sociorum S. Francisci: The Writings of Leo, Rufino and Angelo Companions of St. Francis*, ed. and trans. R. B. Brooke (Oxford, 1970).

Sen, A., *Rationality and Freedom* (Cambridge, Mass., 2002).

*Sermones Discipuli*, see Herolt.

Shepsle, K. A., and Bonchek, M. S., *Analyzing Politics: Rationality, Behaviour and Institutions* (New York, 1997).

Shotwell, J. T., and Loomis, L. R., *The See of Peter* ([Columbia] Records of Western Civilization; New York, 1991).

Silva-Tarouca, K., 'Die Quellen der Briefsammlungen Papst Leos des Grossen: Ein Beitrag zur Frage nach den Quellen der ältesten Papstbriefsammlungen', in A. Brackmann (ed.), *Papsttum und Kaisertum: Forschungen zur politischen Geschichte und Geisteskultur des Mittelalters Paul Kehr zum 65. Geburtstag dargebracht* (Munich, 1926), 23–47.

Skinner, Q., 'Interpretation, Rationality and Truth', in *Visions of Politics, i: Regarding Method* (Cambridge, 2002), 27–56.

Smalley, B., *The Study of the Bible in the Middle Ages* (Oxford, 1983 edn).

Smart, J. J. C., 'Ruth Anna Putnam and the Fact–Value Distinction', *Philosophy*, 74 (1999), 431–7.

Sohm, R., *Trauung und Verlobung: Eine Entgegnung auf Friedberg: Verlobung und Trauung* (Weimar, 1876).

'Wesen und Ursprung des Katholizismus', *Abhandlungen der philologisch-historischen Klasse der königlich sächsischen Gesellschaft der Wissenschaften*, 27 (Leipzig, 1909), 333–90.

Southern, R. W., 'Aspects of the European Tradition of Historical Writing: 3. History as Prophecy', *Transactions of the Royal Historical Society*, ser. 5/22 (1972), 159–80.

*Scholastic Humanism and the Unification of Europe*, vol. 1: *Foundations* (Oxford, 1995).

(with notes and additions by L. Smith and B. Ward), *Scholastic Humanism and the Unification of Europe*, vol. 2: *The Heroic Age* (Oxford, 2001).

Stark, R., and Brainbridge, W. S., *A Theory of Religion* (New Brunswick, NJ, 1996 edn).

*Statuta ordinis Cartusiensis a domno Guigone priore cartusie edita* (Basel, 1510; BL call number 4071.h.5).

Stiegler, M. A., *Dispensation, Dispensationswesen und Dispensationsrecht im Kirchenrecht* (Mainz, 1901).

Stout, H. S., 'Religion, Communications, and the Career of George Whitefield', in Sweet (ed.), *Communication and Change*, 108–25.

Strnad, A. A., and Walsh, K., 'Cesarini, Giuliano', in *Dizionario biografico degli italiani*, vol. 24 (Rome, 1980), 188–95.

Swanson, R. N., *Church and Society in Late Medieval England* (Oxford, 1989). *Religion and Devotion in Europe c. 1215–c. 1515* (Cambridge, 1995).

Sweet, I. (ed.), *Communication and Change in American Religious History* (Grand Rapids, Mich., 1993).

Tambiah, S. J., *Magic, Science, Religion, and the Scope of Rationality* (Cambridge, 1990).

Taylor, C., 'Rationality', in Hollis and Lukes (eds.), *Rationality and Relativism*, 87–105.

Tewes, G.-R., 'Die päpstliche Datarie um 1500', in Bertram (ed.), *Stagnation oder Fortbildung?*, 159–80.

Thomas Aquinas, *Compendium theologiae*, in *Opera omnia*, 42 (Rome, 1979), 1–205.

*Opera omnia... Leonis XIII P.M. edita* (Rome, 1882, etc. [in progress]).

*Summa contra Gentiles* (Editio Leonina manualis; Rome, 1934).

Thompson, A., *Revival Preachers and Politics in Thirteenth-Century Italy: The Great Devotion of 1233* (Oxford, 1992).

Thouzellier, C. (ed.), *Livre des deux principes* (Paris, 1973).

Tierney, B., *The Crisis of Church and State 1050–1300* (Englewood Cliffs, NJ, 1964).

*Foundations of the Conciliar Theory: The Contribution of the Medieval Canonists from Gratian to the Great Schism* (Studies in the History of Christian Thought, 81; Leiden, 1998 edn).

Triantaphyllopoulos, J., *Das Rechtsdenken der Griechen* (Münchener Beiträge zur Papyrusforschung und antiken Rechtsgeschichte, 78; Munich, 1985).

Ubl, K., *Inzestverbot und Gesetzgebung: Die Konstruktion eines Verbrechens (300–1100)* (Millenium-Studien, 20; Berlin, 2008).

Uecker, S., *Die Rationalisierung des Rechts: Max Weber's Rechtssoziologie* (Berlin, 2005).

Van Hove, A., *De privilegiis, de dispensationibus* (Commentarium Lovaniense in Codicem Iuris Canonici I/v; Mechelen, 1939).

Vauchez, A., 'Conclusion', in Klaniczay, *Procès de canonisation au Moyen Âge*, 357–63.

*La Sainteté en Occident aux derniers siècles du Moyen Âge d'après les procès de canonisation et les documents hagiographiques* (Bibliothèque des Écoles Françaises d'Athènes et de Rome, 241; Rome, 1981).

Verger, J., *Les Universités au Moyen Âge* (Paris, 1973).

*Vinaya Texts, Part I: The Pâtimokkha. The Mahâvagga, I–IV*, trans. T. W. Rhys Davids and H. Oldenberg (The Sacred Books of the East, 13; Oxford, 1881; repr. Delhi, 1968).

Vodola, E., *Excommunication in the Middle Ages* (Berkeley, 1986).

Walker, R. C. S., *The Coherence Theory of Truth: Realism, Anti-Realism, Idealism* (London, 1988).

Walz, A., *Compendium historiae Ordinis Praedicatorum*, rev. edn (Rome, 1948).

Warning, R., *Rezeptionsästhetik: Theorie und Praxis*, 2nd edn (Munich, 1979).

Watkins, C. S., *History and the Supernatural in Medieval England* (Cambridge, 2007).

Webb, D., *Medieval European Pilgrimage, c. 700–c. 1500* (Basingstoke, 2002).

Weber, M., *Gesammelte Aufsätze zur Religionssoziologie*, vols. 1–2 (Tübingen, 1988 edn).

*Gesammelte Aufsätze zur Wissenschaftslehre*, ed. J. Winckelmann, 7th edn (Tübingen, 1988).

*Wirtschaft und Gesellschaft*, 5th edn, ed. J. Winckelmann, 3 vols. (Tübingen, 1976).

*Die Wirtschaftsethik der Weltreligionen*, vol. 2: *Hinduismus und Buddhismus*, repr. in *Gesammelte Aufsätze zur Religionssoziologie*, vol. 2 (Tübingen, 1988).

Wetter, F., *Die Trinitätslehre des Johannes Duns Scotus* (Beiträge zu Geschichte der Philosophie des Mittelalters, 41, 5; Münster im Westfalen, 1967).

Wigger, J. H., *Taking Heaven by Storm: Methodism and the Rise of Popular Christianity in America* (New York, 1998).

Wilks, M., *The Problem of Sovereignty in the Middle Ages: The Papal Monarchy with Augustinus Triumphus and the Publicists* (Cambridge, 1963).

Williams, B., *Morality: An Introduction to Ethics* (Cambridge, 1976).

Wilson, B. R. (ed.), *Rationality* (Oxford, 1970).

Winckelmann, J., *see* Weber, M.

Winroth, A., *The Making of Gratian's* Decretum (Cambridge, 2000).

Winston-Allen, A., *Stories of the Rose: The Making of the Rosary in the Middle Ages* (University Park, Pa., 1997).

Worstbrock, F. J., 'Herolt, Johannes (Discipulus)', in *Die deutsche Literatur des Mittelalters Verfasserlexikon*, vol. 3 (Berlin, 1981), cols. 1123–7.

'Piccolomini, Aeneas Silvius (Papst Pius II.), in *Die deutsche Literatur des Mittelalters Verfasserlexikon*, vol. 7 (Berlin, 1989), cols. 634–69.

Wurm, H., 'Decretales selectae ex antiquissimis Romanorum Pontificum epistulis decretalibus, praemissa introductione et disquisitione critice editae', *Apollinaris: Commentarius iuris canonici*, 12 (1939), 40–93.

*Studien und Texte zur Dekretalensammlung des Dionysius Exiguus* (Kanonistische Studien und Texte, 16; Bonn, 1938).

Zimmermann, H. (ed.), *Papsturkunden 896–1046*, vol. 2: 996–1046 (Österreichische Akademie der Wissenschaften, philosophisch-historische Klasse, Denkschriften, 177; Veröffentlichungen der historischen Kommission, 4; Vienna, 1985).

# Index of manuscripts

**BIRMINGHAM**

Birmingham University Library 6/iii/19:
55–6

**LONDON, BRITISH
LIBRARY (BL)**

Add. 24057: 155 n. 23
Harley 3215: 47–8 n. 49
Lansdowne 397: 141
Lansdowne 1201: 124–6
Royal 5.A.i: 118, 153, 161–2
Royal 8.D.iii: 153, 161–2

**MUNICH, BAYERISCHE
STAATSBIBLIOTHEK**

Clm. 4649: 58–9
Clm. 14194: 32–3

Clm. 14892: 34 n. 12
Clm. 28673: 43–6

**PARIS, BIBLIOTHÈQUE
NATIONALE DE FRANCE
(BNF)**

MS Lat. 3736: 81–2
MS Lat. 18181: 82 n. 71

**VATICAN CITY,
BIBLIOTECA APOSTOLICA
VATICANA (BAV)**

Lat. 3994: 5

# General index